Politics of Civil Wars

I0091853

Civil war is one of the critical issues of our time. Although intrastate in nature, it has a disproportionate and overwhelming effect on the overall peace and stability of contemporary international society.

Organized around the themes of contested nationalism, violence, external intervention, post-conflict reconstruction, reconciliation and governance, Amalendu Misra investigates why civil wars have become so widespread and how they can be contained. Particularly noteworthy is its focus on the 'cycle' of conflict, ranging as it does on the causes, conduct and end of civil wars as well as on subsequent efforts to return post-conflict society to 'normal' politics.

Theoretically robust and empirically solid, this book clearly charts the course of contemporary civil wars using case studies from a variety of zones of conflict including Africa, Asia and Latin America to produce the most comprehensive guide to understanding civil wars in an interconnected and interdependent world.

Amalendu Misra is Senior Lecturer in the Department of Politics and International Relations, Lancaster University, United Kingdom. He is the author of *Identity and Religion: Foundations of Anti-Islamism in India* (Sage, 2004) and *Afghanistan: The Labyrinth of Violence* (Polity, 2007). He has travelled extensively along the Gulf of Mexico.

Politics of Civil Wars

Conflict, intervention and resolution

Amalendu Misra

Routledge
Taylor & Francis Group

LONDON AND NEW YORK

First published 2008
by Routledge
2 Park Square, Milton Park, Abingdon, Oxon OX14 5RN

Simultaneously published in the USA and Canada
by Routledge
270 Madison Ave, New York, NY 10016

*Routledge is an imprint of the Taylor & Francis Group,
an informa business*

Typeset in Times New Roman
by Swales & Willis Ltd, Exeter, Devon
Printed and bound in Great Britain by CPI Antony Rowe,
Chippenham, Wiltshire

British Library Cataloguing in Publication Data
A catalogue record for this book is available from the British Library

Library of Congress Cataloging-in-Publication Data
Misra, Amalendu.
Politics of civil wars: conflict, intervention & resolution/Amalendu Misra.
p. cm.
Includes bibliographical references and index
1. Violence. 2. Civil war. 3. Conflict management. I. Title.
JC 328.6.M57 2008
303.6'4—dc22
2007046490

ISBN 10: 0–415–40345–6 (hbk)
ISBN 10: 0–415–40346–4 (pbk)
ISBN 10: 0–203–92734–6 (ebk)

ISBN 13: 978–0–415–40345–0 (hbk)
ISBN 13: 978–0–415–40346–7 (pbk)
ISBN 13: 978–0–203–92734–2 (ebk)

For Noël O'Sullivan

And you, my friends from the latest call-up!
My life has been spared to mourn for you.
Not to freeze over your memory as a weeping willow.
But to shout all your names to the whole wide world!
                                    Anna Akhmatova, 1942

Contents

Preface

The renaissance Dutch philosopher Desiderius Erasmus in one of his works mused, 'war is only sweet to those who never experienced one'. Although it has some grains of truth this mode of argument runs into difficulty in the context of civil war. The logic or illogic behind participation (forced or otherwise) in a civil war is a very complex one. Civil war is often about redressing grievances. Those who are drawn to it may commit to the ideology of conflict while aiming to fulfil a particular objective. War may not be a natural condition. But waging war is a condition that aims to change the status quo. Participants in a civil war choose it because it promises them something better than what they have. It is that promise, the belief in a possibility, which dictates the participants' involvement.

A peasant participating in the civil war might entrust his or her beliefs to it in the hope of better land distribution; a militia might commit to it for the promises of a quick fortune; for a rebel leader this might be a chance to grab power in some form and to those countless people who are a part of it the conflict offers the opportunities for a new beginning. While travelling with a note pad in 1930s-post-civil-war Mexico the English writer Graham Greene encounters a doctor who goes on to describe the virtues of such internal struggle. According to this character, ideas that spawn civil wars and revolution are a good thing. For it provides people with something to look forward to that is different from the stale everyday misery. 'It gives people ambition. Puts money in circulation' (Greene 1985: 126). Civil war, then, is not necessarily irrational, but a product of certain rational intentions (Murshed 2002: 387).

If civil war is all about realising a hitherto unrealisable goal, violence is the midwife which oversees the birth and delivery of that objective. Rebels in civil wars from across conflict zones – as I shall highlight in the course of the discussion – clearly revel in the condition of war. For the lack of a better expression I argue that they are captivated by what one might call the 'narcissism of violence'. The condition of war gives an identity to these otherwise nameless individuals. Civil war is a great leveller of differences. A peasant who picks up a musket in the foothills of the Himalayas and cries out his or her defiance against the government soldiers is at once an equal to those against whom s/he promises his/her fight. Prior to his/her baptism into violence – from the perspective of the state – the peasant was barely a human. Civil war, therefore, has a great legitimating quality.

Subversion against the status quo locks the rebels and violence in a tight constant embrace. Sometimes this embrace eliminates all the peripheral reminders among the participants that they could be from different regions, cultures and religions and are speaking a Babel of tongues. What unites them is a yet to be fulfilled common ambition. They are all fired by the same frustration, entertain copious disdain for the existing law, and harbour a violent desire to overthrow the faraway authority.

A civil war is an intramural revolution. As a revolution it engages in transmitting a certain message. Its confident, optimistic rhetoric, at a time when possibilities of change through appeal, discussion, and consultation have retreated from the political process, is a big part of its appeal. But as this study will underscore at times, it is a vision based on little more than the mystique of protest and a refusal to address in any detail the old question: What is to be done?

Unsurprisingly, those who live under the spectre of civil war on a continuous basis invariably end up with a way of thinking that is dominated by the discourse of the conflict. When this permeates too deeply into the psyche of the people it is often hard to desensitise them. For conflict resolution is about making the affected people move forward: to abandon the signposts of the past that dominated their erstwhile world and embrace something new and challenging. Making people believe in this newness can often be a daunting task. My old friend Cathal McCall who once upon a time taught in an interfaith school in Belfast had this rather peculiar experience. He put a deceptively simple Biblical question to some primary school students under his tutelage as to Who Killed Goliath? Those who came from the Catholic background chorused overwhelmingly it was the Protestant Paramilitaries who killed Goliath. Those who came from the Protestant background shouted it was the Irish Republican Army (IRA).

When a society is caught up in the shadow of such absurd logic and stereotypes, re-educating its members to the actual reality and beyond can be a strenuous, time-consuming and above all a very expensive affair. Yet, given the right amount of commitment and investment in all the three areas, people affected by the narrative of conflict can affirm their faith in an alternative future. My own decade-long study of societies affected by civil unrest and communal strife in various parts of the world has inculcated this belief in me.

While it is easy to ignore other people's misfortunes because some of them are so small, especially against the broader political, ideological and physical landscape, there is no real way of avoiding them. When violence is the dominant theme of the narrative there is no available neutral unaffected space to escape to. Recalling his experiences in the Angolan civil war Ryszard Kapuściński wrote, 'It's wrong to write about people without living through at least a little of what they are living through' (Kapuściński 1984: 66). I cannot claim to have experienced a great deal of the sorrow and tragedy of the dispossessed in countless wars of our times whose story is captured in the following pages. Yet, I have encountered the ugly, violent and chaotic face of civil strife in some brooding landscapes. And, as the reader will realise, some of these experiences have found their way into my analyses.

The chapters in this book are products of my reflections over the years. They grew and assumed their own specific identity during my peripatetic academic sojourns in Belfast, Veracruz, Madrid and Lancaster. In all these places I have had the good fortune of having a steady supply of students known for their intellectual curiosity and stimulation. Their inquiries, hesitations and challenges toward some of my ideas eventually helped me sharpen and polish my arguments. But they bear no blame if I have been unable to live up to their expectations in this book.

AM
San Andrés Cholula

Acknowledgements

Writing is a lonely affair. And I don't particularly thrive when left to myself. Over the years I have accumulated an enormous amount of debt to a great many people, for their love, affection and friendship. Now is the occasion to record their contribution.

I would like to extend my sincere gratitude to the following: to Emily S. Rueb, for her love; to Bhikhu Parekh, from whom I never cease to learn; to Natividad Mateos Lucero, for being there; to Ángel Rivero, Francisco Berlin Valenzuela, Jose Jorge Eufracio, Gurharpal Singh, Gaston Alvarez, Beverley Milton Edwards and Peter Glazer for their constant encouragement; to Mark Lacy, Rakesh Agrawal, Graham Chapman, Triloknath Mishra, Cathal McCall, Chris May, Karin Fierke, Mark Garnett, Julie Hearn, David Mena Aleman, Feargal Cochrane, Clare Coxhill, Pramila Parekh, David Denver, Apurba Kundu, Margaret O'Sullivan, S.G. Pandian, Daphne Glazer, Stefan Andreasson, Maria Eugenia Bonilla and Dionisio Trigo Dominguez for their unreserved and indispensable friendship. Thank you all for looking out for me. Lacking your support and warmth I would have been long lost.

My thanks also go to Caroline Hartzell and Michael Pugh for reading and commenting on the manuscript. Craig Fowlie and Natalja Mortensen at Routledge and copy-editor Jane Olorenshaw have been an indispensable source of support. I am grateful to you all for your unfailing help during the preparation of this book.

Finally, I dedicate this book to Noël O'Sullivan, an admirable individual whose contribution to my academic and personal life has been quite simply immeasurable.

Introduction

Civil wars have been a familiar and persistent feature of human civilisation. Although origins of civil war go back to the days of antiquity[1] – since the time humanity organised itself into settled societies with clear rules and laws – it has defied easy generalisations. The complex nature of civil war makes it necessary to inquire not only into its general characteristics but also into the circumstances behind its emergence and prevalence. Civil wars must be treated as an organism capable of going through the cycle of development, decay and eventual demise. To understand this organism first we need to situate it within a clear framework of interpretation.

Graham Evans and Jeffrey Newman in their *Dictionary of International Relations* have defined civil war as 'a protracted internal violence aimed at securing control of the political and legal apparatus' (Evans and Newman 1998: 54). In their seminal study on the subject Small and Singer described civil war as 'any armed conflict that involves (a) military action internal to the metropole; (b) the active participation of the national government, and; (c) effective resistance by both sides' (Small and Singer 1982: 210). According to Kumar Rupesinghe civil war refers to a 'range of conflict situations' occurring within the defined frontiers of a state and undertaken by various internal actors or parties (Rupesinghe 1998: 25).

One might insist, at this point, that conflict between the state and dissatisfied groups or between groups within the frontiers of a state is a familiar and recurring feature in many societies. How then are we to attribute the title of civil war in one particular context and avoid applying it indiscriminately? Equally importantly when does internal disorder assume the title of civil war? Researchers and monitors observing internal violence generally use the number of casualties to determine the nature of the conflict. The Peace Research Institute, Oslo, and Uppsala University's dataset on armed conflicts has set a threshold of 25 deaths per year as sufficient proof to term an internal dispute civil war (Eriksson *et al.* 2003; Gleditsch *et al.* 2002). Another study suggests that when an internal conflict is between two or more identifiable groups and results in at least 1,000 combat-related casualties, of which at least 5 per cent must be incurred on each or all sides, then it qualifies as a civil war (Collier and Dollar 2001).

Some other scholars have interpreted civil war on the basis of prevailing levels of political violence in a state along a continuum (Cornett and Gibney 2003). This form of theorisation moves away from the conventional measurement of lowest and highest threshold of casualties or war dead and instead attempts to gauge the sustainability of violence. To put it slightly differently, it recognises an internal violence as civil war based on the time scale of the conflict. In this particular framework, the longer the period of conflict the higher the chances of it assuming the title of civil war.

A comprehensive description of civil war, however, would have to be something along these lines:

> A condition where there is prevalence of mass violence, primarily within the confines of a single state. This violence is organised by and conducted between at least two political groups. The resulting mortality has a minimum threshold of 1,000 deaths on average per annum with no more than 95 per cent inflicted by one side.
>
> (Eckstein 1980; Misra 2002; Tierney 2005)

While violence is a common feature of civil wars not all forms of internal violence qualify to be included under this category. Revenge killing based on some ancient tribal codes, mass criminality and looting during a temporary absence of order, piracy on the high seas, ransom abductions for profit and many such events, while they lead to a massive loss of life, cannot be termed civil wars (Keegan and Bull 2006: 2). As John Keegan and Bartie Bull argue, the basic formula for defining civil war is fairly simple: the violence must be 'civil' The very use of the term 'civil' in this context would imply that the violence takes place within a national frontier or territory and is waged by civilians and within that territory (Keegan and Bull 2006: 2). Furthermore, the point of this violence must be sovereign rule: combatants engaged in this violence must be motivated by the urge to seize national power, transform it, or maintain it. Even if the engagement in this violence is not specifically about ousting the government and replacing it with a new government of the rebel group's or insurgents' liking, the motivation must be to change the government's policies in a significant manner (Fearon 2007: 3).

A good working definition that includes several of the arguments highlighted earlier is provided by Nicholas Sambanis. According to Sambanis, a civil war can be defined

> as an armed conflict that has (1) caused more than one thousands deaths; (2) challenged the sovereignty of an internationally recognised state; (3) occurred within the recognised boundaries of that state; (4) involved the state as one of the principal combatants; (5) included rebels with the ability to mount an organised opposition; and (6) involved parties concerned with the prospect of living together in the same political unit after the end of the war.
>
> (Sambanis 2000: 444)

Civil war in the words of Angus Calder, can be 'easily interpreted. It is the battling out of internal differences within one country. This is the narrative of people who having formerly lived side by side on more or less neighbourly terms sort themselves out into groups and kill each other' (Calder 1999: 123).

Our reflection on details of language and interpretation is crucial in understanding civil war in its entirety and distinguishing it from other forms of conflicts or wars. Our interrogation of definitions has allowed us to bear in mind that civil wars are protracted conflicts fought within the internal borders of a state. They are not communal conflicts. Civil war is distinguishable from a *coup d'état*. Unlike national wars, civil wars do not unify the society. It is a conflict in which various factions within the same society or state engage in armed fights against each other. The source of this conflict is often the the existence of differences over the prevailing political culture or distribution of resources. Failure to find an acceptable distributive scale for the delivery of political, social and economic resources between constituent communities within a given state often results in violence. When this violent behaviour and activism is persistent and protracted the situation acquires the character of civil war. In sum, civil wars exacerbate latent tensions and differences, and are fought out amid a total breakdown of social and governmental institutions (Mazower 2001: 134).

A minimalist definition of civil war could be constructed along the following framework: civil war is a war that involves civilians. This simplistic interpretation is highly relevant if we contrast civil war participants against the participants in a conventional war. While a conventional war is fought between regular armies and the battle casualties are armed personnel, a civil war is often fought between irregulars and most of the victims are civilians.[2] From the perspective of a civilian, civil war becomes a reality 'when individuals, groups, and factions discover that representatives of the state such as a policeman, judge, soldier or politician no longer speaks and acts for them' (Doyle and Sambanis 2000: 779).

While there is nothing new about civil wars, as such, there has been a significant character change between earlier conflicts and contemporary ones. We benefit enormously in our understanding of the dynamics of civil war if we divide it into the categories of 'old' and 'new' civil wars. Mary Kaldor (1999) provides a useful contrast when she uses a comparative scale to highlight the qualitative differences between the two. Old civil wars were almost always political in nature. Within each opposing faction, people who participated in in the war were tied together through a common political belief or ideology. This broad political belief not only nurtured a sense of togetherness but created space for clearly articulated demands and operated within a framework of controlled violence. To all intent and purposes the belligerents waged the battle or war within a specific agenda with clearly defined targets. While violence was a part and parcel of these conflicts it was never blatantly glorified. Or, to put it slightly differently, violence was legitimised within that particular political and ideological context and was not allowed as a medium for the furtherance of individual self-interest.

Contemporary civil wars are fundamentally different from those of the the past. Because of the presence of multiple and often competing leaderships there is rarely a commonly defined goal. Absence of a clearly defined hierarchy of leadership makes it impossible to promote a common vision within an all-embracing ideology. In those civil wars which are based on a certain ideal, that ideal or ideology is never clearly defined or thought through. Consequently those participating in it have a very thin understanding of the purpose of the conflict. Without a unifying ideology, a collective goal or leadership to lead them their participation and commitment to this conflict remains capricious at best. Unsurprisingly, the masses in whose name the war is waged are very often its most reluctant participants. Typically such conflict during its course picks up many itinerant participants. A significant portion of these participants participates in it to either eke out a living or make a personal gain.

While this is not true of all contemporary civil wars, many do display this characteristic. In this scenario the conflict provides a convenient façade for many opportunistic actors to engage in predatory violence and exploitation (Berdal and Malone 2000; Collier and Hoeffler 2002).[3] As Charles Tilly eloquently puts it, civil wars fought within an opportunistic framework do not contain a distinct causal logic. Very often the actors involved in the conflict embark on a form of 'coordinated destruction' – a framework of interaction that includes varieties of political violence that generate salient 'short-run damage' (Tilly 2003: 14). The new civil wars, thus, are not only perverse but sometimes operate within an illogical paradigm.

Internal conflict or civil war is the most pervasive form of armed conflict in the contemporary international system (Brown 1996; Licklider 1993). The recurring feature of international society following the end of the Second World War is the continuity of civil wars. In terms of incidence of types of wars throughout the twentieth century and into the twenty-first, intra-state or civil war has been more frequent than inter-state war (Harbom *et al.* 2006: 619; Newman 2004: 180). The casualty statistics surrounding civil wars is both shocking and startling. To suggest that we are in the midst of a worldwide civil war will not be an exaggeration (if we consider the number of people affected by it). For instance, in the first quarter of the twentieth century – during the First World War to be precise – only one out of ten casualties was a civilian. By contrast, in the twenty-first century, nine out of ten casualties of war are civilians. Some estimates put the number of casualties in the civil wars in the post-Second World War period at around 20 million, with another 67 million displaced (Sambanis 2003: 1).

Given the fact that we live in a globalised world, contemporary civil conflicts, which are theoretically intra-state in nature, can have severe destabilising effects beyond the immediate boundaries of the state concerned. In an interconnected world the chance of one particular localised conflict spreading across many sovereign frontiers is frighteningly real. The spill-over effects of civil war could take various forms: from the spread of actual war to the flow of refugees, introduction of new diseases, environmental degradation, as well as weapons-smuggling, human-trafficking, banditry, terrorism and other similar inflammatory activities. A civil war also has the power and potential to alter the regional political climate. The best example one could highlight in this context is the Palestinian refugee presence in Lebanon, Syria and Jordan and their consequent involvement in the Israeli-Palestinian conflict. Similarly the civil war in Afghanistan not only attracted close to a dozen external powers to meddle in its affairs for the promotion of their own national interest, but the war eventually altered the profile of international society by precipitating the demise of the Soviet Union (Misra 2004b).

Civil wars have attracted considerable attention in recent years among academic and policy circles. Both these groups have offered several different explanations and interpretation on the causes of civil war. However, none of their assessments can be regarded as exhaustive or given. In Chapter 1, I interrogate the arguments of some key theorists in the field and ask if we can develop a general theory of civil war. In Chapter 2, I assess the role of nationalism in the formation and break-up of nations and the ensuing conflict dynamics. I also posit that nationalism is a Janus-like creature. It can both unite and divide. I argue that a given society or state falls into chaos and anarchy when there is a short supply of national spirit or there is an emphasis on a particular variety of nationalism.

Given the asymmetric nature of confrontation between groups fighting for the control of the state or between the state and insurgent groups, most civil wars give rise to long-drawn-out armed engagement of which prolonged violence is a common feature. Yet some civil wars can be described as simple exercises in nihilism. The dominant question that Chapter 3 sets out to explore is the logic and illogic of violence in civil war.

Although domestic in nature, civil wars have generated considerable external apprehension and anxiety in recent years. The spill-over of the conflict into neighbouring areas, with problems associated with issues such as human rights violations and genocide and their destabilising impact across the region, has necessitated an external response. In Chapter 4, I examine the response strategy of external actors towards these conflicts within the framework of humanitarian intervention, and in the following chapter (5) I assess their post-conflict state-building initiatives.

While it has its merits, external intervention has its limitations in the reconstruction of a post-war state. To a large degree such engagement only provides an ancillary role: limited to bricks and mortars and construction of highways and buildings. The deeper questions about right and wrong and justice and retribution are issues that constantly plague a post-conflict society. If it is to move forward and rebuild a stable future the affected community needs to engage in some form of soul-searching. What are the possible methods and mechanisms available for the post-conflict society to entertain this catharsis? This question is couched in the framework of reconciliation, which I explore in Chapter 6.

Very often civil wars are all about the reorganisation of the power relationship within a given state. The conflict occurs because a certain group or institutional structure manipulates the power relationship to its sole advantage while excluding others from it. One of the key tasks of the post-civil war society, therefore, is to create a framework that allows everyone a stake in the governing process. An inclusive pluralist process to which each individual and group can belong and which it can appreciate is paramount in the context of post-war governance. I chart this process of post-conflict governance in Chapter 7.

In spite of the best intentions of the international community and the firm resolve of those who suffered as a consequence of the conflict to pronounce 'never again', most civil wars, however, have the nasty habit of making a come-back. Hence a study that is intended to contribute to the understanding of civil war cannot avoid looking at ways of putting an end to it forever. What viable methods would one need to employ if one were to make intra-state wars completely and fully redundant? In Chapter 8, I explore that very question.

Finally, a few words about the style and procedures adopted in this book. Since my topic is vast and I am primarily interested in theories and issues, I have not tried to be thoroughly comprehensive in my selection of examples, and many readers will no doubt think of obvious ones that I have failed to highlight and elaborate. Similarly, when I offer some of my extended lists of examples, I may appear to be partial in my selection of evidences. In this work I have cut across disciplines very freely, and have tried to comprehend civil war through a wide variety of lenses. Rather than accepting one fixed approach I apply an integrative contextual analysis in this book, which aims to examine a range of variables that contribute to and affect the overall conflict dynamics in a civil war. This form of integrative assessment, I would like to stress, allows us a most definitive explanation in our understanding of civil wars and in turn helps us find viable conflict resolution methods.

1   Theorising civil war

Civil war is a complex social phenomenon with many interrelated and overlapping dimensions. Over the years it has attracted the attention of scholars from various fields in the social sciences. And they have often proposed their own sets of theories and explanations on its emergence and prevalence. As a result, while there exists a *mélange* of interpretations on the nature and character of civil war there is no commonly agreed position.[1] Given this complexity it is hard to suggest one particular theory that captures the overall essence of such conflicts. This chapter aims to bring civil wars into the purview of a set of theories. I do this by first examining this phenomenon against the conventional arguments about deprivation and protest. This helps us open up the debate by bringing in two interrelated theories, grievance and greed. Having examined grievance and greed theories I propose that these two theories by themselves do not fully explain the prevalence of civil wars in all situations and contexts. At this stage I introduce a set of variables such as ethnicity, religion and poverty in order to build a comprehensive picture on the theories of civil war.

Civil war is actor-oriented. A given society or state may have deep inherited fault lines capable of destabilising it, but it can only rupture in the event of an intervention by a particular individual, group or regime. In the second section of this chapter I probe the ideological underpinnings behind an individual's participation in political violence. I also ask what motivates a rebel leader to take his/her followers on a collision path with the established government. In a similar vein I enquire into the logic behind a state's violent opposition to group-based demands for equity, fairness or in some instances statehood. Furthermore in order to fully appreciate the dynamics of civil war we need to study it in the context of geography. For example, an overwhelming majority of these conflicts usually occur on the borders and frontiers of states. This is an obvious puzzle. What does it tell us? How do we explain such a peculiarity? In the last section of this chapter I focus on the relationship between topography and conflict. By interrogating a set of variables I suggest why the nature of the terrain in a given state is responsible for conflict promotion.

On the causes of civil war

Relative deprivation and grievance

The reason why at a given time a particular state or society should become the radiating point for violence has no easy explanations. However, on the causes of civil war two main schools of thought dominate. For the sake of convenience I shall define these two as traditionalists and modernists. According to traditionalists civil wars are the ultimate manifestations of the collective grievance of a people (Azar 1990; Gurr 1993; Stewart 2000). This traditional theoretical exposition surrounding the dynamics of conflict has emphasised that civil wars are caused by inequality, political oppression and competition over scarce resources.

Grievance theory further posits that opposition to the national state and the emergence of civil war is directly linked to the perception of long-standing deprivation experienced by a particular group *vis-à-vis* another group or groups within that multi-ethnic, multi-religious or multinational set up. By a simple comparison the individual, the leader or the group as a whole makes a fair assessment of what it really deserves and how that expectation or standard can be met. Following this evaluation the individual or the group realises that it has been consistently and methodically kept underprivileged in relation to other constituent groups or communities. As a redress mechanism against this grievance, it usually follows two sets of strategies to remedy that institutional imbalance. In the first instance, it appeals to the government or the governing structure to amend the rules, which would allow the underprivileged and deprived groups to attain relative equality.

In the event of opposition to this demand, or the failure of the national government to attend to these grievances, the response can force that group to adopt strategies that undermine the authority of the state. This could involve protests, law-breaking, attacks on the state and in the ultimate analysis a civil war where that particular group initiates an armed struggle against the state itself. The discourses surrounding the uprising often highlight the conditions of the community as a whole, both uniting the community and representing it as a unified whole against the authority concerned or the state. Some scholars argue that from this point on the issue of relative deprivation in provoking nationalist militant behaviour is fired not so much by personally experienced deprivation but by a general concern over the fate of the entire community, explained within the framework of 'communal' or 'fraternal' deprivation (Kogan Iasnyi and Zisserman-Brodsky 1998: 212).

While grievance theory is crucial in explaining causes, 'the relationship between discontent and participation in strife both are also mediated by a number of intervening social conditions' (Gurr 1968: 1105). In the absence of variables such as favourable support from within the group, help from outside actors and a determined leadership, a group feeling neglected, left out or facing persecution may find it hard to organise itself into an effective rebel group. Furthermore, while exploring grievance theory we need to stress that in addition to securing equity through the capture of various resource bases, civil wars are often fought over a political objective, e.g., control over the mechanism structure or apparatus of the state or the creation of a new independent unit in the form of a sovereign state. As Buhaug and Gates argue, while these are paramount objectives the nature of these objectives ultimately determines the very character of the civil war. A war over control of the state, for instance, would have an entirely different course and character as against a war of secession (Buhaug and Gates 2002: 418).

Ironically it is not only the poor dispossessed and the damned who, when they find themselves in conditions of abject deprivation, voice their discontent by taking up arms against society. The rich and the affluent, when their position is threatened and challenged, can put the society in peril by using the same 'deprivation' or 'grievance' argument. The use of force in this context might amount to an effort to maintain and preserve the status quo. The civil war in Colombia, which has been raging in the country for the past fifty years and has contributed to the near-total breakdown of societal order and functioning of the government, can be viewed within this particular framework. What started as a simple 'self-defence' strategy soon created a veritable web of complexity and confusion that drew the whole society into a miasma of violence.[2]

Greed

Grievance theory and those theorists who stressed this specific factor in their study (Azar 1990; Gurr 1993; Homer-Dixon 1999; Stewart 2000) dominated the discourse on civil war for the greater part of the 1990s. However, at the turn of the century, this traditionalist exposition about articulation of demands and participation in the conflict within the context of grievance was challenged by a new group of scholars who argued that the previous interpretation of the causes of civil war was too simplistic. These modernists developed a radical new approach to the study of civil war. As some of them put it, 'to explain the outbreak of civil war we need to discover the circumstances which favor rebellion' (Collier and Hoeffler 2002: 7).

By using a sequence of models they argued that 'grievance' is rarely the sole motivating factor for participants in civil wars. According to this school, those factors which determine the financial and military viability of a rebellion are more important than objective goals for grievance (Collier and Hoeffler 2002: 1). The modernists situated the causes of civil war in the framework of 'greed' as opposed to the earlier explanation of 'grievance'. This new theory was built around an economic model of rebellion. As one of the early proponents of greed theory wrote:

> This discourse of grievance is how most people understand the causes of conflict. A thorough analysis of the causes of a conflict then becomes a matter of tracing back the grievances and counter-grievances in the history of protest. An economist, however, views conflict rather differently. Economists who have studied the ultimate manifestation of organised crime . . . . . Rebellion is a large-scale predation of productive economic activity.

> (Collier 2003: 3)

Paul Collier and Anke Hoeffler, two of the early proponents of this theory, have argued that countries whose wealth is largely dependent on the production and exportation of primary commodities such as natural resources and agricultural produce are more prone to civil violence than those which are resource-poor. In their view, the presence of abundant lootable resources, rather than competition over limited resources, ultimately explains the presence or absence of civil war in a given state or society. According to Collier and Hoeffler 'We test a "greed" theory focusing on the ability to finance rebellion, against a "grievance" theory focusing on ethnic and religious divisions, political repression and inequality. We find that greed considerably outperforms grievance' (Collier and Hoeffler 2000: 1). Their assessment of the availability of primary commodities and conflict occurrence led them to conclude: 'to understand the causes of contemporary civil wars one should forget about the political and cultural arguments and focus instead on the greed of rebels and especially on their trade in natural resources' (Humphreys 2005: 510).

As we mentioned above, according to Collier 'rebellion is a large-scale predation of productive economic activity' (Collier 2003: 3). Contemporary civil wars, in this formulation, have more to do with rapacious loot-seeking motivations than with higher ideals such as national consolidation or wars over ideologies. Participants in these conflicts, therefore, it would appear 'have more in common with ordinary criminals than with aggrieved, Fanon-style warriors eager for liberation, revenge, or cultural integrity' (Ron 2005: 444). Viewed from within the greed model those participating in rebel activities or civil conflict are like employees working for a wage, and the source of revenue to pay soldiers is the looting associated with the conflict (Regan and Norton 2005: 322). Put simply, according to 'greed' theory civil conflicts appear in those states where there is not only a breakdown of order but when there is also the potential to profit from the presence of lootable resources (Azam and Hoeffler 2002; Collier 2000b; Collier and Hoeffler 2002).

On another level, while interrogating the central hypothesis of 'grievance' theory that civil strife and violence are caused by social divisions and over identity issues, the 'greed' theorists introduced an altogether opposite argument. According to Collier and Hoeffler:

> Contrary to 'greed' theory social fractionalisation measured in ethnic and religious diversity lowers the risk of conflict. For rebel organisations typically recruit their members from a similar background. Thus diversity and ethnoreligious heterogeneity would make it more difficult to generate a large rebel force in order to maintain cohesion during the war.
>
> (Collier and Hoeffler 2002: 1)

Greed *versus* grievance

Which theory then best explains the causes of civil war? Traditionalists like Gurr continue to have a wider appeal, holding that societies which are poor, weak and heterogeneous in their ethno-religious profile are more likely to get sucked into protracted periods of instability and resultant civil war than those which are resource-rich (Gurr 1994 and 2000). The traditional mode of profiling of states within the framework of 'grievance' and subsequently underscoring their susceptibility to conflict holds true in many contemporary civil war-affected societies. Resource-poor and weak states such as Nepal, the Sudan, Somalia, Sri Lanka and Haiti, for instance, are not in the midst of protracted civil wars because of the potential for groups to engage in looting the precious commodities but because of unaddressed grievances and competition over resources.

In spite of the dominance of grievance in many civil war contexts, over the years grievance theory has encountered sustained criticism from various scholars. According to some critics while 'grievance' was crucial, people did not simply jump into revolutionary fervour because they were discontent. The act of rebellion, in other words, requires effective mobilisation strategies: strategies to facilitate consolidation of grievances and which articulate it as one unified whole (Lichbach 1990). In the final analysis it is the ability to mobilise resources that determines the extent of that conflict (Regan and Norton 2005: 321).

When examining 'greed' theory, one realises it is a useful theoretical framework to explain the dynamics of internal violence in some societies. However, the emphasis on 'greed' is somewhat overstated. The idea of a conflict economy where civil war creates an environment in which various combatants pursue the logic of war for personal economic gains and are not particularly concerned with the larger political objective may be overemphasised. While it may be a useful argument economic greed is not a general phenomenon or overriding explanatory variable in contemporary civil wars. There are myriad factors that contribute to the discontent of a certain group or groups of people. According to Mats Berdal, 'on the central question of causes and triggers of conflict, the conclusion is unambiguous: contemporary civil wars simply cannot be reduced to "resource wars" sparked by predatory designs of governments and/or the actions of greed loot-seeking rebels' (Berdal 2005: 691).

Similarly, as other critics have argued:

> Economic incentives and opportunities may be a powerful force in motivating individuals and groups to engage in civil unrest or internal conflict, yet they only gain prominence when they interact with other social, economic and political grievances, interethnic disputes, and security dilemmas in triggering the outbreak of warfare.
>
> (Ballentine 2003: 260)

The rebel greed hypothesis depends on just one of many plausible mechanisms that could underline a relationship between resource dependence and violence (Humphreys 2005: 208). More importantly, the quantitative evidence that 'greed' theorists underscore to make a case does not always stand up to the challenge. The greed-based war economy logic, for instance, fails to explain the civil war dynamics in the Basque country, Chechnya, Colombia, India, Indonesia, Nepal or Sri Lanka, where ideology and normative objectives have clearly been important in fuelling the insurgency, rebellion and the overall conflict (Newman 2004: 183).

On balance both 'grievance' and 'greed' provide a motives in regulating rebel behaviour in contemporary civil wars. Although critical of the traditionalists, the modernists nonetheless have tried to highlight the symbiotic relationship between 'grievance' and 'greed'. As some of the founding members of this school have put, 'in spite of the relatively low explanatory power of the "grievance" model we cannot reject it in favor of the "greed" model and thus combine the two models' (Collier and Hoeffler 2002: 1). Consequently, one could argue that while grievance-based issues are at the core of the process that leads to civil conflict, in the absence of immediate tangible benefits rebels tend to lose their incentive to continue the protest or fight. In order to regulate that self-interested behaviour and maintain a collective that is so vital to the very existence of civil war dynamics some rebel leaders resort to selective benefits and engage in exploiting the resources available in the war zone (Regan and Norton 2005: 319–36). Thus in the framework of modernists, in those settings where there was 'the opportunity and incentive to loot resources', the dormant or otherwise insignificant 'grievance' issues were brought to the forefront. 'Grievance', in this context, served as a façade to allow for the real motivational factor that is greed.

In the following pages, in analysing a sample of case studies across various geographical regions this study will purport to show that neither 'grievance' nor 'greed' are the sole motivational factors influencing the dynamics of civil war. A combination of the two is often the norm in various conflicts. In addition, while both greed and grievance motivate belligerents, there are many other complex and deep-rooted factors that contribute to the overall conflict dynamics. These factors can be identified as issues related to identity.

Politics of identity

A growing body of scholarship has interpreted the rising levels of civil war across the globe as 'identity conflicts' (Misra 2004a; Seul 1999; Smith 1986). What does this exactly mean and imply? In an identity conflict individuals in opposing faction seek out communal alliance based on ethnicity, language, religion, tribal alliance and so on in pursuit of access to natural resources, territory, security and ultimately political power (Lederach 1997: 8). In such situations the secular civic ideology of the state is replaced by narrow parochial alliance systems. Suffice it to say, when the citizenry of a given state view themselves within such an insular worldview the whole narrative of civic interaction is perverted. In an identity-driven charged political atmosphere the 'local cop becomes the Croatian, Serb, or Muslim cop' (Doyle and Sambanis 2000: 779–80).

Within the context of identity I explore the role of three interrelated rubrics. These are ethnicity, religion and class.[3] As Ted Robert Gurr concludes 'it is ethnicity, faith and class which are the key sources of intra-state conflict in contemporary international society' (Gurr 2000). In the discussion below I examine how these rubrics become the focus of attention and contention during periods of civil disturbance. But more importantly, I enquire why people are so easily persuaded by the logic of division, based on these three identity markers.

Ethnicity

What possible role does ethnicity play in civil wars? Is there a direct co-relation between ethnicity and inter-group conflict as many theorists have pointed out (Gurr 1993; Horowitz 1985; Sambanis 2001)? If ethnicity were a divisive factor how would one counter its power and potency in a competitive multi-ethnic situation? In this section, I aim to explore these very questions.

In a deeply divided society ethnicity is defined in terms of four key components: a concept of a real or imaginary homeland, a shared body of cultural beliefs and practices, a historical consciousness which includes a common past and, crucially, identification with and a biological attachment to a particular body of people with a certain racial background.[4] Ethnicity is often a means-based concept, which provides a necessary sense of solidarity within the social movement (Gilley 2004: 1159). Consequently, ethnic conflicts are disputes between communities which see themselves as having distinct heritages (Kaufmann 1996: 137).

While ethnicity is one of the prime explanatory variables in contemporary civil wars, its emergence can be described as relatively recent. Although conscious of their roots many multi-ethnic societies, in the past, had dissociated ethnicity from their political process. Ethnic association in many of these states had been quasi-voluntary, and there was a certain dehistoricisation of ethnicity in favour of a secular modern identity. Initially reluctant, the citizens in these polities had come to terms with a shared notion of identity that was far removed from ethnic markers. This was especially true of the decolonised world and to some extent among the new nations of Europe that emerged after the Second World War. In fact, a majority of the societies experiencing ethnic conflict in recent years had at one point or the other in their career dismantled ethnic boundaries.

The relevant question here, then, is why communities and nations that had once uncoupled the national self from any narrow identification now celebrate their strait-jacket identity, to the extent of bringing grievous harm to others who are not a part of it? In short, whatever happened to that multi-cultural vision of communal coexistence that dominated the political culture at the beginning of the nation's birth? How do we explain the redrawing of these boundaries? Our interrogation of societies that had once committed themselves to distance from ethnicity but now find themselves in the midst of its divisive influence provides a very simple explanation. To a large extent the resurfacing of ethnicity and labelling of citizenry along ethnic identity lines is for the most part a result of dwindling resources and non-egalitarian politics and policy practices in many societies. In this context, ethnicity succeeds in becoming useful to legitimise access to resources and exclusion of the 'ethnic other' (Azam 2001; Hechter 2000). And when big bad men intervene in such matters the conflict spirals out of control.

According Azam 'individuals sharing a common ethnicity are held together by a bond of "ethnic capital"' (Azam 2001). This facilitates the distribution of resources, which is the key to the group's survival. Organised along the principle of 'who gets, what and when', a common ethnicity enhances the group's solidarity. Any rupture in the process of distribution of resources or competition posed by another group, which is organised along the same principles but with a different ethnic identity, creates tensions leading to the eruption of violence. In times of competition over resources and struggle for political control (in order to dictate the laws of distribution), ethnicity invariably becomes an invaluable tool for mobilisation.

As Lake and Rothchild argue, ethnicity,

> by itself does not always cause violent conflict . . . . But when ethnicity is linked with acute social uncertainty, a history of conflict, and, indeed, fear of what the future might bring it emerges as one of a number of major fault lines along which societies fracture.
>
> (Lake and Rothchild 1998: 7)

In other words, an ethnic security dilemma often creates conditions for intra-group conflict. And in times of crises, it all too easily becomes a shorthand method of creating an enemy image, making the other responsible for every failings in the society or state. The civil wars in the Balkans, in Rwanda, in Sudan can all be explained within this framework.

In spite of the cultural hybridity offered by the forces of globalisation, the politics of ethnicity is far from burned out. Ethnicity is important both to identity and to political conflict (Gilley 2004: 1161). In times of crisis, for many, ethnicity provides a sense of location, of belonging, of refuge, of identity, trust, acceptance and security (Cohen 1999: 5). In a multi-ethnic state ethnic diversity has clear economic, political and social consequences. In such a set-up ethnicity all too easily serves as an organising principle for collective action (Hardin 1997). Hence, as Neal Ascherson puts it, 'People will continue to turn against their neighbours and minorities as political lids come off. Freedom in such suddenly compressed societies will continue to release the worst instincts ("better off without them")' (Ascherson 2004: 106). If the current experience with civil wars is anything to go by, more severe conflicts will occur in states that are ethnically polarised (Lacina 2006: 284).

Religion

How potent is religion as a contributing factor in contemporary conflicts? All religions have both creative and disruptive potential. While they can bond by bringing together the faithful, they can also erect boundaries by labeleing the members of society as insiders and outsiders and believers and unbelievers. When demanded, religion has the same 'crowd-pulling' qualities as other ideologies. In fact allegiance towards a particular religion may be far more potent compared to invented secular ideologies. This power has prompted some critics to refer to religions as 'ideologies of order' (Juergensmeyer 1993). While ideologies such as communism or liberalism are considered man-made and the central tenets of these ideals constructed and improvised by men, religion by contrast occupies a different niche. Given that it is believed to have come down from an unseen power which one terms God, the ideology behind it is rarely questioned. Groups, communities, societies and states have harnessed its organising power since the inception of human history. Unsurprisingly it lends itself to power struggles as easily as do ethnicity, race and language but often with more vehemence (Bell-Fialkoff 1996: 75).

Several studies have suggested that from the 1980s onward there has been a steady growth of religion-inspired political conflicts around the world. During this period religious nationalists were responsible for increasingly more violent conflicts in comparison to non-religious nationalist groups (Gurr 1993; Juergensmeyer 1993; Fox 2004: 715). How does one explain this development? Although religion can be a major source of conflict in some societies the larger question that one needs to entertain, however, is whether it is religion alone or the politicisation of religion that is at the heart of antagonism between communities in a given state or society. Reduction of mainstream civic identities and their replacement with faith-based identities is often at the heart of many contemporary religion-inspired conflicts. When a group tries to control the public space and attempts to transform that hitherto secular space through its own narrative that is full of heavy religious undertones the scene is set for a long drawn-out contest between the dominant group and the others. The conflict is compounded if the group that had filled the secular space with its own religious narratives manages to occupy the governing role in national politics.

In the current context, radical mass conversion into politicised religious identities has become possible because of the prevalent breakdown of order, the absence of security and the general sense of loss that individuals experience in many societies. For a desperate people in a time of abject deprivation religion becomes the only constant source of strength. Subscription to a particular faith and blindly fighting for it tooth and nail can sometimes be seen in the same context as an individual's commitment to the issue of race and racial segregation. One could draw a parallel here by using V.S. Naipaul's reflection on the basis of White racism in the Southern United States as recently as the end of the twentieth century. As he points out, 'for poor white people in the Southern landscape, race is their "only identity"'. He goes on to argue, 'someone well-off could walk away from that issue, could find another cause for self-esteem; but it wasn't that easy for the man with little money or education; without race he would lose his idea of who he was' (Naipaul 1989: 29). Viewed within that framework, someone who fights over religion or sectarianism in a multi-religious setting, it is often found, has little or no other recourse to a secure and settled identity. Religion, in this context, by default becomes the only framework of reference for that individual in a tense and competitive social atmosphere.

However, as I mentioned earlier, the individual commitment to this particularised form of identity does not by itself become an instrument of conflict. It is only when this belief system is invoked, provoked and channelled in a particular direction that it assumes an incendiary character. Some key theorists belonging to the instrumentalist school of nationalism such as Anthony D. Smith and Ted Robert Gurr are of the opinion that power-seeking political elites are notorious for using religion as a convenient tool for their own political aggrandisement (Gurr 1993; Smith 1986). For them, religion becomes an attractive option to rally support when a society is faced with deep economic chaos, encountering problems with social integration and the state itself is in imminent danger of disintegration. In this charged atmosphere the self-seeking political elite embarks upon consolidating its authority by introducing a whole new language based on religion.[5] As these elites recast political adversaries as foes of faith, they acquire the support of those whose faith has become their last resort (Hasenclever and Rittberger 2003: 111).

One could also argue that when political grievances are high and there is no other way to present a consolidated opposition, religion appears to facilitate mobilisation for protest and activism. As Seul suggests, the powerful ability of religion to serve the identity-related needs of individuals and groups explain why some conflicts occur along religious fault lines (Seul 1999: 563). In this context Thomas de Waal's musing on the civil war in Chechnya would appear very apt. He wonders, 'How has it come about that a generation of village boys and girls, born in the atheist Soviet Union, have turned into Islamist suicide bombers and child-killers?' (de Waal 2004: 55). Similarly, the basis of civil war in Kashmir is not the result of economic impoverishment, mass unemployment and other such economic maladies, which often are at the heart of a minority community's discontent. The separatist war in Kashmir is a direct result of the majority Kashmiri Muslims' detestation of Indian political control over their territory.

Another crucial point that one needs to bear in mind while examining the role of religion in conflict dynamics is that the type of religion confessed by a group is often a significant factor in inter-ethnic, inter-group and inter-communal relations (Enloe 1996: 198). An inherent prejudice against that particular religion or a skewed understanding of it from an outsider's perspective might have something to do with the conflict dynamics. In multi-religious India, for instance, the civil conflict is much more prominent where groups are divided along Muslim and non-Muslim identity lines as compared to Hindus and non-Muslims. This form of identification or religious marking is a growing worldwide phenomenon now. It is not only found in underdeveloped and developing non-western societies but is found to be well embedded in many modern developed industrial societies as well. In Britain the inter-group relationship between Muslims and non-Muslims is particularly problematic as compared to the relationship between various groups of non-Muslims. This prejudice against Muslims from across various ethno-racial groups was consolidated following several communal riots in the northwest of the country involving Muslims and the state and a steady stream of cases in which radical Muslims participated in various terror plots.

To sum up, religion brings the faithful together and is self-segregating in nature. Religion serves as the key boundary maintenance mechanism in many religiously divided societies. However, its binding strength is only relative. Those societies which exhibit religious homogeneity are no less immune from forms of divisions. The differences here are played out in terms of sect, language, regional identity, resource-holding or more generally ethnicity (Gurr 1993; Horowitz 1985). While religion has unifying qualities it does not necessarily eliminate differences. In those instances when the religious beliefs of two or more ethnic groups converge and allow them to stand united the differences find manifestation in other areas (Enloe

1996: 201). For instance, in Darfur, western Sudan, those caught up on each side in the civil war belong to the same religious category. As several studies have indicated the killers as well as victims of the genocide there are Muslims (Flint and de Waal 2005; Prunier 2005). Similarly, although united by the common faith of Islam various Afghan groups contested and fought against each other, and the civil war dynamics operated along the lines of ethnicity and tribal identity (Misra 2004b).

Poverty

The correlation between poverty and protest is an established feature of human society. Individuals are easily susceptible to forms of violence against the prevailing system during periods of economic hardship and deprivation.[6] This characteristic is shared by almost all cultures, ethnicities and nations. History is replete with examples of not only states but also long-established empires consumed by revolutions which originated in the economic hardship of its ordinary citizens. If one were to apply the above argument in the contemporary context, one would encounter some familiar truths. Most civil war-affected countries in the twenty-first century are in the low-income developing and underdeveloped part of the world (Murshed 2002: 388).

Some common characteristics that these countries exhibit are deep-rooted poverty, massive unemployment, severe economic stagnation and in many cases the complete breakdown of the economic system. As Fearon and Laitin have argued, low gross domestic product (GDP) per capita is indeed a strong precursor of civil war onset because it proxies for state incapacity (Fearon and Laitin 2003). Some other scholars have gone a step further and have argued that among states experiencing civil conflicts, more severe conflict will occur in economically impoverished and weak states (Lacina 2006: 280). If indeed the symbiosis between economic malaise and civil war is a strong one it would be worth exploring the underlying factors that contribute to the breakdown of the economic system in these specific societies.

In those instances where a minority is in possession of a large chunk of the country's wealth and the majority lives in deprivation, the economic divide 'becomes an engine of potentially catastrophic ethno-nationalism, pitting a frustrated majority, easily aroused by opportunistic politicians, against a resented, wealthy minority' (Chua 2003: 28).

In the worst case the minority may experience genocide if the majority feels that by reducing the number of its opponents it will guarantee a better economic future. As Gérard Prunier puts it:

> The decision to kill [Tutsis], was of course made by politicians for political reasons. But at least part of the reason why it was carried out so thoroughly by ordinary rank-and-file peasants . . . was the feeling that there were too many people on too little land, and that with a few less there would be more for the survivors.
>
> (Prunier 1995: 14)

The relationship between poverty, breakdown of governing institutions and the ensuing internal conflict is by no means straightforward (Chege 2002: 147). While many civil war-affected societies are poverty-stricken, not all poverty-stricken societies experience civil war. Some of the poorest countries such as Bangladesh and Burkina Faso or Bolivia and Burundi – to give a broad sample – have not slipped into anarchy. A counter-argument that one could pose here is that while the latter group of countries have not experienced civil conflict, other poor countries like Sierra Leone and Sudan or Afghanistan and Angola certainly have been experiencing it for a significant period. What then is the correlation between poverty and civil war? Is there any generally agreed theory in this regard?

There are various ways of looking at poverty, underdevelopment and the civil war nexus. What one could argue is that while poverty is a denominator in rousing dissent in a society it can only become a destructive force when accompanied by several other factors. According to Collier 'civil war reflects not just a problem for development but a failure of development' (Collier 2003). Similarly, poverty that contributes to civil war is the outcome of much deeper factors such as the influence of political elites who seek mainly to protect their own position, the persistence of dysfunctional institutions, and the prevalence of practices such as corruption and a long history of exploitation (Easterly 2006). Similarly, poverty by itself does not make people kill, but when poverty is accompanied by deep-seated indignity, hopelessness and unmitigated grievances things take an explosive turn (Chua 2003: 27).

The root causes of the problem of civil war in many underdeveloped countries lay in the systematic destruction of state institutions by a succession of corrupt and inept governments, external support for these regimes, rising levels of public grievance, the involvement of predatory internal actors and finally poverty. While poverty *per se* might not have led to more conflicts between communities, it certainly has social consequences that cause destabilisation, displacement, evacuation and tensions between communities in a deeply divided and economically backward country. Structural inequality has been linked to the mass political violence characteristic of many revolutionary movements in the non-western developing part of the world (Regan and Norton 2005: 320). Poverty and low levels of economic development are precursors to ethnic conflict, and economic antagonism explains much more about conflict at the top level involving politicians, bureaucrats and other policy planners in developing societies (Horowitz 1985: 134–5, and 2001). A decrease in the level of deadly ethnic riot in the West in recent years, as one critic cautiously remarks, may be a result of consistent economic prosperity and the extension of its benefit to all the communities within that given state (Horowitz 2001: 561). Conversely a rapid rise in levels of conflict in Africa has prompted some critics to attribute it principally to declining economic conditions (Holloway and Stedman 2002: 173).

A healthy economic system is very often a guarantor of the smooth functioning of the society. The opposite is true of a chaotic conflict-ridden society. Let me highlight two contemporary states to illustrate this point. Exploring the ideological roots of civil war in the Himalayan state of Nepal, one could argue that the seeds of discontent that kick-started the 'People's War' in the country were sown some four decades ago. A callous, cowardly and corrupt capitalist class comprehensively contributed to class oppression in the country. A system of governance that was supposed to nurture equality did little or nothing on that front. The representatives of the Panchayat, largely from the upper castes, helped themselves to the foreign aid that made up most of the state budget, and did little to alleviate poverty in rural areas (Mishra 2005: 7). The Caribbean state of Haiti has been in and out of a continuous spell of civil war whose roots lie in the economic mismanagement dating back to the Duvalier regimes.

The state, the individual and the rebel leader

The state

Our discussion, so far, has probed the role of non-state entities, forces and issues in the overall civil war dynamics. While our earlier statements about 'greed', 'grievance' and 'mobilisation' and their co-relation to civil conflict provide some answers, the explanation will remain inadequate unless we bring another crucial entity into the overall discussion. Here I would like to open up the debate by exploring the role of the state in civil war. It is worth asking, in this context, why some states fall victim to rebellion and civil war while others do not. The dominant theoretical position in this regard is built around three hypotheses. First, when a state is highly autocratic, there is a considerably lower probability of violent rebellion or civil war. Second, when the political institutions in the state allow some forms of popular participation, the likelihood of rebellion has a corresponding increase (Regan and Norton 2005). Third, ensuring a mechanism for opposition groups to protest about what they see as failed policies of the state allows for some of their anger to be deflected and they are less likely to organise themselves into armed opposition (Regan and Norton 2005: 333). Let us now apply these hypotheses to concrete situations and check the validity of the claim.

Hypothesis 1 proposed that violent rebellion is less imminent when the structure of governance is autocratic. Testing this hypothesis against some contemporary autocratic states suggests this to be the case. Iraq under Saddam Hussein, for example, was a dictatorial state but it had succeeded in capping all forms of insurgency to the lowest possible level. The removal of that regime allowed hitherto divided groups to protest against the state. The new triangular violence between Shi'ia, Sunni and the Kurds speaks as much about the erstwhile dictatorial state's ability to contain the differences as much as it does about the crises brought about by the removal of the regime. Moving on to another empirical analysis, this time Burma or Myanmar, we find that a highly fractured society is held together by the reclusive military junta. The opposition against the military regime in Rangoon was minimal when the former followed a strong-handed technique to quell opposition. In those instances when it introduced a small concession (allowing a democratic opposition, in the form of the National League for Democracy in 1989) the state faced a series of rebellions. When it reverted to the earlier tough autocratic framework it succeeded in establishing a sort of enforced calm and the threat of a countrywide civil war receded.

While a dictatorial regime or government may fend off rebellion through repression it is not necessarily an effective long-term tool or means of political control (Regan and Norton 2005: 334). In the long run the regime responsible for maintaining a strong-handed tactic is bound to encounter fierce opposition leading to the loss of its power and the surfacing of an all-out civil war. Post-Saddam Hussein Iraq, again, is an example in this regard. Zaire (now renamed as the Democratic Republic of Congo) had a peace of sorts under the dictatorial regime of Mobuto Sese Seko. His removal in the mid-1990s allowed for the emergence of opposition but nonetheless plunged the country into a vicious civil war from which it is yet to recover. This validates the argument that highly repressive states have a far greater probability of experiencing a civil war following a regime change (Regan and Norton 2005: 334).

Hypothesis 2 is built around the argument that when a state allows for some form of democratic or popular participation there is an increased likelihood of rebellion. While this argument may not have a universal validity it certainly is true in many instances. A case in point is Indian-administered Kashmir. The central government in New Delhi had continually manipulated the political process in the troubled province. When a new political party came into power at the centre it reversed the process and allowed for transparency and greater levels of democracy in Kashmir. This, however, had a counter-effect. Rather than reduce the opposition against the centre the new-found democratic space allowed the Kashmiri separatist groups to engage in a fierce national self-determination struggle. The province has now been in the midst of a civil war for nearly two decades. And in spite of consistent attempts by New Delhi there appears to be very little window of opportunity to bring the conflict to a peaceful conclusion.

Hypothesis 3 underlines that ensuring a mechanism for opposition groups to protest about what they see as failed policies of the state allows for the deflection of some of their anger. As a consequence of this concession, it is argued, the dissatisfied groups are less likely to organise themselves into armed opposition. A large multinational state such as India has reaped the benefits of allowing a democratic opposition to function in its restive faraway provinces. Although opposition to its rule in the northeastern region has been ever present since the country gained independence some six decades ago, New Delhi nonetheless has succeeded in channelling some of that opposition into the emergence of effective democratic oppositions (Misra 2001). Nigeria is another example where this practice has borne some fruit. Other multinational states such as Spain, Canada and Belgium have reaped the benefits of an open democratic system that allows for the opposition to vent its criticism against the state for its policies without actually going down the path of violent rebellion.[7] This mechanism works best in developed Western states.

The individual

That there is a correlation between the behaviour of the state and opposition to its authority from the citizenry can be hardly denied. Very often conflicts between the state and the citizenry have a very modest beginning in protest movements. These movements usually start their campaign using peaceful means. As the campaign gathers momentum its constituents not only become restless but press for the immediate evaluation of their grievances. This forces the leadership of the movement to demand greater concessions from their opponent (the state, governing structure, or the group at the helm of the power hierarchy). The normal response of the authority at this juncture is not only to refuse to give in to the demands but respond to the opposition by means of violence and repression. Once physical repression finds its way into the process the opposition retaliates by using its own means of violence. Therefore what started as a protest movement metamorphoses into rebellion and possibly civil war (Gurr 2000; Regan and Norton 2005). Thus contrary to popular belief civil wars do not emerge fully formed from the wellspring of discontent but rather move from lower levels of unrest toward large-scale violence and civil war (Regan and Norton 2005: 326).

In their study Regan and Norton (2005) also argue that participation by individuals in civil war may have also to do with fears of state repression. As they put it, when the opposition engages in violence, high levels of state repression become a natural outcome. This, in turn, makes the potential rebel supporters conclude that the probability of punishment is high and approaching certainty. This perceived fear of state repression eventually forces the potential supporters to join the movement in pursuit of protection from random violence or punishment by the state (Regan and Norton 2005: 326). To a large extent individual participation in civil war is also determined by the nature of the rebel leadership. In the absence of an effective rebel leadership capable of consolidating the anger of the masses the conflict may remain sporadic at best and subdued at worst.

Put simply, the rebel leadership's manipulation of the fear, anxiety and grievance of the individual can push a society into the throes of civil war. Throughout history, leaders have enjoyed the trust of the people they represent. Therefore, their narrative and interpretation of a given conflict has the ability to mould the thinking of the masses and eventually lead them in a particular direction. For instance, although most multinational or ethnically divided societies contain the dynamics of conflict, it spirals out of control only when the elites interpret it according to their own vision. A closer inspection of many of the contemporary civil wars across the world revealed that some of these conflicts received momentum and pushed the society into the darkest depths of violence when the elites of that society manipulated their followers to think and behave in a particular way. The stoking of Serbian xenophobic nationalism by Slobodan Milosovic that led to the massacre of thousands of Muslims in the former Yugoslavia is a case in point. The genocide in Rwanda was started by the Hutu elites. In Sri Lanka the Sinhalese leaders too put a wedge between the majority Sinhalese and minority Tamils by their incendiary verbal attack on the minorities. This, as we shall see later in this study, gave credence to Tamil separatism.

The rebel leader

Once in charge, rebel leaders often pursue authoritarian strategies in their organisational principles. This, it is clear, is primarily aimed at consolidating and presenting the group as a united opposition against the state. For the conventional argument suggests that if a group is divided it is weak and can never be an effective opposition. Absence of a united front then would always prevent it from achieving a strong bargaining position. Such military-strategic philosophy is always present when a dominant and powerful leadership introduces itself to the affected group or populace. This is primarily done in order to gain legitimacy in the eyes of the constituency. This strategy, while it allows the key rebel group and its leadership to launch an offensive against the authority, also makes it extremely vulnerable in the long run. For instance, if the rebel movement has consolidated itself as the sole spokesgroup by way of intimidating its other opponents and has silenced the democratic opposition, then the state might attempt to discredit it by questioning the rebel group and its leadership's very legitimacy and show reluctance to enter into any negotiation.

In the second scenario, the rebel leadership may encounter questions about its very existence if it fails to achieve the targets that it had promised to its constituency. An affected population which had put its faith and trust in the logic of that particular group's philosophy and strategies of revolt is easily disillusioned if the conflict goes on for a long time. It begins to calculate the cost to civilian life and liberties and wonders if it should continue supporting the rebel leadership. Once this doubt appears in the psyche of the affected group the conflict takes an entirely new turn. At this juncture, the leadership may enter into predatory tactics, which involves intimidation of the constituency which had originally placed its confidence in the rebels. Now the revolution turns inward. In a desperate attempt to hold on to guns the insurgents and the leadership turn against the group for which they were supposed to be fighting. Examples of such recalcitrant anti-populist rebel behaviour can be found in almost all civil conflicts from Peru to the Philippines and Sri Lanka to Sierra Leone.

In Peru, the rebel Sendero Luminoso or Shining Path leadership that fought a bloody war against the central authorities in Lima (from 1980 to 1995) in the name of the poor, deprived and unrepresented indigenous Indians of the country turned against that very destitute constituency when it failed to make any significant strides on their behalf. From 1980 until his capture in 1992 Abimael Guzman's Sendero Luminoso was responsible for the killing of thousands of poor helpless peasants in its attempt to create a countrywide opposition against the Peruvian state. As the killings grew so did the disillusionment of the peasants. Following Abimael Guzman's capture those peasants who had initially put their faith in Sendero abandoned its philosophy and tactics without so much as a second thought. In Sierra Leone the Revolutionary United Front (RUF) led by Foday Sankoh launched an insurgency in 1991 bent on controlling the government and the country's lucrative diamond fields. Initially supportive of the RUF, the Sierra Leoneans slowly got disenchanted by its approach when Sankoh's RUF followed the tactic of abduction and recruitment of young boys and later forced them to kill friends and family members in this mindless conflict.

Many civil wars acquire a protracted nature not because people at the grassroots level wish to pursue the struggle persistently but solely due to the recalcitrant attitude of the leadership. The Angolan civil war went on for almost three decades owing to the dogged refusal of its main rebel leader Jonas Savimbi to enter into any peace agreement. He was consumed by the logic of insurgency and rebellion. When his trusted lieutenants and supporters tried to persuade him of the futility of the continuation of the armed struggle when there was scope for a countrywide peace dividend Savimbi turned against these very supporters and had them killed in their thousands. As the conservative *Economist* magazine argued in its obituary on Mr Savimbi, the rebel leader 'was not the sole cause of Angola's civil war, but he was probably the most important reason why it lasted so long' (The Economist 2002).

There is no doubting the fact that a rebel leader's self-defined job in a conflict zone is to oppose and fight against oppression, inequality and intimidation. But as recounted in the previous few paragraphs these actors in some of the worst civil war-affected societies pursue agendas which serve their own self-interest. As Burke reflected two centuries back, 'when men of rank sacrifice all ideas of dignity to an ambition without a distinct universally respected object, and work with low instruments and for low ends, the whole composition becomes low and base'.

Geography of conflict

Civil war is almost always about control of territory, the resources within it and contest over the centres of power in the form of capital city, administrative headquarters or financial centres. In all these instances geography is never far away from the discourse on civil war. Yet, there is very little discussion about geography in the definite analysis of civil war. In this section I will explore this particular neglected aspect.

It is the topography of the given state which often dictates the nature of the conflict. Civil wars are most common in large multinational states. These entities with diverse ethno-religious constituencies contain a higher number of peripheral and possibly marginalised groups. Owing to the vastness of the territory and the weak reach of the government in all its aspects of authority (administrative, economic, political and military) in these outlying areas the state remains rather marginalised. When the state, and the groups living in these far-flung areas, find themselves within such a framework of relationship the groups feel very little in common with the state. An inaccessible and rough terrain aggravates state weakness because of the expensive infrastructure investment necessary to control these sparsely populated regions (Fearon and Laitin 2003: 80). The absence of state presence, consequently, provides easy movement to rebels and insurgents (Lacina 2006: 281). This state of affairs invariably leads to a growing divide between the two. Over time, if this condition continues, the centre–periphery divide finds a new momentum through the opposition against the state mostly along the lines of secessionist insurgency (Buhaug 2006; Misra 2002). Once afflicted by this condition these peripheral insurgencies operating on the state's frontiers assume an intractable nature and are remarkably difficult to end (Fearon 2004: 277).

Staying on the topic of topography and civil war we also need to remember that the rebel objective is often dependent on the size of the territory. For instance, countries with a large territory or land mass will witness very few organised attempts to seize power at the centre by rebel groups. This is simply because given the enormity of space the state would have the power and ability to deflate or marginalise rebel behaviour before it approaches the centre of political authority – the capital city. Large multinational states such as India, Indonesia and Russia fit into this category. Although all these states have witnessed occasional attacks on their capital there has never been any serious attempt to seize the power of the state. Since these are multinational states most of the rebel behaviour has tended to be identity-based, involving attempts to break away from the mainstream. In India the civil war in Kashmir is a secessionist war where the logic of rebel confrontation is based on the establishment of a separate homeland. In Russia, Chechens are fighting for independence. In Indonesia too, in Ache and West Papua, the attempt is to break away from the authority of Jakarta.

While large states tend to have identity-based civil wars fought within the centre – periphery divide, small states may have both identity- and non-identity-based civil wars fought primarily over the control of the entire territory. While civil unrest and civil violence leading to civil war in multinational states is invariably geared towards separatism it is less so in political entities which are geographically small. Smaller countries rarely have separatist civil wars. Thus the conflicts in such countries are geared more towards capturing the state apparatus and installing the rebel government. Given the smallness of the territory and the limited wealth it possesses the rebels are not persuaded by the logic of dividing the country; rather the central aim here is to disenfranchise one group of individuals with a certain racial, ethnic or ideological background and appropriate all the resources. The state of Haiti in the Caribbean, which has witnessed several civil wars since the 1990s, falls into this framework of explanation. And so does Timor Leste or East Timor in the Indonesian archipelago.

Medium-sized states with a homogeneous ethno-religious profile on the other hand are more susceptible to countrywide war. Absence of any ethno-religious fissures and actual centre – periphery divide in geographical terms does not support any kind of separatist civil war in such states. The nature of the conflict in these instances is over ideology and the objective of the insurgents is to introduce a completely new order in the form of a new government. Thus the conflict on these occasions is more widespread. According to Buhaug and Gates:

> Rebel groups or belligerents that aim to introduce complete transformation of the political process will try to seize control of the state from their adversary and therefore will fight their wars closer to the centre of power i.e. the capital and other commercial and administrative cities.
>
> (Buhaug and Gates 2002: 421)

States that are considered medium-sized in terms of their geographical area with a relatively homogeneous ethno-religious profile have all fallen prey to rebel attacks on their capital for control of the state. Afghanistan, Somalia and Sierra Leone provide good examples in that direction.

If anything, a study of the actual location or geography of the conflict tells us a lot about the nature and character of the civil war, the rebel objective and the direction in which the conflict will finally go.

Conclusion

The causes of civil war in the contemporary world are limitless. Within a broad framework there are endless variations: every civil war differs from every other civil war, not only in terms of its dynamics, but in projection, goal and overall ideology. Each civil conflict operates according to the logic of its own inherited grievance and seeks to redress it according to the demands of that society and the opportunities that the larger political system offers. Consequently the narrative of one civil war in a given geographical region, culture or setting usually has very little similarity to any other. Naturally one cannot have a standardised formula to assess the nature and character of civil wars.

In spite of this complexity, our preceding discussion underscored several key findings. Exploring the variables that trigger conflict we realised that although division and difference is a norm in most contemporary societies it is competition among a divided constituency over resources, influence and power that creates fissures within that society and eventually leads to some form of unrest. In addition, we also found that those states which are poor, have massive regional imbalances, have autocratic governing structures and are led by corrupt leaders are more likely experience forms of organised violence against the state leading to civil war than those where none of these conditions exists. And finally, identity issues also contribute to conflict dynamics in some divided societies.

A healthy and peaceful society is a self-regulating organism. It is held together by a *modus operandi* called a social contract. It is only when there are fissures in this contract that conflict appears. The early indications of these fissures can be found within the following sets of questions: (a) How do its corresponding members view their associations within that contract? (b) How do they imagine the future of that contract? In the event of an erosion of the egalitarian principle in the contract some groups may try to repair it by opposition, protest and in the ultimate analysis by taking up arms. Equally importantly if the future of that constituency starts to appear very uncertain and indeed so uncertain that they doubt their own safety within the contract (Addison and Murshed 2006: 139) then they may attempt to withdraw from it altogether. These two are the abiding concerns in all civil wars.

On balance one could emphasise that in all societies at all times there exist both the potential for conflict and the potential for peaceful coexistence (Bringa 2002: 216). But, in the ultimate analysis and quite frequently, which of these two components becomes dominant is dependent on what the economically and politically powerful in a society whom we term *elites* choose to stress. Societies that have gone through or are undergoing a radical transition, where state structures and the institutions regulating law and order have disintegrated or are in decay – as was the case in former Yugoslavia, Rwanda, Somalia, Iraq, Afghanistan and so on – have a greater potential for conflict, and they are arguably more vulnerable to spurious ideologies, individuals and organisations that seek to exploit the potential for conflict (Bringa 2002: 216).

Civil wars are also a manifestation of the unsolved debate surrounding the capable and incapable state. The state's failure to live up to its distinct personality – as the sacred institution competent of delivery – often breeds discontent among its citizenry. Many conflicts in the underdeveloped and developing world that escalate into civil wars have often their origin in the disempowerment of a people in its numerous forms. The resolve of that people to turn the tables is what leads to violent confrontations. A state may be engaged in its celebratory mood for its supposed achievements but if the peasants, workers, students, activists wonder if anything has actually been achieved, then the state has a difficult time maintaining its legitimacy. In the next chapter I focus on the role of the state and its central ideology, i.e. nationalism, in order to explain the absence and prevalence of conflict dynamics.

2 Poverty of nationalism

Nationalism is an overarching, all-encompassing ideal that provides a basis for the continuation of communities with both distinct and varied backgrounds to participate in a common political project. It is one of the most crucial ingredients for the successful functioning of a state. It is an ideological movement for the attainment and maintenance of autonomy, unity and identity of a human population (Smith 1999: 37). A political community inherits a particular brand of nationalism through three main progressions. First, a primal origin and a sentiment of commonality based on a shared ethno-linguistic and ethno-religious milieu often create conditions for the emergence of primordial nationalism. Second, communities who had experienced some form of external manipulation of their political process, such as under colonialism, develop a sentiment of unity through the administrative structures of the state and project a unifying national sentiment. The nationalism to which they commit themselves is often described as an artificial construct. Third and finally, some societies deeply committed to rationality and modernism evolve a form of civic association between all the constituent communities of the state. This spirit and sentiment finds its manifestation in what is often described as civic nationalism. Civic nationalism seeks to constitute a sense of common belonging among a diverse populace by means of a common appeal to what Jürgen Habermas has called 'constitutional patriotism' and simultaneously to treat the nation as open to all individuals and communities who come under and accept the jurisdiction of the civic institutions (Habermas 1991; MacCormick 1999). Within the framework of civic nationalism the constituent members construct a framework of 'we' from a population divided by ethnicity, religion, class, language, local and regional interest and numerous other differentiae.

However, there are several ways through which this spirit of nationalism can be lost. When this spirit dissipates dissent becomes the norm and in place of one overarching national sentiment or national identity bound together by one brand of nationalism there appear multiple visions of nationalism. This is a condition, I argue, which can be termed as the failure of nationalism. When that occurs violence becomes the dominant narrative of interaction between groups and communities. Put simply, when nationalism fails civil war appears.

In this chapter I am going to look at the theory and practice of nationalism, and ask if there is a certain ideal that nationalism presupposes. Having done that, I will underscore how that ideal faces erosion and is eventually lost, an event which marks the onset and eventual consolidation of civil war. The thrust of my argument in this chapter is that levels of nationalism and national sentiment determine the level of violence and conflict in a given state. I will use the terms state, nation and nationalism interchangeably but they all aim to convey the same meaning in the discussion that follows.

Objectives of nationalism

One of the stated objectives of nationalism is to integrate groups with varied backgrounds into a unified whole.[1] It does so by allowing every individual and group an equal stake in the collective ideal of national spirit. This collective ideal is manifested in a democratic and participatory nation where every constituent member enjoys what may be called democratic citizenship. The existence of the nation is made possible by the participation of free individuals in this collective called nation. For its part, following the membership of individuals and groups, the nation not only becomes the chief guarantor of security to each member but also maintains a political system that allows for the distribution of goods and services to everyone. The principle of equality and transparency, in this context, acts as the chief motivating factor in the participants' allegiance to the nation and consequently its key ideal expressed in the idea and ideal of nationalism. 'Nationalism', then, 'is the political utilisation of the symbol of nation through discourse and political activity, as well as the sentiment that draws people into responding to this symbol's use' (Verdery 1996: 228).

The above scenario, of course, is an ideal condition. Those who succeed in achieving this ideal condition not only fulfil their obligation as a nation but also succeed in maintaining it. Those that fail to live up to such standards naturally fall prey to civil unrest, violence and eventually civil war. If we were to discover why some societies succeed in achieving that ideal and others do not we need to look at the formation of the nation itself. According to some scholars the 'nation' is not an 'eternal category'. It is the product of a long and complicated process of historical development (Hroch 1996: 79). Those who have gone through this historical development exhibit all the features of a matured nation and as a result, are less susceptible to unrest, instability and civil conflict. The idea of nation, in this context 'is strongly connected to the idea of civil peace, which presupposes the presence of a broad majority that freely bestow their allegiance to the central power and feel that they participate in the polity' (Addi 1997: 111).

A society affected by civil war, by contrast, lacks some of the above conditions, and is characterised by the following features: (a) the nation in question is rather young; (b) because of its relative recent beginnings the consensual value system found here is rather fragile. Let me explore these two issues in detail. Theoretically a young nation is not a liability in itself. Yet, from a practical perspective because of its newness its reach among the citizenry or overall consolidation is never total. This argument is best explained in the context of the newly formed developing and underdeveloped states. In most of the developing world the nation that came into existence following the anti-colonial struggle has failed to maintain either its sanctity or its legitimacy among those who were the very participants in its creation.[2] Why such an anomaly?

To explain this anomaly we need to ask what nationalism demands in this particular environment. The traditional manifestation of nationalism or national ideology was set within the context of one single group. Nationalism in this instance came to be synonymous with the manifestation of that group's goals and aspirations. But many of the post-colonial states which have now fallen victims of civil unrest, violence and wars were multi-ethnic entities which on occasions contained two or more nations. How were they to have a nationalism which would rise above the earlier 'one group-one nation' definition?

To be fair many of these polities initially entertained a form of nationalism that was not specific to one group but was an all-encompassing ideal with several different groups affirming their allegiance to it. Nationalism in such a setting was based on the structural integration and unification of various groups and their nationalities into a unified whole. The success of this unified ideology was dependent on the presence of justice, equality and fairness across the board and the establishment of a national self. In a diverse multi-ethnic or multi-cultural setting it was vital that the state rose above all narrow group or sectarian interest and adopted a model which represented all citizens, equally and served their interests without bias.

The state in question could aim to develop a national ideology or infuse a sense of nationalism through the adoption of a system of equality that was highly transparent. Fulfilment of this prime objective had the ability to nurture a mainstream and unified national identity. Creation of this uncontested national self allowed for the ushering in of what one might call civic nationalism. This new framework, while paying equal attention to all the diverse constituent members in the polity, also presented the state as culturally neutral.

Many states in the developing and underdeveloped world that have now fallen victim to civil wars originally tried to bind the society through this glue of post-colonial civic nationalism. As Kalevi J. Holsti wrote 'the colonial state, an organism that left legacies primarily of arbitrary boundaries, bureaucracy, and the military, was taken over by leaders who believed they could go on to create real nations and master the new state' (Holsti 1996: 71). But as the evidence suggests, the post-colonial nation-state had always had a difficult relation with its constituent members. In the first place, it was not always successful in maintaining the identity of a neutral national self to which everyone could express their uncontested allegiance. Secondly, 'it was unable to make power impersonal or tame the influence of tribal, clan, group-based or clientelist politics. To put it slightly differently, the central power proved powerless to promote a public sphere where a political citizenship of the universalist type could be exercised' (Addi 1997: 120).

As the nation in question was relatively young and was operating on limited resources there were always challenges to its authority. Consequently the original ideal of civic nationalism came to be replaced by group-based clientelist politics. Many of these states, of course, tried to counter such challenges, but most failed in

their efforts. As a desperate last-ditch attempt to reinforce the ideal of civic nationalism, in some instances the state resorted to what one might call imposition of fear
through force. Unfortunately, instead of undermining the power and influence of
the groups opposed to the civic nationalism project the application of force only
made them stronger in their resolve to replace this model. Eventually there emerged
a scenario where every domain of interaction came to be contested within that given
state. The situation was typical of minorities and majorities increasingly clashing
over such issues as language rights, regional autonomy, political representation,
education curriculum, land claims, immigration and naturalisation policy, even
national symbols, such as the choice of national anthem or public holidays
(Kymlicka 1995: 1).

While it is true that failure of civic nationalism was the harbinger of violence and
civil conflict, one needs to remember that people or groups simply do not hurry into
the melee if they are dissatisfied with the dominant ideology or the direction in which
the government is taking them. Failures of the social contract and failures of
development create conditions of deep social inequality which results in the erosion
of the ideology of nationalism. This condition consequently tips the society into an
imbalance and pushes it into the throes of civil war. As Blimes argues, 'when a central government is unable to provide credible guarantees of future security for groups
within the state, a condition of anarchy prevails within it and groups take it upon
themselves to provide security' (Blimes 2006: 537). When there is the demise of the
national self, societies fall prey to the logic of division, use incendiary language and
behaviour against their fellow members and develop a propensity for violence.

Emergence and decline of nationalism

One of the enduring explanations for the causes of civil war is pitched within the
context of decolonisation and nationalism. It is now commonly agreed that colonial
administrative practice often fostered an atmosphere of distrust and division among
the colonised. In some cases it was inevitable, as 'the colonial state brought many
quite separate and distant ethnic communities and categories under a single political jurisdiction, increasing both the scale of politics and the chances of conflict over
centrally distributed resources' (Smith 1991: 131). But in many cases, in order to
prevent the coalescing of unity among these 'separate and distinct communities'
the colonial state introduced the idea of inter-group division. Such divisions and
animosities implanted among the colonised during the colonial period were subsequently carried forward by that particular constituency into the post-colonial phase
(Misra 2004a).

The process of colonisation had effectively denied the 'natives' any authority in
the decision-making process or power play. The process of decolonisation, however, allowed these communities to take control of natural resources, to consolidate
their territory and to establish group autonomy, and so on. Once in power, however,
the new rulers could not distance themselves from the logic of division which their
ex-colonial masters had implanted in their society. This was one of the reasons
why the 'natives', once they assumed power, had difficulty ensuring an equitable

system of governance. The explanation as to why they behaved in this particular manner is fairly simple. First, being excluded from the decision-making process for a very long period of time (often spanning centuries) they had lost the capacity to govern themselves effectively. Second, through a 'divide and rule' policy the colonial administration had implanted the seeds of deep division among various groups which some of them found hard to eliminate.

According to I. William Zartman the civil wars in post-colonial states typically exhibit three key characteristics. In the first phase, the society finds itself in the midst of a deep crisis leading to civil unrest and war owing to the 'decolonisation power struggle' (Zartman 1989: 12). In this scenario, individuals, groups and communities who had once worked, united, against their colonial subjugators fight against each other over political power. Power, to quote Henry Kissinger, assumes the properties of 'aphrodisiac' for these communities and they try and use every possible means to restrict it to their own groups.

In the second phase, if the society as a whole manages to avoid the divisive tendencies associated with power it nonetheless faces other key challenges. The process of decolonisation often leads to national consolidation in the newly independent state. During this phase the leaders try to strengthen their authority by proposing a particular brand of national identity and demand that all the constituent members of the state pay allegiance to that specific brand of nationalism. In a heterogeneous landscape this often proves to be the recipe for conflict. Groups and communities which emerge as minorities in this consolidation drive often find this new arrangement hard to accept. According to Hasenclever and Rittberger, 'if serious political and economic cleavages exist in a nation, it should be easy for political entrepreneurs to give meaning to these cleavages in terms of cultural, ethnic, or religious discrimination' (Hasenclever and Rittberger 2003: 112). When this grievance is channelled through an organised leadership backed by a sizeable constituency of supporters it is seen by the governing community as anti-national and the state begins to impose a process of forced homogenisation that gives birth to sub-nationalism, irredentism and secessionist struggle and eventually pushes the society towards civil war.

Now we come to the third explanation. The euphoria that accompanies decolonisation is at times so strong that some societies do actually ignore any form of disparity or deep underlying division between the constituent groups and communities that make up the state.[3] Those groups or communities who feel disadvantaged in this new arrangement accept the fact that such deficiency is bound to exist in the short and medium term but believe the society and the state as a whole would be able to evolve and move towards a consensual political arrangement in the longer term. Consequently both the majority and the minority community embark on a nation-building initiative in the spirit of true cooperation and inter-communal harmony. The allure of achieving something great and permanent allows these communities to stay together in a tightly forged close partnership.

However, when that given society spends a significant amount of time, energy and effort trying to achieve its target objective and realises that it is not only hard to reach that objective, but it may be impossible to achieve that objective, then it shows strains of fatigue. The first casualty of this failed nation-building process is communal solidarity. When communities that once worked towards those grand objectives find themselves in the midst of failure they look for scapegoats to carry the blame. This creates fissures in the society. Groups who feel most dissatisfied introduce their breakaway strategies. When the power-holding authority or the state tries to oppose these moves conflict ensues.

Such internal contradictions were the key sources of the breakdown of order in various newly independent states in Africa, Asia and Latin America. Very often, in challenging circumstances, these contradictions were played out within a broad range of dissents. In some places it led to the rise of peaceful democratic opposition, in others it manifested in rebel insurgency movements, and in many others it led to an open declaration of secession. Those political units or states which were weak soon fell into disarray and encountered territorial division. Yet, those states which were a bit more powerful and had an organised economic and military machine at its disposal tried to throttle the voice of dissent and opposition. This approach, while successful at the beginning, could never allow the state an all-out victory over its opponents. What followed, therefore, was long drawn-out low-level domestic warfare.

The internal security situation in many newly independent underdeveloped states with heterogeneous ethno-religious profiles became worse during the Cold War years. During this period, in their competition to attract converts to their ideological camp the two superpowers, i.e. the United States and the Soviet Union, took an active interest in the domestic politics of many underdeveloped, developing and fragile states. Their involvement in the internal politics of these states often led to disastrous consequences when groups fought bitter wars against one another (usually with the military and economic support of the superpowers) to control the powerbase.

Civil wars during Cold War

One could argue, as a general rule, most civil wars between the end of Second World War and the end of Cold War had been proxy wars: nasty skirmishes at the margins of a strategically bigger struggle. Given that the United States and the Soviet Union were adversaries, they both influenced and intervened in small internal disputes in various locales around the world from Africa to Central America and Indochina to the Middle East.

Cold War politics created conditions in which superpowers forced tiny vulnerable states to enter into a patron–client relationship. This facilitated the dominance of local strongmen who stayed on in power through external support and remained oblivious to the needs of the citizenry in general or the suffering of minorities in particular. In many instances such repression backed by one of the superpowers created conditions of insurgency and armed uprising for which another superpower provided material and ideological support. Their meddling in domestic issues turned small disputes into raging civil wars affecting not only that particular state but often the entire region and international society. The civil war in Afghanistan,

Guatemala and Vietnam, for instance, not only destabilised whole regions but had a profound effect at the global level.

While it may sound perverse, at another level Cold War politics forced some societies to stay together. Through a vast money and military machine these superpowers often guaranteed the territorial integrity of many countries with deep social divisions. Such interference, while it succeeded in keeping the national frontiers of some states intact, did very little in terms of national consolidation, social cohesion or the promotion of a unified nationalism. The end of the Cold War, which also initiated the end of the patron–client relationship, created a sudden vacuum in many client states. The first casualty of this change in status quo was social cohesion.

Following the end of Cold War, as 'the vast superstructure of conflict retreated, shrivelled up and withered away' (Wendt 1994: 165), conditions allowed for the small and medium-sized local conflicts to raise their head. In many of these societies individuals, groups, and communities with contesting identities and ideologies were bound together within the framework of an externally sponsored political and, frequently, economic order. The absence of these two key pillars in that given society precipitated old rivalries. In the new changed climate old animosities resurfaced at the slightest provocation and divisions were easily reinforced.

Globalisation, the state and civil war

Some contend that most civil wars – whether involving ethnic groups, ideological factions, or any other social category – have a way of manufacturing their own inevitability (King 2001b: 168). While there is some truth in this, the argument I would suggest is overstated.

Traditionally the states and their citizenry functioned within a symbiotic relationship. This symbiosis can be explained in terms of the duty of the state to achieve certain objectives on behalf of its citizens. The citizens, on their part, were obliged to recognise the authority of the state in lieu of the services provided by the latter. As John Gray put it 'now, as in the past, the legitimacy of states was based on the premise as to how far they meet vital needs of its citizenry' (Gray 2001). In the twenty-first century, however, national consolidation and state maintenance – where the state is a relatively modern institution – has become an expensive affair (Orr 2002). The demands placed on the state were simply enormous. When the dominant institution of society lost its capacity to perform in some instances it lost its legitimacy. In those situations where a certain group in the population harboured a long-standing grievance, the dialectics between governing and the governed was altered forever. This condition not only led to the breakdown of order and a new interplay of power and counter-power but also precipitated the rearrangement of the dominant narrative of nationalism.

A large number of societies experiencing civil war situations are those where the state has been unable to deliver (Berdal and Malone 2000) or are either unable or unwilling to carry out their end of the 'social contract'. But how did the state come to be in this scenario in the first place? Although there are several explanations as to why the state has become a moribund institution in some settings, it is important that we first of all study this problem from the perspective of globalisation. I use the neo-liberal theory to underscore the correlation between development and stability as well as anti-globalisation theories to assess the latter's key assumption that the challenges posed by globalisation have precipitated the conflict potential in many weak and vulnerable states. In this context I will examine the validity of the argument that 'civil war is actually caused because of unexpected global economic pressure and the concerned society's incapacity to meet it'.

The liberal economic theory has been consistent in its argument that the greater the economic affluence of a society the smaller the chances of it encountering either inter-state or intra-state conflict. Cross-national quantitative studies over the past fifty years or so have overwhelmingly proved that to be the case. The relatively stable economic condition in the western world and the consequent social stability in those regions also validate that argument.

In addition, liberal theory has also proposed that an increased interconnectedness with the larger global economy can assist states with deep ethno-religious and other forms of fault lines to avoid instability in those areas. Although it has its critics the basic thesis behind this theory appears to work in most cases. In an engaging quantitative cross-national study Quan Li and D. Schaub showed that socio-political stability in a given state was directly affected by the level of foreign direct investment, capital inflow, foreign trade, and so on (Li and Schaub 2004: 254–5). In sum, the greater the respectability of a given state in the international or global economy the greater the chances it had of escaping the threats of internal socio-economic instability which are often the forerunners of civil unrest and war. For globalisation's enthusiasts, the cure for group hatred and ethnic violence around the world is more markets and more democracy.

This correlation between the levels of economic integration of states into the global economy and the resultant stability or instability is also recognised by such bodies as the US Central Intelligence Agency (CIA). In one of its annual reports it predicted that 'regions, countries, and groups feeling left behind by the processes of economic globalisation will face deepening economic stagnation, political instability, and cultural alienation. This, in turn, will foster political, ethnic ideological, and religious extremism, along with the violence that often accompanies it' (CIA 2000). Building on the theory of economic conditionality and internal conflict the World Bank too elaborated how a combination of fiscal decline, dependency on primary commodities, lack of foreign investment and low per capita income in poor countries puts them at high risk of civil war (World Bank 2003: 2–4). But there have been arguments that highlight the exact opposite view.

That there is a direct link between externally imposed economic doctrines and breakdown of political order in a given country where it is introduced is a widely shared view. According to this argument, 'when global economy pressures governments to engage in rapid political and economic reform, ethnic and sectarian entrepreneurs mobilise around ethnic or religious differences in an attempt to grab or restore positions of power and wealth' (Lipschutz and Crawford 1995: 1). Similarly, as Richard Sandbrook and David Romano have put it:

Market liberalisation owing to the demands of economic globalisation, not only heightens the insecurity and uncertainty of certain groups but also may deepen existing social cleavages (and create new ones) by widening the gap between the rich and the poor the winners and losers the haves and have nots while circumscribing a state's capacity to deliver valued services and patronage.

(Sandbrook and Romano 2004: 1014)

According to this school of thought, "globalisation – understood as external and internal market liberalisation – generates conditions in poor countries that are conducive to the emergence of extremist movements, instability and conflict" (Sandbrook and Romano 2004: 1007). Globalisation, in its attempt to create a wider interconnected world economic system, in fact does the exact opposite.[4] Critics contend that economic globalisation precipitates conditions for the emergence of extremist movements, which are often forerunners of armed insurgencies. Put simply, the pursuit of free market democracy produces highly combustible conditions (Chua 2003: 28). How valid is this argument? What is the relationship between globalisation and armed groups running around looting shops and businesses and terrorising people (a familiar scene on our television screens these days)?

The apprehension of some theorists that globalisation is responsible for

the weakening of former national identities and the emergence of new identities – especially the dissolution of a kind of membership known as 'citizenship', in the abstract meaning of membership in a territorially defined and state-governed society, and its replacement by an identity based on 'primordial loyalties', of ethnicity, 'race', local community, language and other culturally concrete forms

(Friedman 1994: 86)

has proved to be an abiding reality in the twenty-first century. The question now that is being increasingly asked is why have individuals and groups developed such parochial interests? One could stress this has happened because of the declining power of the state especially in the economic domain. For example, in the earlier mode of state-led national capitalism, governments or regimes were in charge of economic decision-making process, which facilitated the establishment of a vertical relationship between the governed and the governing. The loyalty of the citizenry towards the state was unquestionable as the state was the prime actor in the economic decision-making process.

In the current context global deregulation of the market has encouraged a tendency for certain kinds of capital to become more footloose. As a consequence state functions have been drastically undermined in order to pay back debt and attract international capital and investment through low tax rates. While this new mode of interaction is a common affliction across the states in the international system, it appears to have a far greater adverse effect on small and medium-sized underdeveloped and developing states and their economies. Resource-starved and often mismanaged African states have been rendered particularly vulnerable by such deregulation of the market. The cutbacks introduced or imposed on these economies are at times so severe that it leaves a state absolutely powerless (Carmody 2002: 54–5). In the opinion of some scholars economic liberalisation has not only increased the level of conflict and intra-group violence in Africa but also in various other parts of the world. According to Roland Paris economic liberalisation has

> fostered an atmosphere of economic insecurity that strained intergroup relations in the vital period leading up to a genocide (in Rwanda) and the violent disintegration (of Yugoslavia); and which appear to be reproducing conditions that have traditionally spurred conflict in places such as Nicaragua, El Salvador and Guatemala.
>
> (Paris 2004: 167)

Other critics such as Ulrich Beck also share this sentiment. According to Beck 'economic globalisation weakens weak states and advances their breakdown, thereby also advancing civil wars' (Beck 2005: 18).

The forces of economic globalisation, then, have severely curtailed the traditional role of the state and in the process affected the relationship between the citizenry and the state. Almost everywhere, the rise of the market and the decline of ideologies of the right and left have signalled a loss of faith in the capacity of the state to remedy social and personal ills (Gottlieb 1999: 119). The inability of the state to provide for its constituency has in turn forced individuals and groups to replicate some of the role of the state and fend for themselves. In the underdeveloped part of the world the decline of the state and scepticism of the citizenry over its very presence has created a 'profound crisis of governability'. As one critic puts it 'it is no wonder that severe breakdown seems to be a feature of an increasing number of states in Africa (Kirby 2006: 91). While this condition has undermined the legitimacy of the state it has also forced groups to compete against each other over a limited and often fast-shrinking resource base.

Economic constraints brought on by globalisation have also meant a reduction in social services, cuts in civil service personnel and continued corruption at all levels of the governing structure in many African states. This has amounted to both desperation and destitution for parts of the general populace. Pushed out of the social safety network of the state and ignored by their leaders, the populace in many of these places has been made to feel truly neglected. Consequently, they have assembled under what one might call the old tribal and ethnic umbrella. As Castells argues:

> Because tribal and ethnic networks are the safest bet for people's support, these have become the instruments with which the masses learn to fight against the state. They are organised around ethnic cleavages, reviving centuries-old hatred and prejudice. No wonder this provides succour to banditry and genocidal tendencies resurface as Africa's disconnection from the new global economy is further consolidated.
>
> (Castells 1996: 135)

If anything, our analysis above suggested that economic globalisation does not produce a uniform socio-economic condition for everyone in a given society. According to some critics, contrary to the general thinking about the improvement of conditions for the masses, globalisation only aids a few. Very often it produces a hierarchy of social relationships which favours one group over the other. In those scenarios where the economy is traditionally dominated by a certain ethnic minority the opportunities provided by the market forces through globalisation widen inter-group rivalry and truly establish the power of a market-dominant minority. This framework bestows the market-dominant minorities, along with their foreign investor partners, with the opportunity to control the crown jewels of the economy, which are often symbolic of the nation's patrimony and identity (Chua 2003: 28).

While there is some truth in the argument that economic globalisation precipitates conflict in a fragile state the opposite can often be true in some cases. As the foundational precept of neo-liberalism goes, societies which are better integrated into the global economic system are more likely to adhere to global norms such as democracy, due process of law and prosperity and general peace.[5] Similarly, states untouched by forces of economic globalisation or not effectively entwined with the global economic processes are likely to exhibit greater degrees of internal weakness and instability. That there is a direct correlation between the constancy of a state and the corresponding level of peace is not an entirely new finding. This is a familiar feature of international society. But what is interesting is the way in which individuals or citizenry have been reacting to the changes occurring within the state.

In the end it is the relative capacity of the state as I pointed at the outset which dictates the conflict dynamics. The higher the capacity of the state to look after its citizens' needs the lower the chances of discontent and its eventual metamorphosis into a full-scale internal conflict. As one scholar has observed, 'countries whose citizens enjoy high levels of economic well-being and have access to various forms of benefits offered by the state are less likely to experience multiple civil wars than countries with low levels of individual welfare' (Walter 2004: 372). As a corollary one could stress that 'wealthy states are better able to initiate costly reforms to reduce grievances of marginalised groups or simply buy off the opposition' (Buhaug 2006: 696).

The relative lack of economic capacity of the state, in other words, becomes the object of discontent among the citizenry. And where this relative poverty and lack of opportunity are linked to inequality and corruption the situation turns volatile and the opportunity costs of rebellion become very high indeed (Collier and Hoeffler 2000; Duffield 2001; Paris 2004). Put simply, poor and underdeveloped states begin their career with a disadvantage. Thus they are particularly predisposed to conflict (Buhaug 2006: 697). As Ignatieff has put it:

> when individuals live in stable states they do not need to rush to the protection of the group. It is the erosion of state authority and inability to provide public goods that creates the condition of social vulnerability. It is this Hobbesian fear

following the disintegration of the state that produces ethnic fragmentation and war.

(Ignatieff 1999: 7)

It is against this background that rival versions of nationalism emerge as opposed to the old confident all-encompassing and all-embracing secular civic nationalism.

The sense of belonging, which is the foremost ingredient of nationalism, is crucially dependent on economic well-being and favourable economic conditions. In a wealthy state with a well-grounded system of equitable distribution of wealth and services the issues about ethnicity, language, religious and regional differences (often the catalysts in inter-communal division in poor countries) find very little voice. Nationalism or the absence of opposition against the state is made possible by the presence of plenty. Poverty of nationalism is more likely to appear in those scenarios where economic opportunities are in short supply. The legitimacy of nationalism within a given state suffers a setback if it encounters intractable economic conditions. Thus we need to treat conflicts and civil war conditions in the underdeveloped and developing parts of the world not as temporary anomalies but rather as intractable conditions reflecting deep-seated flaws and weakness of states (Gray 2001).

Before we move on to the next section, it would be instructive to inquire if globalisation contributes to civil wars from some other perspective. Here I would like to stress that, thanks to globalisation, now it is possible to wage intra-state wars from a distance. This aspect of globalisation, however, is less examined and needs further exploration.

Although civil wars are primarily intra-state in nature many contemporary civil wars display a transnational character (Gleditsch 2007: 293). These are often termed 'networked wars involving multiple actors in polyarchical and mutating relationships' (Duffield 2001; Goodhand 2007: 304). Thanks to economic globalisation, large-scale movement of people and communities across national frontiers, availability of new channels to transfer funds and resources, and new and effective modes of communication made possible by revolution in telecommunications technology have given a new dimension to civil war. All this has meant the leadership and decision-makers may not be actually in the field or conflict zone to direct the insurgency undertaking.

A case in point is the low-level insurgency and civil conflict in the Pakistani port city of Karachi. Since the late 1970s the Muttahida Qaumi Movement (MQM), a party of Muhajir, an Urdu-speaking Muslim linguistic group, has been engaged in armed sectarian violence for the preservation of the economic and cultural rights of that community. Since it was banned in the 1990s by the Pakistani government the leadership has moved to London. Although branded as a violent terrorist front by many international bodies such as the UNHCR and the United States Department of State, it has been successfully raising its violent campaign from outside Pakistan. Observing its violent campaign methods, some have argued MQM to have mastered the politics of 'telephone terror'. Thanks to the developments in global communication technology its leader Altaf Hussain is alleged to have been conducting the insurgency in Karachi from London over telephone and the Internet.

Similarly, despite the complete collapse of the state and the absence of institutions of governance in some parts of the world, conflict persists and this can only be attributed to the forces of globalisation. For instance, Chechnya and Somalia, while devoid of any credible governing structure and the complete absence of a formal economy, have nonetheless 'continued to support parts of the population and, more importantly, fund the warlords', consequently maintaining the civil war dynamics. The prevalence of the money order economy in the case of Somalia or the successful smuggling operation in Chechnya is made possible because of the development in economic globalisation and transformations in the telecommunications network. These stateless states and their inhabitants 'may exemplify a trend whereby national groups that are apparently "anarchic" and outside the mainstream of the world economy can survive or prosper mightily by exploiting the cracks in that system' (Lieven 2000: 150).

Between conservative and liberal nationalism

Octavio Paz wrote:

> All of us at some moment, have had a vision of our existence as something unique, untransferable and very precious. Much the same thing happens to nations and peoples at a certain critical moment in their development. They ask themselves: What are we, and how can we fulfill our obligations to ourselves as we are?
>
> (Paz 1985: 9)

For the most part civil war is about attempts by a group, a community or nation to find its own identity in the larger landscape. It ensues as and when that particular people tries to entertain their own unique vision.[6] This vision, very often, has to do with carving out a separate space, identity, ideology and finally nation for that group. 'The more emotional, radical and discriminatory a nationalist discourse, the deeper it digs the trench between "us" and "them", the more effective it is in mobilising its audience' (Maiz 2003: 257). However, since this challenges the overall mainstream narrative that is present within that political entity, the authorities or the state try to suppress it. This ultimately leads to an altercation whose end product is civil war.

But should the territory of a state remain frozen permanently? Should a particular brand of nationalism, which emerged at a given time in that nation's history, remain uncontested and unchallenged? Should everyone in that nation be forced to remain committed to the national ethos even if it does not fulfil his or her needs? Here one could argue in favour of those contesting the original version of nationalism. In defence of this new thinking one could argue, since global political structures change constantly with socio-economic and modernising forces, the 'current' state may not be the final form of political structure.

Consequently, all nations ought to have the right to forge their own brand of nationalism and their destiny.

Although this is a valid line of argument such reorganisation of the state structure in order to allow suppressed voices of nationalism their due space is very problematic. To reshape a given state is fraught with challenges where there is an acute demand for autonomy and independence by a particular group owing to their unmet grievance and an historical claim to a particular territory. For it is well known that the old framework of geographically concentrated homogeneous communities have become a thing of the past. Thanks to both modernisation and globalisation every state has now a mosaic of cultures, ethnicities, religions and nations. Given this heterogeneous profile, no wonder that when a multinational state finds itself being confronted by such forms of nationalism its response is usually negative. A given state or polity's negative response in this regard is couched in three interrelated frameworks of explanation. First, adherence to the sacredness of the state's authority and frontier. Second, fears of a balkanisation of territory – demand for self-hood or autonomy, which would start a precedent, which the state or the regime feels it would be unable to fulfil. Third, and finally, the concern for those citizens or minorities who find themselves in a region with a restive nationalism with which they do not identify precipitates internal violence. These three interrelated factors have been instrumental in the clash between the state and autonomy-seeking groups across the developed, developing and underdeveloped states.

One of the fundamental problems plaguing many multinational states in the non-western world is related to the challenges involved in developing a political structure that is responsive to the needs of a diverse population without being subservient to the interest of any particular cultural, linguistic or religious group. By and large most of these states happen to have what one might call a state-forming ethnos, an ethno-religious majority, which also controls the political authority. Nationalism in this context has a majoritarian flavour that is heavily shaped by the dominant or majority community.[7] In this framework the minorities find themselves in an obviously disadvantageous position, often in the cleft stick of either denying their own identity for the sake of full citizenship or asserting their identity at the price of non-recognition or non-participation as full citizens (MacCormick 1999: 127). If this were not enough this particular brand of conservative and hegemonic nationalism with its absolute commitment to the sacredness of sovereignty permits very little room for those wanting a peaceful separation from the mother unit.

Caught between the dominance of an ideology that is discriminatory and the constant need to have their own specific narrative about their identity and autonomy, minority groups often confront the state either for greater recognition of their identities or for autonomous spaces. As a response mechanism the state often engages in what one may call an 'assimilation drive'. Many insurgent nationalist movements in various civil war-affected zones appear in response to the strong-handed assimilation strategies of that multinational or multi-ethnic state. Karl Deutsch offers a credible theory in that regard. According to Deutsch's mobilisation-assimilation theory, 'if the rate of social mobilisation in a multiethnic or multinational state is greater than that of assimilation to the dominant culture, the balance in a state system is disturbed and resurgent nationalism is likely to emerge' (Deutsch 1961: 493). In this tug of war between the nationalism of the state and the separatism of the disgruntled community, violence becomes a natural outcome. And the state liberally uses its war machine to suppress the opposition and the insurgency.

A thinking person's response, in this context, would be to ask why states or regimes continue to pursue policies of violence while fully aware that this practice or resistance to the demands of a restive community would only result in a long-drawn-out conflict and destruction of the existing order? This behaviour can be explained within the context of the sexuality of the state. The state, to its custodians, or in our context the rule-making authorities, is a sacred entity. Any form of resistance to its authority even by default is considered an attempt to violate that sacredness. According to some scholars 'despite the fact that modern states and their inter-state structures were recent inventions, state elites and their supporters portray them as something "natural" that cannot be changed or modified' (Jalata 2001: 389). It is this dogged commitment to the sacredness of the state, its authority, control over an inherited territory and consequently all those living within it, which is often the root cause of dissent, resentment, opposition, rebellion and eventually the breakdown of the state.

Refusal to retreat from the status quo or allow the restive groups the 'right to exit' is also couched in the larger argument surrounding the future of groups that would become a new minority should the group fighting for autonomy be allowed to secede. The separatist nationalism of a particular group often sits uncomfortably with the other minorities within that area. As a rule, a group that strives for its self-determination, its separation from a larger and/or stronger entity, is likely to follow a hard-line policy and oppress weaker and smaller communities that are either on the same territory or part of it (Psalidas-Perlmutter 2000: 238).[8] For instance Ibo separatist nationalism, which led to the bloody Biafran civil war in the 1960s, ignored the rights of around forty other minority groups such as Efiks, Ijawas, Ibibios, Annangs, Kalabaris, Ogojas and others. In India the Sikh nationalism in the Punjab in the 1980s and the Kashmiri Islamic separatist nationalism of the 1990s ignored the rights and interest of the Hindu, Buddhist and other minorities. The argument that a minority claiming separate statehood renders the future of new minorities extremely volatile gains further credence if we assess the fate of minorities in other conflict zones, such as Gypsies in Kosovo, Muslims in Tamil-dominated northern Sri Lanka and Bodos in Assam and so on.

Given this complexity, the state in many instances has used the twin argument of the inviolability of state sovereignty and its responsibility to protect minorities in order to oppose any nationalist sentiment or counter narratives of nationalism. In this framework, in the eyes of their respective states, the Ibos, the Sikhs of Punjab or the Kashmiri Muslims in Jammu and Kashmir did not have legitimate national aspirations. The most obvious objection to allowing a separatist or secessionist nationalism was based on the premise that this would eventually lead to the break-up of the state 'creating new minorities and groups stranded on one side of the line or the other, for whom the *status quo ante* was better than the new dispensation' (Mayall 1999: 486).

All states claim forms of unitary nationalism. But it is only in those nation-states where there exists complete ethno-religious and linguistic homogeneity that this ambition becomes more or less successful. Adherence to what one might call conservative unitary nationalism, where there is little national consciousness, is responsible for minority uprisings, conflict and civil war. The states that remain faithful to the old conservative nationalism posit that self-determination is not a mechanical principle indiscriminately applicable to all groups whatever their social, economic, ethnic, religious or regional context. This hard-line view of nationalism, however, has not deterred groups and communities from seeking their autonomy. A confrontation between these two forms of nationalism has made conflict inevitable in many contexts.

In the non-western world erosion of state sovereignty and that of the capacity to deliver has made a serious dent in the ideology of nationalism. This in turn has allowed many groups and communities with a different vision or identity (as opposed to the mainstream) to contest and challenge the old established ideology of nationalism. Such uprisings have gained certain legitimacy owing to the failure of the state to attend to the disaffected groups' everyday needs and requirements. Or in some instances, the state's preferential treatment of the majority community while ignoring the minority during lean times precipitated the decline of faith in mainstream nationalism. Such response strategy has also facilitated the emergence of group-specific and community-based identity formations with their own alternative narratives of nationalism. In sum, erosion of faith in the state and its ideology is at the heart of many civil wars in many underdeveloped, developing non-western societies.

Some multinational states have now embraced the full remits of what one might call liberal nationalism as a safety mechanism to guard against insurgent nationalism. These are mostly developed western states where the concept of statehood has undergone significant transformation. For instance, in the not so distant past the United Kingdom and Spain were committed to conservative nationalism and therefore had responded against the separatist nationalism of the Irish Republican Army (IRA) or Basque Euskadi Ta Askatasuna (ETA) respectively rather violently. Their adoption of liberal nationalism, however, has allowed them to be more open about the reorganisation of state power and consequently mainstream nationalism. As Yael Tamir puts it, within the context of liberal nationalism 'the move from the centralised nation-state, anxious to present itself as representing a homogenous nation, to regional or international organisationations explicitly multinational, in many ways has ensured the minorities their rights' (Tamir 1994). Put simply, adoption of this liberal framework has neutralised any secessionist or anti-state and alternative versions of parallel nationalism in these polities.

It is worth asking in this context what ideological characteristics lead to some nationalisms being liberal, pacific and democratic and to others being violent, xenophobic and authoritarian (Maiz 2003: 260). To go back to the title of this chapter: all multinational states are currently experiencing what one might call a 'poverty of nationalism'. But the consequences they encounter owing to this deficiency could not have been more varied. The lack of or absence of an old-fashioned national mainstream nationalism in the developed world has made separatist nationalism somewhat irrelevant. In addition, the creation of supranational identities such as the European Union and the gradual renunciation by the state of its absolute sovereign authority in favour of regions and nations within that superstructure has made claims for separate statehood by distinct nations an anomaly. However, in the non-western setting we have now a slow march of a new form of nationalism that, unlike 'modern' nationalism, which aimed at state-building, is intent on state disintegration (Kaldor 1999: 39). The results of this are a miasma of civil strife over large swathes of the non-western world.

Conclusion

Nationalism is a political principle (Gellner 1983). At its most positive pole nationalism represents a self-assured, confident and above all a successful and forward-looking polity. At its most negative extremity it leads to a condition of total loss of rationality and the slow decline of that polity into a Hobbesian state of nature. In a world of political and cultural pluralism, where states and ethnies operate with rival conceptions of the nation and its central ideology, i.e. nationalism, conflict is a natural outcome (Anthony Smith 1999: 41). For nationalism to work well 'the people' have to affirm their faith in its central ideal and regard themselves a unified political community. When questions such as 'Who are "we the people"?' are asked by some constituent members of that political community, when there is little sense of a unified political community, and the political world is organised largely around a system of unequal distribution of power and authority, nationalism becomes an object of derision, loses its legitimacy and is deeply contested.[9]

Much of the history of contemporary civil war-afflicted societies is a history of failed nationalism. Equally importantly most of the contemporary civil wars appear to be concentrated in the post-colonial societies where nationalism is of recent origin and has only a tenuous hold over its citizenry. State structures in the former Yugoslavia, in most of Africa, in a majority of states in the Middle East and in parts of Central America and Southern Asia were all artificially created or cobbled together in the wake of Empire with no coherent and shared vision of national identity or nationalism. Unsurprisingly owing to this poverty of nationalism few of these have evolved into fully fledged nation-states.

While it is easy to dismiss these entities as failed or incapable states owing to the overwhelming chaos and violence in which they find themselves this also tells another story. In this context, one could argue that civil wars in the history and politics of these states are symptomatic of their aspiration to construct a legitimate and all-encompassing nationalism. Creating a successful nation with a shared national identity and unifying nationalism always extracts immense amounts of suffering and sacrifice from the citizenry of that state. Eventually, in a few rare occasions, a handful of polities ever manage to realise this undertaking. However, those that do nonetheless go through bloody periods of extreme levels of violence and conflict.

Even the most successful nation of our times, the United States – in order to reach the level it has – had to undergo an exceptionally savage civil war. Or take India: the largest democracy and a relatively successful non-western nation has been perpetually at war with its diverse communities to forge a common mainstream nationalism since it emerged as an independent nation some sixty years ago.

In the end, as John Gray reminds us, constructing homogeneous nations from the patchwork of tribes, clans, ethnicities and contesting faiths is an immensely destructive affair. For most part, if history is our guide, nationalism, nation-building and ethnic cleansing go together (Gray 2001). In the next chapter, I am going to explore the logic and illogic of violence in the context of civil war. I also examine the circumstances which transform normal human beings into expert killers and condition them to partake in a mass celebration of cruelty and savagery: in which son turns against father, mother against daughter, neighbour against neighbour and community against community in a landscape devoid of any human values.

3 Erotics of violence

Violence is central to all civil wars. Civil wars generate 'savage temptations'. Civil wars and violence are often synonymous with each other. As I emphasised in the introductory chapter it is only when there has been the presence of a certain level of violence in a given conflict that it succeeds in qualifying as a civil war. For the participants in a civil war violence is the means through which they aim to realise their ultimate goal. And it is usually the tenacity of the parties to the conflict and their ability to sustain violence over a period of time which dictates the final conflict outcome.

While violence is central to all civil wars it occupies a somewhat complex position in the overall discourse. Violence in the context of civil war is often condemned. It is considered illegitimate. While they themselves indulge in unregulated violence, the participants in a civil war constantly accuse their rivals of unrestrained cruelty. Although violence and civil war are like conjoined twins they share an incongruous relationship. How do we make sense of this contradiction?

The answer to this paradox may be found if we contrast civil wars with conventional inter-state wars. The dialectics of violence in civil war is different from normal conventional war between states. Unlike conventional wars, which enjoy a certain degree of legitimacy, civil wars often lack general approval. The violence that accompanies civil wars often lack popular endorsement. A conventional war is often a national affair. It raises the national passion for the event. The onus falls on the entire citizenry to rally behind it. Going to war with another external actor or power in an inter-state war for some is a moment of celebration. It is a great legal event. Such conventional wars allow its participants to engage in what might be called 'lawful killing' of other people. Violence is valorised in this context. Violence and the accompanying killing are to a great extent a matter of national pride in such wars. Or as one critic puts it, on these occasions, murder and bloodletting is 'sanctioned and legislated by the highest civilian authorities and the general populace' (Bourke 2000: 1).

Civil war, by contrast, does not elicit any of the above feelings. If a conventional inter-state war is like two separate families toughing it out in the battlefield, civil war is like siblings within a family falling out and resorting to extreme measures to establish their authority. Violence is internalised here as the members engage in an intramural struggle to establish their own supremacy over the other. Civil wars are to all intents and purposes irregular undeclared wars within the perimeters of a given state. And, as such, the killing and mayhem that goes on as a part of the overall dynamics is never fully legitimised. In inter-state war combatants draw a rigid distinction between legitimate killing (of enemy combatants) and illegitimate killing (of defenceless civilians) (Bourke 2000: 365). A civil war, on the other hand, blurs this traditional divide between combatants and civilians. Killing in a civil war is clandestine in nature. It is all about ambush, taking the rebels by surprise, and there is very little provision for face-to-face combat that one would otherwise encounter in an inter-state war. And even when there is killing there exists a sustained attempt by the state, rebel groups or individuals to deny their complicity in the killing. Why such oddity one might ask?

My enquiry, in this chapter, is laid out in four interconnected sections. I begin by exploring the basis of violence within the state. I then analyse the psychology of violence, by focusing primarily on the behaviour of individuals, groups and institutions. Next, I pursue the issue of genocide, which undoubtedly is the lowpoint in any civil war. To this end, I offer a simple explanation on the logic and illogic of cruelty within a socio-psychological framework of prejudice, insecurity and power projection. In the last section, I examine the use of personalised forms of violence by individuals and inquire if there is a certain degree of eroticism associated with violence; but more importantly if the civil war provides the perfect tableau to experiment and engage in that desire. I conclude by underscoring the effects of violence on the psyche of those who have undertaken it and those over whom it was exercised in the context of such intramural struggle.

The state and violence

The Weberian notion of the state being in complete and absolute control of power does not apply in many non-western multinational states. Most civil war-affected states are characterised by their weakening hold over the monopoly of violence (Kaplan 2000; Misra 2002; van Creveld 1991). As Giddens points out, in such states, 'it is almost always the case that significant elements of actual or potential military power exist outside the control of the central state apparatus' (Giddens 1987: 57). In a scenario in which the 'monopoly of the means of violence eludes the state' the state gives in to the temptation of using its superior military strength to subdue dissent and subjugate those challenging its authority. When this occurs the result is wanton mayhem and anarchy.

All else being equal, war and violence are more likely to occur when the national leaders believe that offence is easier than defence (Walt 1996: 37). The option of using force appears attractive to the leaders concerned for two reasons. First, they believe that the state has the monopoly over the use of violence and that it is legitimate. Second, use of force promises greater benefits, as it is simpler to gain a decisive victory over the opponents and less cumbersome than entering into phases of dialogue, negotiation and reorganisation of the existing power structure. The existence of a legitimate institution of violence in the form of armed forces also compounds the problem.

As Giddens argues, the presence of such an institution and the doctrine of militarism amounts to:

> A proclivity on the part of those in higher echelons of the armed forces and in other leading circles outside to look first of all for military solution to issues which could be solved by other means; and the readiness of the lower ranks to accept such solutions unquestioningly creates a condition of free and uncontrolled use of violence.
>
> (Giddens 1987: 328)

As countless examples of civil wars across the world suggest, when the state gives in to the temptation of responding to an internal problem through its armed forces it only makes a bad situation worse.

The level of opposition on the part of the state in defending the status quo has a direct bearing on the dynamics of violence. If the state is perceived to be unusually aggressive its opponents will be more willing to use force to reduce its dominance and power to moderate its aggressive aims, seek out more autonomy, or to eliminate it entirely (Walt 1996: 19). The converse is equally true. For instance, if the state or the power-holding authority realises that the insurgents are highly organised, antagonistic and capable of using superior methods of armed resistance then the state would respond accordingly: to subdue, marginalise or eliminate it. However, for the insurgents to assess the behaviour of the state in such scenarios and calculate the extent to which the state will go in its use of violence to quell opposition, and for the state to gauge the level of future armed resistance that the insurgents can offer, is not decided at the outset of this confrontation. For both the state and insurgents to work out their respective strengths, weaknesses and willingness to use violence is calculated over a long period of time. The result, therefore, is an ever-increasing circle of violence. The longer both actors take to calculate the capability of the other the greater is the level of violence.

When both these parties enter into such a chapter in their encounter the real substantive issues that led them to this confrontation in the first place are ignored. The only objective goal becomes the production and reproduction of violence with the sole aim of presenting the opponent with maximum humiliation and harm. Unlike inter-state wars the targets in an intra-state conflict are very hard to pin down; consequently the use of violence becomes indiscriminate. The state, on its part, profiles every village or community within the vicinity of the rebel-held areas as potential insurgents. Unable to find the exact location of the insurgents it embarks on an indiscriminate and blind use of its arsenal. As a result of this witchhunt many innocent bystanders encounter horrendous levels of state-led violence. The rebels, on their part, in order to respond to this disproportionate use of force, engage in indiscriminate killing of civilians whenever they find a window of opportunity. In recent years, the Russian killing spree in Chechnya and the Chechen hostage-taking and killing of innocent Russians (including hundreds of school children) are cases in point.

Although it is never a level playing field a civil war often prompts the oppressed and the oppressor, the victim and the perpetrator, and the underdog and the tyrant to take recourse in identical methods of violent engagement. The prime objective behind the state's use of indiscriminate and retaliatory engagement is simply to maintain its monopoly over the use of violence. From the perspective of the victim community, expressions of such mimetic violence serves a clear primary purpose i.e. reduction of the threat from the 'other'.

However, once entrenched in this framework the victim community may actually come to embrace the seductiveness of violence and engage in the same orgy as its adversary. For instance, the IRA, which started as a resistance movement (against both the British state and the Protestant paramilitaries), was easily persuaded to adopt the same torture techniques as its archrivals in the civil war. The Sri Lankan civil war, which started in 1983, between the government in Colombo and the rebel Liberation Tigers of Tamil Eealm (LTTE) has long since been operating within the framework of killing and revenge killing. This inevitably leads us to inquire into the psychology of violence from the perspective of non-state actors or rebels in civil wars.

The psychology of violence

Is there a psychological explanation to wanton violence in civil conflicts? The shortest answer to that would be an overwhelming and uncontested 'Yes'. While substantive issues such as ideology, competition over resources and ethnic divide are key determinants in a given conflict, socio-psychological factors too contribute to the overall conflict dynamics in many settings. The social identity theory, for instance, while recognising the importance of resource distribution and the resulting clash between groups in a given society, also introduces abstract factors such as esteem, status and prestige in contributing to a particular discourse in inter-group relationships. In an already divided society such discourse tends to portray the 'other' in negative stereotypes, which eventually fosters deep-seated prejudice which is carried forward by the respective members of the group (Misra 2004a). According to some observers, exposure to the existence and dissemination of such discourse at an early stage in an individual's life can impair him or her for life and programme that individual to harbour antipathies and animosities against members of the opposing community. This worldview, it is argued, can be easily provoked, especially at a time of anxiety over one's own place within the larger society (Adorno *et al.* 1950).

Then a society finds itself in the midst of an intractable group divide, the psychological repertoire about the 'other' or adversary group dominates its everyday agenda (Bar Tal and Teichman 2005: 13). Such preoccupation can be found in all conflict zones across the world. The early acquisition of a negative repertoire about the rival group, in the context of an intractable conflict, some argue, occurs through unintentional learning. The recipients, mostly children, absorb the cultural climate of conflict that is part of the everyday life and that dominates prevailing beliefs, attitudes and emotions in the society as expressed through various channels (Bar Tal and Teichman 2005: 13).

My half-a-decade-long stay and the ensuing experience in the troubled British province of Northern Ireland confirm my belief in the above argument. In spite of the peace process and the relatively violence-free atmosphere of the early 2000s the divided communities of Northern Ireland were deeply embroiled in negative stereotyping and harboured incalculable prejudice against each other. Reproduction of this inherited prejudices at times found its manifestation even among these university graduates. In some of my undergraduate and graduate seminars local students not only made irrational claims about the 'other' but also in some instances refused to be in a particular classroom on the grounds of fear of 'intellectual intimidation'.

At a different level and in a much more pronounced setting of inter-face areas this prejudice was replayed in terms of children as young as eight years of age throwing stones and Molotov cocktails at their neighbours, who belonged to a different sectarian group, during a flare-up.[1] When this form of hate is acquired, it becomes a powerful psychological collective force that is easily evoked by an encounter with the group label (Bar Tal and Teichman 2005: 73). Hence at times of communal violence each sides to their inherited prejudices and exchanges anger and animosities often in the most brutal manner.[2]

Labelling or negative stereotyping may appear banal but nonetheless has some deep epistemic justifications from the perpetrators' perspective. Negative stereotyping allows the perpetrator a self-constructed moral high ground as against the 'other'. It allows that particular individual or group to engage in a one-sided debate about 'good' and 'bad' and one's responsibility. Very often an alluring unsubstantiated myth that portrays 'the other' in a poor light allows the ethnic homophobe or rioter a context in which to operate.[3]

In Rwanda, for instance, over decades and centuries a culture of Tutsi superiority over Hutus was cultivated 'inflating the Tutsi cultural ego inordinately and crushing Hutu feelings until they coalesced into an aggressively resentful inferiority complex' (Prunier 1995: 9). This sense of 'inferiority' in the face of a minority that claimed 'superiority' ultimately forced some Hutus to be openly anti-Tutsi and racist. The Coalition pour la Défense de la République (CDR), an extremist Hutu party, party to the genocide, advocated in its commandment that 'the Hutu, where they may be, must be united, show solidarity, and be preoccupied with the fate of their Hutu brethren. The Hutu must be firm and vigilant in their enmity against their common Tutsi enemy' (Magnarella 2000: 16).

Similarly, as Norman Cigar points out in the context of the Balkan civil wars, 'well before the actual breakup of Yugoslavia influential figures in Serbia had begun to shape a stereotypical image of Muslims as alien, inferior and a threat to all that the Serbs held dear' (Cigar 1997: 19). The drift towards such ethno-cultural determinism was encouraged because it conformed to the protagonists' own ethno-nationalist agenda (Allen 1997: 33). In the run-up to the killing of Bosnian Muslims many areas under Serb control continually broadcast spurious propaganda that dangerous Muslim extremists were hiding in their cities, preparing to seize the town and commit genocide against the Serbs.

Such carefully choreographed propaganda, when fed incessantly to a people who in many cases had been prepared for it by their own cherished historical myths, rumours, unsubstantiated facts and imaginary threats, easily serve to transform neighbours into 'the other', 'outsider', 'usurper', 'alien' and 'the enemy' (Danner 1997: 9). Very often such prejudice has a purpose. The prejudice that a person or group harbours allows that person or group a clearly defined goal. As several studies have suggested such cognitive framing of the adversary group with negative stereotyping, delegitimising labels and outright prejudice frees the framers from moral restraints, and the continuation of such a mindset over a period of time eventually provides them with an epistemic justification of degrees of violence from riots and pogroms to ethnic cleansing and genocide (Bandura 1999; Bar Tal and Teichman 2005; Misra 2004a).[4]

Every individual or group that raises a machete or a Kalashnikov against his or her neighbour during civil strife goes through a change of heart. This process can be sudden or slow. But the logic or illogic of this act is always tenuous. As Michael Ignatieff argues, the identity marker that motivates the individual to engage in violence against someone who until that particular moment was a part of the same landscape is only relational. A Serb in this instance is someone who is not a Croat or a Croat is someone who is not a Serb (Ignatieff 1999: 37). The Hutus who lived a parallel life with their Tutsi counterpart were not profoundly different from the latter. But if the differences were so superficial and held together by relational comparisons how did Serbs and Hutus manage to engage in genocidal practices?

To step into the realm where an individual can easily slit the throat of the neighbour, a doctor can kill the patient without remorse, or a priest can hand over the faithful to a killer mob outside the church, requires indoctrination into an ideology. A participant in a civil war has his or her conscience blighted by a perpetual twilight. That twilight presents the participant an ambiguous vision where it is hard for him or her or a given community to distinguish between myth and reality. That misunderstood hallucinatory state of mind is often responsible for perpetuating the worst violence. The Chinese during the Cultural Revolution of the 1960s, the Cambodians under the Pol Pot regime in the 1970s, the Serbs under Slobodan Milosovic in the 1990s lived in a collective twilight and ended up massacring their own fellow citizens. As Michael Sells says, for Serbs 'the national mythology, hatred and unfounded charges of actual genocide in Kosovo and imminent genocide in Bosnia had shaped into a code: the charge of genocide became a signal to begin genocide' (Sells 1997: 3).

The wanton lust for inflicting violence on 'the enemy' assumes sadistic proportions in some conflict scenarios. Administering pain or subjecting the 'other' to torture and humiliation in these instances implies a deep affirmation of power, which the perpetrator until that moment did not have. It is this desire to transform the supposedly mortally threatening enemy to a mere subject, methodically reducing him or her from human to nonhuman (Danner 1997: 7) which appeals most to the perpetrators of violence in these scenarios. Here the image of the enemy is conflated in order to allow the perpetrators to engage in what might be called pleasure-seeking violence. Instances of these forms violence are very common, indeed.

All civil wars create conditions for some groups to engage in this personalised lust for violence. But the most widely documented of these is the bloody savagery of the *Shankill Butchers* of Northern Ireland. During the height of the conflict in the

1970s this gang made regular trips to Catholic areas of the city, kidnapped innocent unsuspecting individuals, ferried them to remote locations and murdered them after employing very slow barbaric painful torture methods. As Martin Dillon, one of the few scholars who have studied this group, writes 'at the time the attitude of Protestant paramilitaries like *Shankill Butchers* was that if you could not get an IRA man, you had to kill a Catholic' (Dillon 1989: xviii–xix).

Clearly, for some, this conflict had become recreational. Violence was ritualised. And all normal rational explanation and understanding about the enemy had been blurred. Enemy in this context had simply assumed the image of 'the other'. Put simply the otherness was the explanation of the divide and there was no attempt to participate in the rational discourse surrounding the overall politics of conflict. As Dillon explains 'within the Protestant paramilitary mind there was a crudely held belief that Catholicism, Nationalism and Republicanism were in some way inseparable' (Dillon 1989: xix). Hence every Catholic was by default an enemy. Thus s/he had to be eliminated. Such stories were familiar in other landscapes such as South Africa under the apartheid regime. Every black man for the white supremacist was an anti-nationalist and had to be eliminated. As some Afrikaner ex-security police admitted in the post-apartheid phase:

> We blindfolded them (our black captives) and took them to a stone quarry outside the town. We hung Subject No One upside down from a tree branch and lit a fire under him. When his hair burned he screamed a lot and then he told us everything. The other two also confessed. After that, we shot them. Our report said they had resisted arrest.
>
> (quoted in Storey 1997: 788)

The danger behind this crude recreational violence is that it regularises the desire for violence among the perpetrators. Seeking out sadistic violence on 'the other' becomes insatiable for this individual or group. Violence seduces the paramilitary, the thug, the butcher. And before long the entire community become participants in this project. As one of the ex-genociders in Rwandan civil war commented: 'a genocide – might seem extraordinary to someone who arrives afterwards, but for someone who got himself muddled up by the intimidators' big words and the joyful shouts of his colleagues, it seemed like a normal activity' (Hatzfeld 2005: 220). That there is a direct correlation between a crowd, the desire for violence and its subsequent uncontrollable character is a well established theory. According to one critic 'once violence has penetrated a community it engages in an orgy of self propagation. There appears to be no way of bringing the reprisals to a halt before the community has been annihilated' (Girard 1977: 67).

The reasons why and the mechanisms by which normal people turn to pure evil are very complex. I would like to stress four key points here. First, a *culture of obedience* may oblige the masses to follow their leadership and engage in violence. Second, *institutional complicity*, where the state apparatus is used to single out minorities, is likely to encourage individuals to participate in mass violence. In such circumstances, the system creates situations which facilitate ordinary individuals in becoming thoroughly violent. Third, if a society is *structurally uneven*, where there is a constituency which feels socially and economically ostracised, and the situation is marked by deep deprivation, then that group finds itself within the easy reach of the incendiary logic of mass violence. Given the importance of the event or situation those participating in it could be defined as situationally specific killers. Fourth and finally, the overwhelming reason behind the celebration of violence is *psychological*. Individuals with early child-hood negative experiences and hateful representation of rivals, when faced with a particular situation, may become 'deviant' and assume the role of mass murderers or genociders.

Genocidal violence

Labelling and negative stereotyping, when taken to extremes, manifest themselves in ethnic cleansing and genocide. When and how 'prejudices' and 'negative stereo-typing' become an organised ideology intent on doing utmost harm is not hard to locate. Many deeply divided societies practise forms of ethnic, religious, racial and other forms of segregation. When this segregation is institutionalised and receives the support of the ruling regime this practice assumes the form of an organised ide-ology. Many contemporary genocides that resulted after a short-lived or prolonged civil war have had a sustained ideological basis. In Rwanda, for example, the Belgian colonial authorities introduced a framework of systematic division between the Hutus and Tutsis while letting the former harbour ancient grudges against the latter (Tabara 1992: 179–85). Bosnian Muslims who experienced eth-nocide at the hands of their Serb leaders had a long history of institutional antipa-thy.[5] Contrary to the general belief, adoption of this ideology and its application is not a random development in the *body politic* of a state going through a chaotic phase but is very often premeditated, well rehearsed and anchored in the policies of that given state.

Now let me open up the discussion by asking what is exactly genocide and why is it important in the context of civil war. According to the 1948 United Nations Genocide Convention, genocide means any of the following acts committed with intent to destroy, in whole or in part, a national, ethnical, racial or religious group, as such:

a   Killing members of the group;
b   Causing serious bodily or mental harm to members of the group;
c   Deliberately inflicting on the group conditions of life calculated to bring about its physical destruction in whole or in part;
d   Imposing measures intended to prevent births within the group;
e   Forcibly transferring children of the group to another group.

My earlier proposition that genocide is never random and is usually premeditated has its basis in a certain ideological imagination. Although it appears grossly repug-nant, like many ideologies, genocide offers the possibility of an alternative future to a given community. In the context of civil war, then, where no overarching authority can promise security and fear is all-pervasive, those caught up in the violence are mobilised on the basis of exclusive and very often chauvinistic identity groups (Lyons 2005: 43–4). Owing to their own anxiety and fears, marked by a psychological state of unease, individuals and groups seek out bonds with those with a similar background. As insecurity grows violence facilitates the process of ethnic outbidding and outflanking which in some instances mutates into genocidal practices. As Barbara Walter notes, 'Hutus picked up machetes and killed their neighbouring Tutsis not only because they hated each other, but also because they feared their own life would be at risk if they failed to do so' (Walter 1999).

The systematic attempt to annihilate a community and ethnic mobilisation are equally possible outcomes of the often fragile but coercive nature of the postcolonial state and its attempts to integrate into a 'territorial nation', a polyethnic society (Smith 1991: 137). In an ethnically, racially and religiously divided society, where there is an absence of homogeneity and where a dominant group feels that homogeneity can be brought back by getting rid of the divide through extermination of the 'other', genocide becomes a practical tool. The chaos and anarchy of civil war allows for the emergence of a vicious all-consuming violent space for this appalling ideology and its equally despicable converts.

To understand why some perpetrators commit 'genocide' we have to understand what they thought they were doing and why they thought it was justified (Freeman 1995: 214). According to one observer,

> However narrow, materialistic, or downright criminal their own motives may be, those engaged in genocide cannot operate without an organised ideology behind them. At least, when operating collectively, they need an ideology to legitimise their behaviour, for without it they would have to see themselves and one another as what they really are – common thieves and murderers. And that apparently is something which even they cannot bear.
>
> (Cohn 1967: 64)

The spurious ideology that converts these people from loving family men to butchers is often presented to them in the garb of nationalism. Since the difference between groups of individuals in a given society, as I said earlier, is often only relational, an externally induced idea about superiority, patriotism, fear and such would appear to provide the overwhelming motives behind the individual's participation in violence, carnage or massacre.

Mass participation in genocide also has its basis in the framework of reward and punishment. As Pamela Oliver's thesis suggests, 'if everyone cooperates no one gets punished, but if everyone defects, everyone must be punished. Thus positive incentives are given to cooperators' (Oliver 1984: 125–6). Fears of extreme consequences beyond their control often drive citizens to support violence in order to avoid becoming a 'victim' (Walter and Snyder 1999: 266). An individual in such situations has little or no independent choice and is made impotent by the larger social situation around him, and it is the 'fear which causes citizens to act on ideas and claims they believe are more likely to be false than true. This is not irrational, but a rational response to the huge cost of being wrong' (Walter and Snyder 1999: 294).

Genocide is not always the work of the uneducated, uncivil, violent and deranged.[6] Genocide has an abiding appeal for those who are modern and educated. According to Michael Freeman,

> When leaders of modern state bureaucracies bear grand designs and are eman-cipated from social constraints, we have the recipe for genocide. The design legitimates genocide. The state bureaucracy is its instrument. The paralysis of society encourages it. The conditions propitious to the perpetration of geno-cide are thus special, yet not exceptional. They are neither immanent in, nor alien to modern society.
>
> (Freeman 1995: 208).

It is a 'modern phenomenon that includes those cases where we know that mass death of a cultural group was premeditated and the basis of that targeting was exclu-sively the existence and membership of that cultural group' (Smith 1991: 31).

According to Zygmut Bauman 'modern' genocide is genocide with purpose. It is a means to an end. The end itself is anchored to a grand vision, of a better and radi-cally different society (Bauman 1991: 91–2). An ethnic pogrom or genocidal war is waged not because the community or regime waging it feels superior, but because it doubts its own superiority and the consequent violence is an attempt to square it in social Darwinist terms. It might appear that in some ways evolutionary heritage is responsible for endowing communities with an inherent tendency for in-group amity and out-group hostility.[7] Coupled with matters of high and low culture and contest over economic space, elite conspiracy and spurious history laced with provocative myths can indeed create a situation where the tendency is to cling to those close to us and react with unreasoning hostility against those who are different (Ferguson and Whitehead 2000: xvi).

If civil wars are about the formalisation of the victor's superiority over the van-quished, genocide in that particular framework would appear as the final 'ritual of purification' to create something wholly sacred and uncontested. It is characteristi-cally an 'engineering' project of social control (Bauman 1991). It is also a part-spiritual and part-political project which constructs and introduces an image of a people along the lines of: pure and impure, legitimate and illegitimate, us and them, and finally, insiders and outsiders. This narrative when examined in the context of multinational states by opposing groups ultimately lays the groundwork for ritual violence.

Let us concentrate on three contemporary events, i.e. Rwanda, Bosnia and Darfur, in order to assess the validity of the above argument. Reflecting on Rwanda, Christopher C. Taylor has suggested 'the violence that occurred there cannot be reduced solely and simply to the competition for power, dominance, and hegemony among antagonistic factions' (Taylor 2002: 139). Much of the violence followed a cultural patterning, a structured and structuring logic, as individual

Rwandans lashed out against a perceived internal other who threatened, in their imaginary, both their personal integrity and the cosmic order of the state. By engaging in a 'hypernationlaist rhetoric' that inferred that Tutsis were a threat to Hutus own existence (perhaps based on Hutu perception of inferiority) the latter finally embarked on the swiftest genocidal mission ever undertaken in human history. The killings, in the end, were a form of massive ritual of purification intended to purge the nation of 'obstructing beings' (Taylor 2002: 139).

The genocide in Bosnia-Herzegovina was introduced and enforced within the framework of the creation of a sacred Serbia. The declaration of Bosnian Serb leader Radovan Karadžic ' that 'Serbs cannot live with Muslims and the Croats, for there is too much hatred. Centuries old hatred, that the Serbs feared the Muslims. Thus they cannot live together. Because of genocide committed against the Serbs in the past, they have to defend themselves' (Bringa 2002: 197) was a subtle message telling the Serbs to respond and rise up in a particular manner. True, there was a Serb institutional genocidal campaign against Bosnian Muslims and Croats during the Balkan civil war in the early 1990s. However, as Tim Judah puts it, politicians and militias could not have succeeded in their project if there had been no embers to fan (Judah 1997: 309).

While moving to our third and final case, of genocide in Darfur, the northwestern region of the Sudan one encounters a similar exercise in supremacist ideology. The Arab militias accompanied by the Sudanese military have been systematically killing their dark-skinned non-Arab fellow citizens in an attempt to free the land for the Arabs themselves.

The intent and subsequent participation in genocidal practices by a particular community is not always impulsive or idiosyncratic in its response. Very often it is a reflection of centuries of successive disappointment, humiliation and vengefulness. The massacre of Bosnian Muslims by their Serb detractors, Hutus by Tutsis and Armenians by Turks all fit into this narrative. The longing to rescue the image of a 'glorious', 'unadulterated', 'uncompromised' past can at times be found to be at the heart of much ethno-communal violence which sometimes translates into genocide.

When a community is in doubt of its own position in history and unsure of its future it embarks on a journey where the minority become the enemy by default. They assume the position of fifth columnists intent on undermining the position of the majority community. The Bosnian Muslims and Croats who, for reasons of history, lived in Serb-dominated areas were easy targets in the civil war. The same may be said of members of the Tutsi minority in Rwanda in areas that were occupied largely by the majority Hutus. Thus when a Serb militiaman was engaged in killing his hapless civilian Bosnian Muslim neighbour he was not only trying to consolidate the dwindling nationalist vision but was also engaged in a repeated exercise in triumph, in satisfying and vanquishing an accumulated paranoia (Danner 1997: 8).

Not all civil war-affected societies, however, resort to mass extermination of a part of their constituent population. In the event of a group's or community's inability to undertake projects of physical elimination of the 'other' it may encourage and adopt additional tactics to achieve the intended goal of purification of the society from 'undesirable' beings. Subtle cultural differences can in some instances lead a community to go an extra length to produce a genuine genetic distance or assimilation. Take the case of the sterilisation of the gypsy population under Nazi-occupied Europe. In our times, the rape of Bosnian Muslim women, although variously interpreted as a strategy to humiliate 'the other', or to claim a reward in the face of death,[8] it overwhelmingly sought to produce children of Serb blood, a strategy which would eventually erode the Muslim population (Allen 1997).[9]

Contemporary ethnic cleansing and genocidal practices are inherently misogynistic. According to Naimark 'the ideology of integral nationalism identifies women as the carriers, quite literally of the next generation of the nation. Not only do women constitute the biological core of nationality but are responsible for transmitting the culture and spiritual values of a said nation and national community' (Naimark 2001: 195).

In those situations where the conflict is all about 'shaping the nature of the political' women serve as easy targets. Sexual violence against women is commonplace in most civil wars. In its extreme form such sexual violence translates into organised mass rapes. Such events have been documented from various conflict zones (such as in East Pakistan/Bangladesh, Bosnia, Cambodia, Haiti, Kashmir, Peru, Sierra Leone, Somalia and Rwanda) over the past four decades. In all these instances the 'strategic' use of rape was both a means of political control and a weapon to break the narrative of national imagination. During the civil war in East Pakistan (Bangladesh, 1971), for instance, an estimated 200,000 Bengali Muslim women were raped by the West Pakistani Urdu-speaking Muslim soldiers. In addition, around 25,000 women were forcibly impregnated in order to crush the demand for a separate homeland for Bengalis. As Susan Brownmiller documents, a whole female Bangladeshi population – 'girls from eight and grandmothers of seventy five – had been sexually assaulted by Pakistani soldiers' (Brownmiller 1993).

The institutional logic in this context was fairly simple. The campaign of mass rape by Pakistani soldiers was conducted within a clearly defined socio-biological project. 'Pakistani soldiers were told that Bengalis were relatively recent converts to Islam and hence not "proper Muslims" – their genes needed improving' (Ali 2007: 7). This coordinated and often state-sponsored mission supports Naimark's argument about the transformation of the biological core of nationality. Interestingly, following its independence the Bangladeshi society excluded the newly born children of the rape victims from the national narrative. In many instances these children were killed by their mothers and a vast majority was encouraged to give away these children for adoption overseas.

Given such complex notions associated with the role of women in the national narrative they often become potential targets in ethnic war zones. The supremacist ideology that prompted Urdu-speaking Muslim West Pakistani soldiers to go on a rampage of rape and defiling of women was played out again in the civil war in western Sudan. This misogynistic vision was translated into the mass rape of the dark-skinned Sudanese in Darfur on a regular basis and became a recognised feature of the conflict there. Since the inception of civil war in 2003, women and girls in Darfur belonging to Black African tribes (such as Jebel, Massalit, Misseryia and Zghawa) have been singled out by their Arabic-speaking light-skinned Janjaweed opponents and subjected to systematic rape, gang rape and abducted into sexual slavery (Sutton 2006: 10). According to an Amnesty International report, the campaign of sexual violence by the Janjaweeds against the Black Africans of the Darfur region has been committed in coordination with the Sudanese govern- ment soldiers and air force, 'in a systematic manner with total impunity and with the full knowledge or acquiescence of the government army' (Amnesty International 2004; Sutton 2006). On its part the Sudanese government has justified rape as a suc- cessful method of political and social control because it introduced terror among the victim population (Kristof 2006a; Prunier 2005).

In those civil wars where men are subjected to sexual violence in its various forms the logic behind the employment of such methods again rests on the larger narrative of nation, nationalism, national identity and overall social control. Actions such as castration of male members of a given ethnic or religious community, forced sodomy between two members of the same enemy community and occasional male-to-male rape by the hegemonic group are all couched in the logic of humiliating the entire victim community and delegitimising their claimed political space. Stories of male castration, rape and sodomy abound from contemporary conflict zones stretching from Rwanda to Bosnia and Darfur to Iraq. As Miranda Alison argues in her assessment of the civil war in the former Yugoslavia,

> The evidence of male-to-male rape and other forms of sexual torture commit- ted during the Balkan wars, including castration and forcing male prisoners to rape or perform sexual acts on other prisoners, illustrates how male-to-male sexual violence is both gendered and ethnicised, acting to feminise victims and homosexualise their ethno-nationality whilst masculinising perpetrators and their heterosexualised ethno-nationality.
>
> (Alison 2007: 86)

A decade since the end of this brutality in the Balkans there have been endless new reports of extreme male sexual violence in Darfur. Here the narrative of male sexual violence has taken the shape of castration of male children and infants by the Janjaweed militias. What explains this development? In this fiercely competitive landscape of ethnicities the policy of castration has a very disturbing logic. For, in instances such as this, 'the castration of a single adult male member or child of the ethnically defined enemy represents the symbolic appropriation of the masculinity of the whole group' (Alison 2007; Zarkov 2001). The Arab Janjaweed sexual humiliation of a man of non-Arab ethnicity, therefore, operates along the principle that the victim is not only a lesser man, but also that his ethnicity is a lesser ethnic- ity. And by the same definition his claim to the shared political space is both questionable and illegitimate.

Locating the explanation of institutional violence in the context of civil war not only helps us to understand its motivation and its justifying ideologies but also shows how various forms of command and control which would include such broad categories as extermination, subjugation, deportation and assimilation were fashioned according to context-specific imagination and the requirements of the dominant community. In the end, there are four key motivational factors behind every genocide. They are:

a   to eliminate threats from competing groups;
b   to spread terror among the opposite side or enemies;
c   to acquire rapid wealth; and finally
d   to implement an ideology (Chalk and Jonassohn 1990: 29).

There is nothing mindless about ethnocide, genocide or complete annihilation of one group of the other within the context of an intramural civil strife. Plenty of groups with rational or irrational grievances are motivated to eliminate the other. But these motives have to be situated within an institutional structure that is prepared to see it through.

'Ethnic cleansing' or 'genocidal projects' rarely succeed in eliminating the group it originally had set out to eliminate. As Anthony Smith has suggested,

> The interesting point about genocide and genocidal actions, at least in modern times, is how rarely they achieve their stated goals. They rarely extinguish *ethnies* or ethnic categories. In fact they may do the opposite, reviving ethnic cohesion and consciousness, or helping crystallise it.
>
> (Smith 1991: 31)

What it really succeeds in doing is that it creates a cycle of violence, which allows for the victim community to appropriate the logic of the oppressors. In other words, the oppressed community undertakes the very tasks and strategies that its oppressor had used against it.

Initial replication of violence by the oppressed community serves merely as a survival strategy. However, once the community finds some degree of success in its efforts it embarks on a journey, which aims to exact revenge against its oppressor. To situate this argument in some concrete examples we have to look at the operational strategies of some oppressed groups that had experienced forms of 'ethnic cleansing'. The initial Tutsi reaction to the Hutu-sponsored genocidal project was to look for ways to escape the violence. But subsequently it started its own campaign of terror, which was as clear and methodical as its adversary. Similarly, as the Serbian atrocities in Kosovo escalated many ethnic Albanians broke away from Ibrahim Rugova's non-violent resistance movement and formed the Kosovo Liberation Army (KLA). Once in existence, the KLA embarked on a 'tit for tat' strategy that oversaw a campaign where Serbs were subjected to the same degree of humiliation and violence which Kosovo Albanians or Kosovars had encountered earlier at the hands of the Serbian perpetrators.

Logic and the illogic of violence

Once upon a time civil wars were fought predominantly over ideologies. The French Revolution, the American Civil War, the Soviet Revolution or the Spanish Civil War were all great ideological wars, which had a purpose – to introduce a new social order bound by a certain value system. Other great civil wars that preceded them in the twentieth century were over national consolidation fought in the aftermath of decolonisation. The aim of the participants fighting post-colonial civil wars was to establish a certain narrative of who they were and how they should conduct themselves while bound together within a political frontier. Most civil wars until this particular period in history were fought over both ideology and politics. Those who participated in these wars gained a degree of legitimacy no matter which side they belonged to. Even violence had sacredness to it. It was both collective and collectivised. The participants used violence in the name of and for a higher goal.

'Oh, what a relief to fight, to fight enemies who defend themselves, enemies who are awake!' wrote André Malraux in his celebrated work *Man's Fate*. This interpretation captures the legitimacy of the use of violence and the civility of civil war. Today's civil wars are a far cry from the above mode and rarely capture the sentiment that Malraux was celebrating. It is not only that the participant in present-day civil war lacks any legitimacy but also that in the twenty-first century both the overarching ideology and politics which predominantly conditioned the intra-state conflict of the past and thereby gave it the title of civil war is largely absent in many instances. In most contemporary civil wars, the narrative of combat and the description of the enemy is often watered down to a stage where it is hard to identify the enemy: thus the violence that is perpetrated by a militia or rebel is indiscriminate, aimless and above all not anchored to any particular ideological goal. Or as Kaplan put it 'there is less and less politics in Liberia, Sierra Leone, Somalia, Sri Lanka, the Balkans and the Caucasus, among other intra-state conflict spots' (Kaplan 2000).

Some societies or communities enter into a phase of violence in order to make a political point. However, it may so happen that the violence overshadows the ultimate political agenda and operates only within the narrative of counter-violence. Violence in such situations can become highly 'unpolitical' (Balibar 2001: 26). For instance, at its height (2006–7) the sectarian violence in the Iraqi civil war was propelled mostly by revenge for past killings and fear of future ones and was far removed from the original desire to achieve specific political goals.

The search for revenge by one particular individual, group or community may not always be based on the principle of rationality. There are no significant clear boundaries or markers that pit the combatants against one another in some conflicts. Michael Ignatieff teases this out very beautifully in his work *The Warrior's Honour*. When he pressed a Serb paramilitary in Croatia during the height of the Balkan civil war as to what made him different from his enemy counterpart, the Croat paramilitary, the only thing that the former could articulate and think of was 'the cigarettes they (the Croats) smoked' (Ignatieff 1999: 36–7).

In many ways the notion of collective violence which characterised the earlier civil wars has metamorphosed into what one might call individual or private enterprise. Thus as some observers have suggested 'many acts of violence which on the surface (and to an external/outside observer) appear to be generated by exclusively political or ideological motivations, ascriptive or not, turn out on closer examination be of a completely different nature' (Kalyvas 2002: 13). These, they argue, are often 'caused not by politics but by personal hatred, vendettas and envy' (Harding 1984: 75). This personalised violence often has very little to do with the collective goal.

As Robert D. Kaplan, covering the Sierra Leonean civil war, narrates, one of the coup leaders Solomon Anthony once having come to power began to shoot the people who had paid for his schooling, not for some higher ideological reason, but 'in order to erase the humiliation and mitigate the power his middle-class sponsors held over him' (Kaplan 2000: 1). Use and proliferation of this form of self-regarding intolerance and self-satisfying violence has greatly reduced the constituency of supporters of civil wars in many conflict landscapes. Privatisation of violence and the absence of any ideology have made some of today's civil wars little more than mediaeval thuggery and butchery.

Civil wars often create a condition in which plenty of people view the conflict as an opportunity to gain or settle old scores (Hart 1998: 306; Kalyvas 2002). To consolidate this argument further, at the height of the Northern Ireland conflict some inhabitants in the troubled province denounced their neighbours to paramilitaries not because they believed in the larger cause of Unionism or Republicanism, but because the climate offered that particular individual a chance to settle personal scores. And getting the 'dirty work' done became a familiar pattern during these trying times. This particular feature in the conflict, however, was not something very new to the landscape. Traces of such individual manoeuvres in the politics of the conflict go all the way back to the Irish Civil War in the 1920s. According to Peter Hart (1998), during the Irish Civil War of 1922–3, 'an "informer" was not someone with a deep ideological aspiration or commitment to the cause but rather someone with a grudge, a grievance, or with people or property to protect'.

Localised violence in contemporary India between Hindus and Muslims that often claim thousands of lives but never fall in the category of civil wars, as they don't have a nation-wide appeal, is another interesting case in point (Misra 2004a; Nussbaum 2007). While the narrative of conflict between these communities is often religion and a contested history, most participants use the occasion to engage in large-scale violence to further their personal ends. Neighbours turn against their neighbours as the ambiguous climate provides a perfect cover to exact revenge on the neighbour or procure financial rewards by eliminating the family next door from their property.[10] Stathis N. Kalyvas provides a very profound argument in this context. According Kalyvas,

Individuals [who] are often willing to denounce their neighbours in order to gain material or other benefits are, under normal conditions, unlikely to murder them, either because they are repelled by an act that transgresses the established normative order in times of peace, or because they are deterred by the sanctions associated with murder in normal times – or both. Denouncing personal enemies when a political actor or ideology assumes all the costs of violence, abolishes sanctions or even replaces them with moral and/or material benefits unfortunately becomes an attractive option.

(Kalyvas 2002: 13)

Plenty of Hutus in the Rwandan civil war became killers of their Tutsi neighbours owing to pressures of material conditions. As one of the killers later recounted 'if you proved too green with the machete, you could find yourself deprived of reward. If you went home empty-handed, you might even be scolded by your wife or your children' (Hatzfeld 2005: 33).

However trivial it might appear, at some level one could comprehend the logic of illogic in an individual participant's role in a conflict. The Serb militiaman's reference to the cigarettes that his enemy Croats smoked or the private massacre undertaken by Solomon Anthony in Sierra Leone were both anchored in something that the individual could identify with. There are, however, spectres of civil war which defy any such private reasoning. Take for instance the atrocities committed in the Liberian civil war in the name of Juju spirits. Militias high on cannabis and other drugs went about butchering masses of innocent civilians throughout the course of the conflict. As Robert D. Kaplan's somewhat skewed interpretation suggests 'in places where western Enlightenment has not penetrated and where there has always been mass poverty and ignorance people find liberation in violence' (Kaplan 2000).

Civil war is about the celebration of violence. It breaks the conventional barrier between 'fair' and 'unfair', 'legal' and 'illegal', 'just' and 'unjust', and 'right' and 'wrong'. It creates conditions for total senseless butchery and instigates members of a previously united community to reach out to each other through vicious means. As Bourke puts it, 'ordinary people placed in extraordinary situations act in ways they would not usually contemplate' (Bourke 2000: 365). Similarly, reflecting on such individually mediated violence Primo Levi, for instance, has suggested, when it comes to

> finding a clear answer, with the wisdom of hindsight, we feel torn between two judgments: did we witness the rational development of an inhuman plan, or a manifestation (so far unique, and still poorly explained) of collective madness? A logic bent on evil, or the absence of logic? As often happens in human affairs, both possibilities of this alternative coexist during such periods of madness.

(Levi 1988: 34)

In the end, there is no epistemological answer as to why seemingly sane people with ordinary lives become expert at killing their neighbours and other countrymen. Why, indeed? Because once upon a time that individual's family, clan, tribe or community was hunted by another. It's a close circle of revenge, in many non-western societies. Revenge, as Freeman argues, 'may be motivated by glory, but it is not reducible to it. One may to seek revenge to protect one's reputation, but revenge may be sweet itself' (Freeman 1995: 212). Some civil wars appear and

continue just for the sake of exacting revenge. Kapuściński captures this beautifully. Concentrating on the mindless killings in the Congo in the 1960s he tries to
find the answers to the senseless butchery around him. 'People ask why the blacks
beat the whites in the Congo. Why, indeed? Because the whites used to beat the
blacks. It is all about revenge. What is there to explain? People give in to that
psychosis and it deforms and kills them' (Kapuściński 1987: 113).

Such reflection has gained credence in the work of many social scientists. Rajeev
Bhargava, for instance, argues, 'all societies remain at the edge of barbarism. None
is able permanently to cross the threshold of minimal decency. Indeed, many societies sustain their own decency by directly perpetrating evil upon other societies'
(Bhargava 2000: 63). Similarly, as René Girard put it almost three decades
ago, 'once violence has penetrated a community it engages in an orgy of self-
propagation. There appears to be no way of bringing the reprisals to a halt before the
community against whom it is directed is annihilated' (Girard 1977: 67).

Conclusion

As Carl von Clausewitz's gentle meditation tells us 'no one starts a war without first
being clear in his mind what he intends to achieve by that war and how he intends
to conduct it' (Clausewitz 1982: 11). The civil wars of the past, therefore, were
about reformation, converting the society to a brand new ideology, starting everything afresh, and at times introducing a recalcitrant minority to a new way of interaction such as making everyone equal by the abolition of slavery or creating a new
mainstream identity through communism. In short they were about regenerating
the society. Contemporary civil wars, by contrast, are devoid of any of these grand
designs or ambitions. Present-day conflicts tend to be driven by some ill-defined
religious or political dogma and some form of nationalism. And only occasionally
are they truly about the defence of a community's identity and autonomy.

With an ever-increasing concentric circle of mindless violence erupting in the
non-western context the international institutions as well as individual actors have
developed a deep 'concern fatigue'. Thus while a decade or so ago there was an
immediate response by the international community to the private tragedies of
some faraway people as exemplified by the humanitarian interventions in Somalia,
Haiti, the Balkans, Sierra Leone, Liberia, East Timor or Congo to name a few, many
other civil wars in the twenty-first century do not elicit the same level of empathy.
If anything, there is now a steady erosion of the collective international conscience.
Thus genocide continues as a matter of course in Darfur and the killings of over a
million Iraqi civilians have just become statistics.

It is the privatisation of violence in contemporary civil wars, absence of any
coherent ideology in such conflicts and finally the absurdity of their emergence and
growth that has meant there is diminished level of concern among the international
community over these developments. This take on violence, as I would argue in
the next chapter, has a direct effect on the politics of external intervention and
non-intervention in contemporary civil wars.

4 Impasse in intervention

Any coherent attempt to bring about an end to the nightmarish state of affairs in a civil war situation must begin with a discussion about external intervention. Over the past decade and half the growth of often very brutal civil wars across the world has led to an increasing feeling among the international community that 'something has to be done' (Hanlon 2006: 60). Intervention, in this context, has become the response strategy to limit the carnage produced by such conflicts. As a policy undertaking intervention has come to imply rearranging the framework of interaction in a society in the midst of anarchy. Such an undertaking also involves the explicit aim of bringing this chaos-ridden society back into the fold of the international community.[1] External intervention in the context of a civil war, as I shall highlight in the discussion below, is based primarily on four key objectives.

The first one is built around the argument about the sanctity of human lives. As Michael Walzer puts it 'the moral standing of any particular state depends upon the reality of the common life it protects', because owing to civil war 'if no common life exists, or if the state does not defend the common life that does exist, its own defense may have no moral justification' (Walzer 2000: 54).[2] Since these conflict-ridden states are marked by their gross violation of human rights and human lives, there appears to exist sufficient *a priori* legal and moral condition for an external actor to intervene on behalf of the international community to rescue those affected by this condition. Such interventions are invoked for the primary purpose of protecting the nationals of the target state from widespread deprivations of internationally recognised human rights (Murphy 1996: 11–12). The underlying assumption here is that human rights and the sanctity of human life has primacy over any notion of state sovereignty. Given that 'a liberal ethics of world order subordinates the principle of state sovereignty to the recognition and respect of human rights' (Michael Smith 1999: 272) prima facie such intervention would appear to have both a moral and a legal mandate.

The second condition for intervention in the domestic affairs of a sovereign state relates to the degree to which an area of local anarchy affects the overall interests of those surrounding it. A civil war and breakdown of order in a particular part of the world creates what Keohane would term zones of conflict, which would prove inimical to the zones of peace (Keohane 2002). Should a zone of conflict appear to be sufficiently threatening to the life, liberty and interest of those living in the zones of peace the situation might warrant a response in the form of diplomatic, humanitarian or military intervention or all at once. Armed intervention in this context assumes prima facie the legitimate introduction of strategic violence in order to achieve the central normative goal i.e. peace.

Apart from the sanctity of human lives and overall peace in the international systems arguments, one could add a third economic argument in the discussion about intervention. As some studies have suggested, the contagion effect of civil wars is not only limited to the flare-up of domestic conflict in the neighbouring states but can also lead to depression in economic performance and growth in states in the immediate vicinity of the war-torn state. Such regional economic implications have made it imperative and all the more vital for the international community to intervene in the conflict (Murdoch and Sandler 2002).

The fourth guiding principle on intervention rests on what one would like to term the self-obligation of states. Confronted by the horrors of genocide in Rwanda and its own moral failings in not preventing it, the international community took a decisive interest in civil wars and intra-state conflicts around the world. The new self-imposed responsibility taken on by the international community or individual actors has led to a series of high-profile interventions whose prime objective has been to end the savagery of civil war in one particular setting and bring these societies back into the fold of civilised international society. Troubled by the abject disregard for human lives in the civil war in Sierra Leone Britain decide to make a unilateral armed intervention in the conflict. Similarly France undertook a high-risk intervention in Ivory Coast earlier in the decade to prevent the society from sliding towards anarchy.

Contemporary unilateral as well as multilateral intervention has its basis in two high-profile international doctrines. The first one is the Chicago Doctrine (1999) which articulated the responsibility of an individual actor or group of actors to undertake an intervention enterprise when faced with a conflict of immense proportion. Tony Blair, the former British Prime Minister, one of the key architects of this doctrine, argued 'there are occasions when nations must be prepared to intervene in the affairs of other nations when they feel that there is an emergency civil war situation. For the world simply cannot stand by idly when such conflicts present themselves'. The Chicago Doctrine eventually provided the rationale for another multilateral intervention undertaking. *The Responsibility to Protect* document of the United Nations introduced in 2000 provided firm ground rules for such undertakings. In the contemporary period these two initiatives have contained the key legal and moral doctrines behind all unilateral and multilateral intervention undertakings.

Although one of the best available mechanisms to counter and cap civil war is the strategy of intervention, it is not without its fair share of problems. It has variously been chastised as 'ineffective', 'counterproductive', 'negative', 'pursued by actors interested in the promotion of national self interest' and so on. As those critical of non-intervention would argue, even when intervention is valid because of apparently clear-cut reasons of right and wrong, there is still a good chance that some or all of the international community would doubt the viability of and rationale behind such undertakings and project their own concerns (Crawford 2002; Fierke 2005; Haas 1999; Ryan 2006). Why has an apparently altruistic endeavour received such an array of accusations?

The discussion that follows brings under scrutiny the politics that surrounds the issue of intervention. It examines the success and failure of intervention as a conflict resolution strategy. It also inquires, since civil wars are a familiar and persistent feature of contemporary international society, why there is no selective interventionist response to these conflicts. Following on this assessment the discussion throws light on what one might call viable intervention, and in the process highlights the dangers of preventive intervention. I conclude by suggesting that for an intervention to work and rescue a society there must be long-term post-conflict peacekeeping and state-building initiatives built into the overall strategy of intervention. But let us first return to exploring the exact meaning of intervention.

Interpreting intervention

According to R.J. Vincent, intervention is

> an activity undertaken by a state, a group within a state, a group of states or an international organization which interferes coercively in the domestic affairs of another state. It is a discrete event having a beginning and an end, and it is aimed at the authority structure of the target state. It is not necessarily lawful or unlawful, but it does break the conventional pattern of international relations.
>
> (Vincent 1974: 13)

External intervention in civil wars can be defined as 'convention breaking military and/or economic activities in the internal affairs of a foreign (third) country targeted at the authority structures of the government with the aim of affecting the balance of power between the government and opposition rebel forces' (Regan 2000, quoted in Collier *et al*. 2004: 272).

Intervention is also a clear and determined introduction of

> the threat or use of force by a state or states, in the affairs of a third country, for the sole purpose of preventing or putting a halt to a serious violation of fundamental human rights in particular the right life of persons, regardless of their nationality.
>
> (Verwey 1992: 114)

Broadly, intervention can refer to any one or the following purposes: 'humanitarian assistance, deterrence, prevention, punishment, peacekeeping, war-fighting, peace-making, nation-building, and rescue' (Haass 1999: 50).

Intervention from the perspective of an external actor(s) becomes imperative 'where, a population is suffering serious harm, as a result of internal war, insurgency, repression or state failure and the state in question is unwilling or unable to halt or avert it'.[3] Humanitarian military intervention can be understood, as Ulrich

Beck points out, from the point of 'cosmopolitan responsibility, which abrogates the total obligation of states within the national space and the total retirement beyond national borders, that makes such interventions possible' (Beck 2005: 8). It is claimed to have a dual purpose: to rescue minority victims of ongoing barbarities in a civil war setting and, on the other, to quarantine majority perpetrators with the stated aim of civilising them (Mamdani 2007: 6).

Thus it could be interpreted as a 'new "voluntary imperialism"' underpinned by the interest and obligation of some 'post-modern states' to bring 'order and organisation', to a pre-modern world in which 'chaos is the norm'; (Cooper 2005: 465). Intervening in other states' affairs, therefore, has not only been legitimised but those with power and capability are expected to take on such responsibilities.[4] Thus under this new arrangement 'human rights must be guaranteed and applied beyond the borders of national sovereignty, even *inside* individual states and possibly *against* their will' (Beck 2005: 8).

According to Barbara F. Walter, intervention is a viable method of conflict termination in a deeply divided society.

> [For] groups fighting civil wars almost always choose to fight to the finish unless an outside power stepped in to guarantee a peaceful agreement. If a third party did not intervene, these talks usually failed. If a third party agreed to enforce the terms of a peace treaty, negotiations always succeeded regardless of the initial goals, ideology or ethnicity of the participants.
>
> (Walter 1997: 335)

In the context of intervention it is worth asking how we categorise external actors or interveners. These can be put in three groups. In the first category (a) are major power and/or their allies acting to gain or deny strategic advantages *vis-à-vis* an opposing major power (a scenario familiar during the Cold War years). In the second group (b) are neighbouring countries or kin states with concerns of their own that intervene in the affairs of their neighbour either to promote or protect their own national interest. In the third grouping (c) are interveners displaying asymmetric characteristics where a major power intervenes in a non-major power's internal conflict in strictly offensive defence in order to offset likely long-term threats. The neo-colonial intervention and the global war on terror fits into this category (Harbom and Wallensteen 2005: 628). On occasions, if one chips away the grand strategies and heavy details that surrounds intervention then one encounters the human element behind the whole enterprise. Often times it is a single external individual who towers above everything else in the discourse and practice of intervention. This individual's position, authority, legitimacy and the degree of trust that he or she receives from the belligerents in a civil war are a key determinant in the outcome. Thus an individual can be a powerful intervener in some civil wars.

There are two main dimensions to contemporary international intervention in civil wars. Intervention could imply peacemaking efforts (mediation) in the conflict or it could be in the realm of peacekeeping (military intervention). Both could be waged independently depending on the nature and character of the civil war.

Peacemaking intervention through mediation is preferred in situations where there is: (a) a relative balance of power between the combatants; (b) both sides have a long history of warfare; (c) the actors have reached what is often called 'combat fatigue'; and (d) have informally indicated their willingness for some form of external mediation effort to break the impasse in their conflict. The mediation-intervention that follows is purely a voluntary act on the part of the intervener which neither has any rational self-interest in it nor has the capacity to enforce a ruling through its mediation. In effect, mediation ties the motivation to intervene explicitly to efforts at conflict management (Regan and Aydin 2006: 741).

The success of an external intervention to terminate a civil war is dependent on two other interrelated factors. Military intervention or the use of force often necessitates: (a) peace-keeping operations, which in turn can lead to (b) nation-building responsibilities. As von Hippel points out 'the success and failure of each component directly impacts the others' (von Hippel 2000: 168). Our earlier analysis underscored that conflicts which exhibit gross disregard for human lives are likely to attract some form of intervention. However, should the intervention be limited to ending the war the society might not be able to achieve its full peace dividend. In this context it becomes imperative that the intervener has a sound long-term plan that pays adequate attention to both peace-keeping and peace enforcement and the nation-building initiatives.

A majority of interventions, in our times, fall in the category of peace-keeping as opposed to peace-making. Peace-keeping intervention involves some form of military intervention. This may be undertaken either through an institutional multilateral military intervention such as under the aegis of the United Nations, African Union or European Union. Alternately it could take the form of unilateral humanitarian intervention (UHI) primarily introduced and overseen by one such actor; for instance the United States. Military intervention becomes imperative in situations where: (a) there is the absence of balance of power between the combatants; (b) the situation is marked by a heavy loss of civilian lives by one or both sides; (c) the conflict threatens to spill into neighbouring region; (d) the external intervener(s) see no other alternative to cap the conflict bar some form of military undertaking.

In the final analysis whether and how an external third party intervention (both military and non military) can influence the trajectory of a civil war depends on several complex and interlinked factors. These may include: (a) the type of actor the intervener is; (b) its motivation(s); (c) the international position of the intervener; (d) the strategy it employs; (e) the nature and character of the dispute and disputants; and finally (f) the level of trust that the disputants have in the intervener (Fierke 2005; Khosla 1999).

Thinking through thoroughly

Implicitly or explicitly, all interventions involve the assertion by the interveners that what they are doing is the right thing to do (Rubinstein 2005: 527). Today, war is seen to be a civilising force, killing people only as the unintended consequence of restoring human rights and a framework for protecting the vulnerable (Chandler

2002: 171). In the ultimate analysis, however, for an intervention to bring an end to an internal conflict one must take into account what Josef Joffe calls the four necessary preconditions (Joffe 1992: 33).

Josef Joffe and four criteria of intervention

1   There is a moral imperative for action.
2   There is a national interest involved, especially if military action is included.
3   There is a reasonable chance of success.
4   The intervening state has full domestic support.

A viable interventionist strategy that ensures lasting peace, according to some scholars, should have both elements of peace-keeping (military engagement) and peace-making (negotiation) process built into it. A military victory through external intervention often creates only a level playing field for the combatants. For these combatants to move out of that conflict dynamics there has to be a sustained effort on the part of the intervener to collaborate in the rebuilding of the trust through empathy among the erstwhile enemies. Contemporary civil wars, one could argue,

> need a peace process, or step-by-step reciprocal moves to build confidence, resolve knotty issues such as disarmament, and carefully define the future. Peace process, then, is an intricate set of steps danced by the parties in conflict – often choreographed by third-party interveners – in which they falteringly attempt to exchange war for peace.
>
> (Sisk 2004: 253)

An external military intervention can put a temporary halt in the exchange of violence between the belligerents in a civil war. This is, however, only the first phase of intervention. The real task of intervention begins in earnest when the external actor involved in the enterprise is faced with the task of introducing a lasting peaceful solution to the problem. This is the second stage of the intervention undertaking and one of the most difficult ones. In this phase it becomes imperative that the external intervener create conditions which would allow the ex-combatants to occupy a common platform and help them resolve their differences within a mutually agreed framework.

With intervention comes responsibility. If an external or international military intervention is aimed at rescuing a society or state, those entrusted in the intervention duties must make sure their removal of the regime concerned or governing structure has the ability to provide an alternative responsible government in the immediate aftermath of their intervention. For removal of one set of actors, however bad and violent they may have been, creates instant and volatile power and a security vacuum. If the interveners do not have a clear governing structure to replace the previous regime the ensuing vacuum has the danger of being appropriated by many new self-serving rebel groups and insurgents. Thus, instead of doing good, the intervention in this context is likely to be negative and counterproductive. The intervention by US and its allies in Iraq to remove the Ba'athist regime of Saddam Hussein – instead of unveiling lasting peace as it was promised at the beginning of this undertaking – was in fact responsible for committing the state to the worst violence in its history and the resultant civil war.

The lesson to learn from such intervention is fairly simple. Without a second plan of action whose primary aim is to install a credible regime in the immediate aftermath of intervention the overall conflict dynamics stands to be transformed from bad to worse. The civil war in Iraq, in fact, started in earnest following the removal of Saddam Hussein's regime and the resulting power vacuum.

Preventive intervention

The US and allied military undertaking in Iraq falls within the category of what one might call preventive intervention. This is rather a new development in the international system. This strategy, although not very well articulated within the doctrine of intervention, nonetheless focuses on intervening in a simmering conflict within the sovereign borders of a state before it spirals out of control. According to Richard N. Haass 'the temptation to undertake preventive intervention mounts as an emerging threat materialises and as the likelihood of conflict grows. Preventive intervention becomes more attractive if conflict is seen as increasingly probable on decreasingly favorable terms' (Haass 1999: 130). The success of such preventive intervention, however, depends on the intervener having a very sound understanding of the problem and an alternative strategy. As I highlighted earlier, in the absence of such a strategy, instead of stemming the conflict the intervention might actually cause it to flare up. Prior to its implementation, preventive intervention must fulfil four preconditions. Let us assess them in turn.

First, it is pertinent that those undertaking preventive intervention should be absolutely sure that the emerging conflict in a given state will lead to a civil war situation unless addressed through some form of intervention. Second, the interveners should have a clear road map on intervention – it ought to specify how this has to be conducted and the exit strategy. Third, there has to be a clearly thought-out plan for post-intervention reconstruction. Fourth, interveners should display a sustained commitment to resolving the problem. If the intervener or the interveners ignore any of these clauses the project meets failure. Given the high level of logistical work and commitment that goes afterwards not many interventions in the contemporary period can be put into the preventive intervention category. Most contemporary interventions tend to be undertaken following the outbreak of a conflict or attract intervention when the conflict has spiralled out of control.

While the strategy of preventive intervention is relatively new and has been discredited owing to the fiasco in Iraq there have been instances where such an undertaking has borne a positive result. Take the EU, US and NATO preventive intervention in Macedonia as an example. In 2001 Macedonia appeared on the brink of a civil war when a guerilla army sprang out of the ranks of the ethnic Albanians, who make up to 25 percent of the population (*The Economist*, 21

October 2006a: 54). This tripartite preventive intervention in Macedonia – just when the conflict was flaring up – put a firm lid on the behaviour of the belligerents. Under pressure from such superior forces the parties to the conflict sat down for peace negotiations, which produced the Ohrid Agreement. Almost six years since the peace agreement there has hardly been any serious disruptive development in Macedonia. Preventive intervention in Macedonia was a success because the interveners were conscious of their roles and obligations.

The counter-argument that one could put here is if Macedonia was a success why did these actors or the international community not follow similar strategies in other conflict zones before the violence reached the tipping point and led to an all out civil war. Darfur in Sudan is a case in point. So is the Democratic Republic of Congo. The response to that could be framed along the following lines. Unilateral or multilateral intervention to resolve a civil war is always guided by some degree of rational self-interest. There is invariably an interplay of altruism and national interest in all forms of intervention by external actors. Actors are generally reluctant to commit themselves to intervene in a faraway conflict situation if there is no tangible reward to be gained.

The reason why the EU, NATO and US intervened in Macedonia was because a civil war in that particularly volatile region of Europe appeared to undermine the security and stability in the whole of Europe and also by default the interest of the United States. Since an impending crisis was not beneficial to any of these actors and, in fact, directly contravened their overall security, they were forced to take notice of the situation and do something about it before it escalated out of control. In this context one would like to stress the rationale for intervention in Iraq was undertaken while keeping in view the threat perception described above.

Obstacles to intervention

Intervention is an ideal condition. In order for it to succeed it not only requires that the interveners follow a clear framework of engagement but it also depends on the attitude and perception of those on whose behalf such an enterprise is undertaken. For it is vital that the constituency for whom a third party engages in such a task appreciate the overall sentiment of the outsiders. There are several complex questions that crop up when we bring under scrutiny the response and responsibility of those on whose behalf intervention is undertaken. These are: What if a society is warlike and celebrates violence? What if that society considers perpetual conflict as a way of life? What if this particular society is vehemently opposed to any form of external intervention (even the most altruistic one)? What role does the international community have in this context? Should it intervene? Should it not leave this society to its own savage devices?

The answers that arise from this interpretation are equally complex. The sceptical position in this regard would be 'if that particular society is warlike and celebrates violence and regards this as a way of life and a part of its culture' then the international community has very little responsibility. The prevailing chaos in Somalia for nearly two decades and the relative lack of interest in rescuing it from the throes of violence fits into this category. The liberal response, however, is somewhat different in this regard. It posits that most of the anarchy and chaos that can be found in civil war locations across the globe is often the product of external meddling in the affairs of that state in the past. Thus it is imperative that the international community intervenes in such conflicts not only on moral grounds but because it is also required to undertake such a mission in order to redeem itself from its past complicity. While it may appear that there is a strong convention in favour of intervention in conflicts the argument about non-intervention has been steadily gaining ground in recent years. As one of the established scholars in the field has argued 'intervening everywhere (either by a multilateral body such as the United Nations or unilateral actors like United States and Britain) is not an option' (Haass 1999: 123).

The reluctance of a third party to get involved in other people's conflicts is often guided by several interrelated factors. Before undertaking an intervention there may be a desire on the part of the intervener to calculate precisely how long it will take, what it will accomplish, and how much it will cost (Haass 1999: 96). If the outcome calculated prior to the intervention is on the minus side for that particular intervener then it may not commit itself to such a project. Similarly at times responsible powers or states with the required military and economic strength may not necessarily feel weighed down by the moral argument about 'the responsibility to protect' which is the precursor to humanitarian intervention in a crisis situation. And those states or powers which do feel a certain degree of responsibility often lack the political, military and economic might that forms the basis of a successful intervention. In addition, any form of liberal-leaning attitude 'to do good' is compromised by something called a 'realist vision'. While most twenty-first-century states define themselves as liberal states their foreign policy is often guided by a 'realist vision' built around the politics of realism.

Within the realist tradition there is not only a strong emphasis on non-intervention but also a resistance to such undertakings. Opponents of intervention enterprise often see it as turning foreign policy into social work and feel these undertakings gravely undermine the national interest of the intervener. No leader or regime seeks to put its citizens or soldiers into harm's way simply to 'protect and preserve' the interest of the destitute population of a third country. If and when a state or groups of states do decide to intervene, as we have seen, it is invariably guided by the 'promotion' of some form of national interest or interests or a 'liberal feel-good factor'. Thus major states generally decide if, when and how to become involved with civil violence in the simpler terms of their dominant national and global security agendas (Lacina 2004: 191).[5]

Legal and moral constraints

The unwillingness to get involved in other people's sorrows during the outbreak of communal violence, delayed interventionist measures in civil conflicts and half-hearted strategies to deal with the problem once we are in the war zone have given rise to plenty of scepticism over our commitment to peace. Critics often stress that, 'while the key global actors and the international community is prepared to fight wars within hours, it seems virtually unprepared to fight for peace' (Colletta and Nezam 1999: 7). The reason why the international community or individual actors have been indecisive and unsuccessful in their stated objective of 'responsibility to protect' is very complex indeed. The narrative of intervention in this regard is dominated by complex political, cultural and legal issues. Let me examine these in turn.

Intervention as a conflict resolution method in the context of civil war has encountered 'crises of legitimacy' owing to the absence of trust among the constituency where this strategy is employed. In the non-western world western (and especially US) intervention has generated intense suspicion. Many regard this as a strategy of neo-colonialism by stealth. Given that these societies are deeply divided and that external actors trying to find a resolution often support the claims of the victims in order to bring about parity in the society, such moves have been discredited by the hegemonic group as a 'divide and rule' policy. Worse still, where intervention aims to support one of the stricken communities the other naturally claims foul play.

Similarly, moving on to the cultural constraints, as Robert Rubinstein argues,

> interveners may appeal to impartial standards or claim that interventions uphold universal human rights or a consensus of the international community. But, how people organise themselves in relation to an intervention, as well as the meaning that they both give and take from the intervention, results in large measure from social and cultural dynamics.
>
> (Rubinstein 2005: 530)

A case in point is the multilateral operations in Somalia. While initially the interveners in the Somali civil war saw their mission as strictly humanitarian, i.e. the distribution of food to a famine-affected populace, many Somalis by contrast believed that the operation was (a) intended to convert the Muslim population to Christianity; (b) an attack on their communities; and worse still (c) attempts at undermining the tribal elders, regional warlords and political leaders.

At another level on those occasions where there exists a sound reason for intervention to alleviate the suffering of a people caught up in a domestic conflict, it is the ineffectiveness of international law that prevents such an undertaking. As Brian Urquhart argues, it is because

> International law is often challenged by the caprices and diverging interests of national politics that it still lacks the authority of national law. With a few important exceptions international law remains unenforceable; when it collides with the sovereign interests or ambitions of states, it is often ignored or rejected.
>
> (Urquhart 2006: 12)

The impotency of international law also stems from the fact that the United Nations itself in its Charter made such a provision when it came to the sovereign rights of individual states. Article 2 Paragraph 4 of the UN Charter, for instance, explicitly lays down the rule that the member states shall refrain in their international relations from the threat or use of force against the territorial integrity or political independence of any state in any other manner inconsistent with the Purposes of the United Nations (UN Charter 1945: 4). Blanketed by this security provision some individual states have thwarted any external interference let alone intervention in their domestic conflicts. The civil wars in Chechnya and Kashmir provide a snapshot of the power of individual states such as Russia and India to avoid international scrutiny and condemnation for their actions in their respective conflict zones.

The recurring question that arises in the context of ineffectiveness of intervention as a conflict resolution mechanism in the face of deep tragedies is a deceptively simple one. It can be phrased along these lines: Should international law and the larger international society permit individual actors to intervene militarily in the affairs of a third state in order to put an end to deep human suffering or tragedies of comparable scale without the approval or authorisation of the United Nations Security Council? Currently there is no generally agreed consensus that allows for individual states to undertake a military campaign in a third state in order to cap or stop the continued atrocity there. Having said that, I should also like to point out that in spite of the absence of this 'consensus' individual actors such as the United States have resorted to what might be called unilateral intervention.

Unilateral intervention to end deep-seated conflict within the sovereign frontiers of a state has assumed familiarity in the wake of military interventions in Kosovo/Serbia and Iraq. Such undertakings have, however, led to strong legal and political debates. Opponents of such intervention have often cited the illegality of such endeavours. Tony Judt, a commentator on contemporary international affairs, argued in one of his engaging essays 'those of us who opposed United States' invasion of Iraq should ask the propriety of 'preventive' military intervention (Judt 2005: 14). Judt's predicament about the US intervention in Iraq is a very simple one. He wonders why the international community regarded the US invasion of Iraq as illegitimate and the precursor to the one in Serbia as legitimate? For both were similar cases where the prime motive was to rid the country and populace of an evil dictator.

If we move beyond the legal issues surrounding the debate on unilateral intervention we are faced with another question which relates to the 'actual motivation' behind such undertakings. Opponents of unilateral intervention have consistently laid stress on the 'selective approach to intervention'. They argue that, while less severe conflicts such as Kosovo and Iraq received immediate third-party intervention, conflicts of far greater proportion such as the genocide in Darfur was ignored (Goodman 2006: 107). Such an approach completely ignores a 'need-based' intervention initiative. Paul Kagame the president of Rwanda, sums up this sentiment very lucidly. According to Kagame,

> We said to them, 'Solve this problem for us. We have had genocide. Here is a situation that is going to repeat. We are going to see genocide taken to its completion. Help us. Not a single person, country or institution stood up against

this with us ... My advice is that when you have problems, try to sort them out, because the international community never comes, or if it comes, it comes in the wrong way, at the wrong time.

(Quoted in Kinzer 2007: 26)

Interventions and the strategic environment in which they are implemented are very complex indeed (Regan and Aydin 2006: 754). On balance, one could argue that, 'external efforts to broker a settlement are inherently weak. Multiple barriers confront mediator-interveners, such as international norms of non-interference that prevent "entry", a lack of leverage, ethnical dilemmas, and co-ordination problems' (Sisk 2004: 249). Even when some external actors do attempt to broker peace in intractable conflicts and are motivated by genuine concern for the victims, the disputants are likely to drag their feet and perpetually postpone a settlement and continue fighting. The twenty-five-year civil war in Sri Lanka is a case in point.

In spite of the shortcomings highlighted earlier, intervention as a conflict resolution undertaking would appear to be constantly evolving. From the modest beginning of humanitarian relief aid-related intervention in civil war zones during the Cold War years, it became synonymous with military and peace-keeping undertakings from the 1990s onwards. Of late the remits of intervention have been broadened further by bringing on board issues relating to criminal justice in civil war-affected societies. Thus within the broad remits of intervention one could now include the intervention by the International Criminal Court (ICC) in bringing to justice the perpetrators of violence during and after the civil war. How relevant is this legal body's rulings in civil war settlements?

As with any new policy undertaking, ICC's remits of intervention has aroused its fair share of criticism and suspicion. While it is too early to make any conclusive argument for or against the powers of the ICC we nonetheless need to bear in mind that its rulings have created complex conditions. Two specific rulings need elaboration to set the argument in context. In early 2007 the ICC issued warrants against the leaders of the Lord's Resistance Army (LRA), which has been fighting against the Ugandan government for the past 20 years. However, prior to this warrant, as a gesture of reconciliation the Ugandan government, which was involved in peace talks with the LRA at the time, had granted amnesty to those very culprits that ICC had indicted. Although both the ICC and the Ugandan government were trying to put an end to the conflict in their own separate ways, a non-complementary strategy in approaching the problem did more harm than good in this particular situation. Such unilateral legal intervention without exploring the repercussions can be counterproductive. On those occasions where it (ICC) tried to intervene without prior consultation with the existing regime it faced outright rejection of its authority. For instance, the Sudanese government rejected the ICC's jurisdiction entirely when the latter tried to indict one of its ministers on charges of genocide in Darfur. An assessment of the civil war in Uganda and the Sudan and the ICC's intervention has raised some complex questions.

In light of this, some critics have argued that, far from bringing about peace, reconciliation and an end to the conflict, such an approach is very likely to hinder the chances of sustainable peace between the government and the insurgents.[7] Looking at it from another perspective, one could also argue that such legal interventions are representative of liberal fundamentalist values. In the context of liberal fundamentalism there is a belief that legitimacy of states depends on whether or not they are liberal democracies in the sense that they are following the prescriptive ideal of liberalism as espoused in the West. According to one critic an interventionist global justice system that aims to try war crimes must have its ideas of justice informed by cultures other than that of the West. Therefore, the ICC cannot hand out justice in Sudan as if it were Surrey (Dowden 2007: 12).

On balance . . .

At one level defining the remits of intervention is problematic and on another its implementation is hugely contentious.[8] Consequently, there have been as many critics of intervention in civil wars as there are supporters. According to its critics interventionist projects are futile as they attempt to save perpetually recidivist societies at a great cost to western lives and funds (Luttwak 1999). Added to this are other sceptics who argue that military intervention in a given society often turns a bad situation to worse. The US interventions in Afghanistan, Somalia and more recently Iraq are cases in point. On all these occasions interventions have been counterproductive in the sense that they ended up hurting the people they claimed to be helping. According to some of these sceptics (who would prefer to be categorised as pragmatists),

> nurturing hopes of an external intervention among those in the insurgency who aspire to victory and reinforcing the fears of those in the counter-insurgency who see it as a prelude to defeat are precisely the ways to ensure that the conflict becomes intractable and gets out of control like Iraq.
>
> (Mamdani 2007: 6)

Thus they argue for 'strengthening those on both sides of the conflict who stand for a political settlement to the civil war as the only realistic approach. And suggest, solidarity, not intervention, as the most realistic and pragmatic approach' (Mamdani 2007: 7).

While it has its drawbacks, a complete abstinence from intervention can be catastrophic, indeed. In poor, underdeveloped, ethnically divided regions with an absence of democratic culture civil war in a neighbouring state spreads far too easily into the as yet uncontaminated state or society. The progress of a civil war can be equated to that of a forest fire. Left unattended it can get out of control and create incalculable damage to a whole wide region. This analogy comes alive in several recent studies on Africa (Flint and de Waal 2005; Prunier 2005). As one observer put it, 'the western (read US) failure to intervene early in Rwanda allowed the genocide in 1994 that claimed perhaps a million Tutsi lives' (Powers 2001). But that was only the beginning. That chaos in turn infected Burundi and especially Congo, which collapsed into civil war. Some 4.1 million people died because of the Congo war, mostly from hunger, disease, tribal insurgency and chaos (Kristof 2006b: 13).

The contagious effect of civil wars as a result of non-intervention can also be found in vivid detail in another locale – this time in West Africa. For years, the international community remained passive in the fate of the low levels of violence in the Liberian civil war. This non-interference not only allowed for the civil war to fester and get out of proportion in Liberia but also succeeded in spreading to neighbouring Sierra Leone and then Ivory Coast and later Guinea. Finally when the international community did intervene, thousands of lives had already been lost in Liberia, Sierra Leone and Guinea. In addition, the economy and lives of people had been shattered and will take generations to repair.

Violence, as we have seen, unless countered with effective mechanism at the initial stages of its eruption, has the propensity to grow out of control. Thus small conflicts, which do not receive adequate attention, linger on, fester, and eventually rapidly escalate into civil war. Our (western and international) failure to attend to the issues surrounding some conflicts then leads to larger and uncontrollable levels of violence. Our initial inaction therefore results in genocide and the highest level of loss of civilian life in a conflict. Reflecting on the politics of non-intervention, a critic points that, 'because nobody in the western community or the international institutions such as the UN were concerned to stop the killings in Darfur when they began in 2003, the conflict metamorphosed to genocide, and also succeeded in spreading to Chad and Central African Republic (Kristof 2006a: 21).

To prevent this small affliction from becoming a life-threatening disease is a relatively simple task – the commitment to engage and intervene in scenarios before the conflict gets out of control. Therefore, if the international community were to limit the threat of civil war it would have to have some form of pre-conflict engagement strategy. According to David Leonard and Scott Straus, 'given that the chances of a conflict increase after an initial outbreak of violence, the most efficient way to deal with civil conflict is to prevent it from occurring in the first place' (Leonard and Straus 2003: 45). This argument, while valid for most conflicts, has special significance in the context of Africa.

Ever since decolonisation almost three-quarters of the African states have experienced civil war in one form of another.[9] While seeds of many of these conflicts are homegrown, inappropriate external meddling has also contributed to this phenomenon. Given Africa's underdevelopment and insularity from major global decision-making processes, the rest of the world has consistently ignored its woes and misfortunes. If there was a mechanism for ensuring security in Africa – sponsored by an external body such as the United Nations, European Union, NATO or the western powers as a whole, then minor conflicts can be managed effectively before they assume civil war proportions.[10] The efficacy of this argument can be felt in the context of the prolonged civil wars in Africa. The external community has been fairly indecisive in terms of its response strategy on many of the conflicts there. This lack of commitment for intervention (humanitarian or military) has produced untold woes and suffering for those caught in the conflicts.

In the opinion of David Leonard and Scott Straus, 'were there to be a pre-emptive intervention strategy that guarantees security in any African country it would substantially cut down the conflict situations, create an incentive for good governance and democracy and eventually help preserve peace' (Leonard and Straus 2003: 197). Another critic who shares this view is Sir Brian Urquhart, a former UN Under Secretary General. According to Urquhart, the need for a UN-sponsored and managed permanent 'fire engine' responsible for attending to conflicts is long overdue. In his opinion, it is high time the UN had its own 'permanent force' that it could deeply quickly to stop conflicts before they spin out of control (Urquhart 2006: 17).

Such thinking is not very new. The UN's founding fathers had envisioned some kind of international army to respond to such occasions, but all proposals for a standing UN force have floundered in its sixty odd years of existence – partly because of political objections to giving the organisation too much power, partly because of the practical difficulties of recruiting, training and paying for such a force (*The Economist* 2007: 21). The introduction of a permanent UN force and endowing it with long-term military capability is definitely linked to the 'question of political will'. At the heart of this debate lie questions about, 'Who will risk their soldier's lives, and their valuable military assets, in a faraway conflict?' (*The Economist* 2007: 21). Meanwhile, those organisations that are trying to do the UN's job in some local conflicts are overstretched and gasping for survival. The African Union (AU), which has deployed peacekeepers in several African locations, is desperately short of resources.[11] But there are not many takers for its pleas for help. While preventive peace-keeping is a sure path to conflict reduction this path is replete with obstacles.

Our interventions to 'protect the unprotected' mirror our interests. That the principle of intervention is based on enlightened self-interest on the part of the intervener is not an exaggeration. There has always been this familiar argument about the resource potential of the state in chaos and the corresponding level of interest in intervening among external actors. There is, yet, another dimension to the above argument. As Ulrich Beck points out, 'the willingness to intervene grows accordingly when the risk of civil war for neighbouring states and the neighbours of neighbouring states grows' (Beck 2005: 17). The EU's delayed intervention in the Yugoslav civil war testifies to this argument. Most western European states remained passive despite the carnage in Yugoslavia for a long time. And only when the threat of refugee inflow and a general level of chaos started permeating their secure borders did they decide to rise to the occasion.

The hesitancy of western powers to commit peacekeepers in the civil war-affected region of Darfur in western Sudan, while no such reluctance was expressed when sending troops to Afghanistan, is another case in point. From a realist perspective one could argue that Darfur promised no rewards in terms of promotion of national interest of the western intervener: for their national security and safety of the citizenry was not affected by the civil war in a faraway corner in Africa. The absence of consensus involving a strong-armed military intervention in Darfur until mid-2007 was primarily because Darfur had no interest for the west. According to Mahmood Mamdani there was no major agonising over Darfur because Darfur is a place without history, Darfur is a place without politics, Darfur is simply a dot on the map. It is simply a place, a site where perpetrators confronts victims (Mamdani 2007).

Conclusion

Civil wars are notoriously savage situations which need effective responses. While they demand some form of external intervention, once that process is set in motion it throws up several other complications. Given the complexity of civil wars and the wide range of mandates of the interveners it is clear that there is little agreement on what kind of interventions are appropriate (Hanlon 2006: 21). Every intervention leaves behind a long trail of falsification and justification in its wake. Intervention always involves claims about legitimacy, standing and authority (Rubinstein 2005: 528). Interventions do not always produce the desired result: while some succeed others are discredited. As we found out in our earlier discussion, there are a number of crucial factors which determine the final outcome. Very often while using the limited available legal ground some actors push through intervention to emphasise the gravity of the situation and the need to have such an undertaking. However, encouraging aggressively minded states to justify force as an exercise of humanitarian intervention can facilitate conditions of intramural struggle of incalculable proportions.

Such unilateral interventions by individual actors rarely produce a positive outcome. The US and its allies intervention in Iraq, Ethiopian intervention in Somalia and Indian intervention in Sri Lanka have all contributed to transforming a situation from bad to worse. Thus, instead of restricting the remits of civil war they have encouraged its incendiary growth. Then there is this issue of local culture in the overall politics of intervention. It is often observed that in their interventions the external actors tend to forget the large diversity of local civil societies, creating many counter-effects on the way (Pouligny 2005: 495).

Not all intervention in intra-state conflicts, however, can be discredited. If anything, there is strong evidence to suggest and confirm that international attention focused on a civil war and leading to some form of intervention can, in fact, be a crucial and detrimental factor in terms of conflict resolution or success or failure of the attendant peace process (Hampson 1996; Misra 2004a). Putting aside legal and moral considerations, coercive measures when combined with astute diplomatic strategies as part of an overall approach can prove highly effective in containing civil wars. As David Wendt puts it, 'although peace itself can sometimes be elusive' it is not an impossible goal. 'Success', from an interventionist's point of view, 'consists in being in the right place at the right time to grasp it' (Wendt 1994: 175), and most important of all is the willingness to have the commitment to see the commitment through.

Given the issues involved, it is hardly surprising that there is little neutral territory in the complex and politically supercharged debate on intervention. Does intervention put to an end to long-running conflict, as its supporters would have us believe; or does it irrevocably destroy the fragile socio-political fabric of a society once and for all? Did intervention bring democracy and free political participation in those societies where the system was marred by autocracy and tyranny, or did it simply remove the old political leaders and replace them with a new regime which continued with the old policies? Did the new system of governance give each member of society a stake in the overall framework, or did it only enable the old guards to assume new positions albeit in new garbs? Most important of all, did the intervenors fulfil their promise of financial and other forms of support until full recovery of that society, or did they abandon it to its fate? Although this mode of interpretation might appear to be highly reductionist and to paint a picture of simple binary opposites, these are often the issues which come up in post-interventionist and post-war states. In the next chapter I explore some of these questions.

5   Responsibility to rebuild

Tasks for Sisyphus

State is one of the most important victims in a civil war. While some intra-state conflicts lead to a complete collapse of the state, some others experience relatively less severe an impact. But in either of these instances the state is a casualty. When the state's position and strength are compromised everything else within its territory is affected. For it is the only institution that provides the main scaffolding for the legitimate use of authority and it stands as a guarantor of individual liberty.

Rebuilding of the state in the violent aftermath of civil war, however, is a huge undertaking. A post-war society in this context has very little energy and resource at its disposal to restore the institution of the state. This deficit has necessitated the involvement of external actors willing to take on the responsibility of ending the cycle of violence, and help reinstate the authority of the state (Wallensteen 2007: 148). This particular task of externally mediated state-building in post-civil war societies is based on what one might call an international liberal peace agenda. As one critics suggests, 'the aim of liberal peace, in this context, is to transform the dysfunctional and war-affected societies that it (international society at large) encounters on its borders into cooperative, representative and, especially stable entities' (Duffield 2001: 11). This endeavour to transform warlike societies into peaceful political entities serves a twin purpose. First, it allows the affected population to escape the large-scale human rights violations and violent conditions they find themselves in following the breakdown of order. Secondly, reconstituting a healthy, effective and self-assured polity without the vestiges of conflict ensures stability, peace and prosperity for those around it and by implication for the wider international society.

It is generally agreed that civil war-affected states are characterised by various degrees of state failure (Clapham 2002; Misra 2004b). Thus our overall discussion on rebuilding the state needs to be couched within the framework of state failure. In this chapter, I attempt to look at ways in which a failed state can be rescued. With that objective in mind, I concentrate on the issue of state reconstruction and nation-building in post-conflict societies. However, an explanation as to what these two concepts really mean is crucial at this stage. State and nation are two distinct entities. State refers to a political and institutional being united by a clear command structure and capable of autonomous decision-making based on its possession of sovereignty. When a state loses these faculties, we tend to regard this unit as being a weak, failed or collapsed state depending on the level of erosion. The nation, by contrast, is a much more complex entity. A nation is composed of a people's cultural preferences, historical memories, linguistic practices and religious beliefs, further united by a common vision for the future.[1] Yet the state and nation are mutually inclusive concepts. It is often difficult to imagine one without the other. For a nation is widely understood to be a community invested in a state (Moore 2001). Successful nation-building, therefore, to a large degree depends upon successful state-building (Kolstø 2006: 730).

One needs to highlight, at this point, the specific meanings of 'state-building' as well as that of 'nation-building'. As some scholars have argued,

> State building pertains to the institutional, economic, and military groundwork of functional states, the 'hard' aspects of state construction. The nation building, on the other hand, concerns the 'soft' aspects of state consolidation as the development of a common political identity among the inhabitants through symbols, propaganda, history writing, and the cultivation and 'invention' of traditional and national customs.
>
> (Kolstø 2006: 729–30)

Nation-building can also refer to the consolidation of viable degrees of unity, adaptation, achievement, and a sense of national identity among the citizenry (Bell and Freeman 1974: 11).

Successful nation-building requires the layering of loyalties from its constituent groups and individual members (Etzioni 2004b: 3). Thus a viable post-civil war nation-building enterprise would imply organising a state structure that can administer its territories effectively while allowing its constituent citizens to live together in a safe and secure environment despite their inherited differences. In the following pages I will use state- and nation-building in the same breath. For, as I suggested earlier, they go together and one cannot have one without the other.

Civil war and state reconstruction

State-building has become the cure of choice for the epidemic of civil war and state failure that has convulsed the developing world since the end of the long imperial peace of the Cold War. From an external intervener's perspective, state- as well as nation-building initiatives can have a unilateral or multilateral dimension or both. In simple terms a state- and nation-building initiative is akin to the Rotary Club adopting a poor, underdeveloped, deprived and divided village in India or Africa and turning it around by making it a success story. Rebuilding such a failed unit at the macro level requires both consistent involvement and long-term economic investment. In addition, this is possible only if the external actor is economically powerful and has a deep moral voice. In the absence of these two key factors, the possibilities of the endeavour or undertaking being misunderstood in the target area remain high and the whole enterprise risks being undermined.

Contemporary nation-building efforts – with a few exceptions – overwhelmingly refers to rebuilding war-torn societies.[2] A more correct term for describing such initiatives should be state or nation *re*building. For one is not referring to the construction of brand new states and nations but the aim of reshaping them. By its very definition state-rebuilding would imply reconstituting the entity where it has developed maladies. It also presupposes the fact that the given entity and its constituent members had at one time embarked on a nation-building effort but without much success. In fact, their failed nation-building efforts resulted in civil strife and internal war. The situation, therefore, calls for some form of external tutoring, intervention and expert advice, i.e. deliberate efforts by external actors to reshape the political, cultural and economic framework of a given society with the explicit aim of making it a success in the model of other viable states. Given the enormity of the task and the challenges involved, very few external actors have felt adequate to undertake such undertakings.

State-building is perhaps the most intrusive form of external intervention there is. It is the massive external regulation of the policy-making of another country (Dempsey and Fontaine 2001: 59). In most instances external military might becomes a necessary component of state-building (Ottaway 2003). Given the sensitiveness and enormity of the task it is often undertaken by key international institutions or major powers. Contemporary debate about state reconstruction is linked to the roles of the United Nations and the United States. Apart from sanctioning armed interventions in third countries, and undertaking that mission unilaterally or multilaterally, these two actors have also shouldered the bulk of the responsibility for rebuilding various war-torn societies to different degrees. Thus a discussion about reconstruction of a post-civil war state needs to be situated within the context of the roles played by these specific actors. Let us examine their post-civil war state-building initiatives in turn.

Intervention for state-building has a long history (Krause and Jütersonke 2005: 450). Ever since its inception the UN has been at the forefront of conflict resolution and war termination in societies beset by internal violence. This undertaking has necessitated some degrees of state-rebuilding in the aftermath of the conflict. In its nearly 60 years of nation-building efforts it has sought to transform unstable polities into peaceful, democratic and successful states. It considers nation-building as an effective means of terminating conflicts, insuring against their recurrence, and promoting human rights and democracy. With this aim in mind it has rigorously tried to replace brutal intra-state conflict with what one might call a liberal peace agenda. The supporters of the UN's nation-building efforts point out that where it was involved, seven out of eight societies were left peaceful, and six out of eight of these states embraced democracy (Dobbins *et al.* 2005). This particular initiative of the UN has been replicated by some individual actors. The role of the United States in this context has been very crucial indeed.

Since 1945, the United States has undertaken eight state-building operations (Germany and Japan after the Second World War, Somalia, Haiti, Bosnia, Kosovo in the 1990s and Afghanistan and Iraq in the early twenty-first century).[3] Contrary to general belief, the US has been a reluctant player in nation-building operations. Its first big success in Germany and Japan was followed by a long gap of almost a generation. When it finally reengaged in this activity in the 1990s, it was with utmost reluctance. The botched attempt to rescue the Somali state from warlords forced the US to remain inert with regard to the needs of Rwanda.[4] It also remained initially passive with regard to the Balkan state-building project.

Given that the US emerged as the sole remaining superpower in the aftermath of the Cold War and that multinational bodies such as the UN were beset by internal problems there was a natural expectation by the international community of a greater and more visible US involvement in post-conflict state-building activities. Its modest involvement in various crises – while it paraded its moral and military supremacy around the world during this period – naturally attracted heavy criticism. The reluctance to commit to state-building enterprises and get involved in other people's misery was a product of a certain degree of isolationist thinking in the upper echelons of power in Washington and was shaped by the pressure put upon it by the domestic lobby. Following its debacle in Somalia the US electorate was deeply sceptical over its interventionist and state-building role in faraway trouble spots. This mindset was very much apparent in the 2000 presidential election.

While bowing to public anxiety George Bush expressed concern and alarm over the US role in such initiatives and promised to adopt a hands-off approach. This pre-election promise and the rhetoric on an isolationist approach that followed, however, was difficult to implement in the policy programme. This was guided by two key considerations. First, its claims of supremacy at all levels of international politics forced it to try to live up to its role as guarantor of peace and security. Secondly, many of the conflicts required direct US participation both in resolving them and in rebuilding the state because of the US's own complicity in its ruination in the past. Both Afghanistan and Congo provide important pointers in this regard. In the new geopolitics of world order it has simply become impossible for the US to ignore the responsibility of rebuilding these states, as their well-being is dependent on the future well-being of the US. Under these circumstances the state- and nation-building undertaking, it appears, is now firmly grounded in US foreign policy. Now let us make an evaluation of it.

An examination of the US role in rebuilding war-torn states would suggest that on those occasions when the United States has decided to become involved in such projects the decision has always been couched in rational self-interest. In addition, the US intervention-led reconstruction initiative has remained highly selective and for that reason it has been intensely politicised. A comparative examination of various US state-building initiatives in post-conflict societies would put this argument in perspective. For instance, while Afghanistan and Iraq have received sustained involvement, the needs of other failed states such as Haiti and Somalia have been completely ignored.

A critical assessment of its role further suggests that in the twenty-first century, an imperialist America is less concerned with the need-based state-rebuilding approach. Assured of military pre-eminence the US has failed to take into its confidence the society on whose behalf it is engaged in nation-building activities. But most unfortunate of all it has transformed the nation-building undertaking into a form of neo-colonial hegemony in the host society. For this and other associated reasons that I highlighted earlier, much of the world no longer sees the US as a credible actor in resuscitating post-conflict states. Thanks to its failed state-building enterprises in Afghanistan and Iraq as at the time of writing and its complete disregard for the needs of other post-conflict states such as Haiti and Somalia the US has lost some of its credibility as an actor capable of rescuing war-torn states.

While at one level Washington's botched state-building initiatives can be attributed to its pursuance of rational self-interest in faraway places, such missions have also been undermined because of complex domestic pressure on what is primarily a foreign affairs undertaking. As Francis Fukuyama puts it,

> In the United States, there has been an ideologised debate over nation building. Some conservatives are opposed in principle to nation building because they do not think it is feasible and do not like the idea of open-ended and expensive commitments to what they regard as a kind of international welfare. On the other hand there are those international financial institutions – with strong roots in the United States – who argue its feasibility in terms of infrastructure and capacity building and ultimately assuring the security and development in the United States.
>
> (Fukuyama 2005: 134)

In spite of various criticisms levelled against them, actors such as the UN and US would appear to remain faithful to the task of rebuilding war-torn states. While some of the state-building initiatives (undertaken by an individual actor) have been partly based on national interest, overall these actors have been committed to these undertakings on the grounds of humanitarianism or altruism. If one were to produce a comparative balance sheet on successful state-building undertaking the US would appear to have a relatively lower success rate than the UN.[5]

Critics have consistently argued that given the proximity of US national interest to the state-building undertaking many of these were bound to end in failure (Dempsey and Fontaine 2001; Fearon 2007; Ferguson 2004). This, however, is a simplistic argument. State or nation rebuilding as I underlined earlier is an extremely complex undertaking. There are a multitude of factors which can undermine and mar an external state-rebuilding exercise in a third country. In the next section, focusing on Afghanistan and Iraq, I show that to be the case.

Afghanistan and Iraq

The primary focus of post-conflict state reconstruction and nation-building relates to freeing the society of anarchy and chaos, the twin factors responsible for fragmenting the society and pushing the state to the abyss. The commitment to construct a new peaceful and viable entity, then, rests on building order. This, however, is a heavy responsibility for the external actors. On those occasions when the international community or groups of actors demonstrate the will to undertake nation-building, they are not always able to figure out how it should be conducted and who should shoulder the burden (Ottaway 2002b: 16). This undertaking is made all the more complex in post-civil war societies where the lines dividing the communities are too pronounced and there exists little or no sense of national unity or identity.

Our test cases of Afghanistan and Iraq underline the fact that a state created by past colonial designs is more likely to exhibit signs of decline and eventual failure than those which evolved through natural progression. Consequently any state-building efforts in such situations would be very challenging, indeed. Both Afghanistan and Iraq are products of colonial state-building enterprise. The competition between the British Raj in India and Tsarist Russia's expansionist policies southward eventually created Afghanistan, whose emergence can be compared to that of a fragile mountain following the collision of two continental plates. Iraq too had an equally inauspicious beginning when the British cobbled together an ill assortment of nationalities into one single administrative unit. This mode of state-building has led critics to argue that the greater the difference between the pre-colonial political entities and what the colonial powers tried to impose, the higher the rate of failure (Ottaway 2003: 21).

Critics and scholars of post-conflict reconstruction constantly refer to Germany and Japan to make a case for externally aided nation-building enterprise. True, these two are success stories. However, while making such a case they tend to over-look two critical factors. First, these two were not states affected by civil war. Second, the inter-state war which ruined the German and Japanese states never made an impact on the social fabric. Given their unique homogeneous identity both Germans and Japanese remained passionately committed to a sense of national unity and consequently common national aspiration when the US-sponsored state-building initiative started in earnest following the Second World War in these two states.

As a recent study by the think tank Rand Corporation highlights, 'nation-building is not principally about economic reconstruction; rather, it is about political transformation.'[6] This broadly refers to an appreciation of the rule of law, values of democracy, liberal outlook and worldview, commitment to multicultural ethics within the country and its expression outside, and so on. In pluralistic societies with a long history of communal divide the aim of nation-building is critically linked to fostering social, economic and political institutions and attitudes that will prevent these societies from sliding back to the politics of antagonism and conflict.

If we turn to two recent cases where a state/nation-building enterprise is introduced to the maximum possible extent we encounter a disappointing level of development in this area. If we were to concentrate on the issue of political transformation in Afghanistan and Iraq we are faced with the uncomfortable reality that very little has changed in terms of the actual transformation of ideas and attitudes about who they are and their place in the post-war society on the part of the citizenry in both countries. A comparative approach again is helpful in this context. The reason why Germans and Japanese could embrace the new ideology of change at the war's end was not only the complete and utter defeat of the wartime leadership but also the complete delegitimisation of the old ideology by the general citizenry. This commitment to making a clear break with the past won them friends abroad and the new resolve galvanised the nation-building initiative.

The commitment of Afghanistan and Iraq in this framework is not so reassuring. The citizenry in Afghanistan and Iraq are yet to fully discredit the old leadership. The narrative of a contest between good and evil here is far from established. A sizeable populace in both countries associate the West with evil. Hence their discredited regimes, i.e. that of the Taliban in Afghanistan and the Ba'athist government in Iraq, are paraded as defenders of the faith and given an elevated martyrdom status. This alternative reading of history has proved to be the main obstacle to forging a new post-war ideology of national consensus in both countries.

Hypothetically, even if the divided communities in Afghanistan and Iraq express an absolute commitment to create a unifying nation and sacrifice their differences to a centripetal bureaucratic state they are unlikely to succeed in their endeavour in creating a successful state on the models of Germany or Japan. It is impossible to comprehend let alone expect the international community to offer the same degree of economic aid that went on to make both Germany and Japan the shining examples of externally aided state- and nation-building enterprise. Furthermore, Gary Dempsey, a critic of US nation-building enterprise overseas, asserts that the reason why Germany and Japan became success stories and Afghanistan and Iraq are unlikely candidates to do so are couched in the fundamental practical differences between these two groups. In his assessment,

> Germany had a strong tradition of rule of law, property rights, and free trade before the Nazi era. Japan's elite embraced an honorific culture that respected and obeyed the wishes of the victor in battle. Afghanistan and its neighbours, in contrast, have little in the way of either liberal traditions or cultural attitudes that are agreeable to massive foreign investment.[7]

In the end Afghanistan and Iraq not only lack this goodwill but also are incapable of mobilising resources internally or extracting revenues from their own economic activities.

Viable reform

There is unanimity in both scholarly and political circles that civil war-affected states are a danger to themselves and the international community. This anxiety over security explains the frenetic attempt to rescue these entities from the quagmire of chaos. A stable state in a post-conflict setting is dependent on both internal and external security. In a post-civil war state the resumption of fighting is never a distant possibility. Failure to arrive at a viable compromise in the post-conflict setting as part of the state-building initiative is one of the key reasons why most enterprises do not take off.

The responsibility on the part of the outsider or intervener in charge of post-conflict reconstruction here is to make sure that the old equation is not replayed in the new setting. The task now is to set up institutional structures in such a manner that each or all the parties or groups feel true partners in a common project where their investment is appreciated and recognised. In addition, this mode of interaction is heavily dependent on the availability of opportunities for exercising freedom in its entirety. For instance making space for political freedom without placing due emphasis on economic freedom can have an adverse effect on the overall project.

Economic freedom in this context would imply creating life-sustaining opportunities for the entire citizenry. As I underlined in Chapter 1 many societies get drawn to the logic of violence owing to the absence of equitable distribution of wealth and lack of economic opportunities. The task here, therefore, is not only to make these opportunities available to every individual but also to make sure that the wide inequality between various groups or between regions is reduced, in order to create an egalitarian economic order. As numerous studies have pointed out, it is through the offering of egalitarian economic freedom across the post-war state that internal security can be achieved.

Does state-building enterprise kick-start economic regeneration in the target country? From an external intervener's perspective the answer could be an overwhelming Yes. According to one scholar, 'for post-civil war countries, economic development can be seen to be the best way of breaking the "conflict trap" of poverty, underdevelopment and war' (Collier 2003: 53). While one cannot deny the importance of economic sector reform one needs to be cautious while introducing these reforms. Some sceptics, for example, have argued that these reforms rarely take into account the actual needs of the post-war society, and that external agencies involved in state-building initiatives are there for the purpose of furthering their own interest.

In addition, they have stressed that external economic assistance as part of the state-building package can do more harm than good. Francis Fukuyama for example argues that in certain respects economic reconstruction can become the enemy of development over the long run (Fukuyama 2006: 7). For instance, in spite of billions of dollars poured into Cambodia, East Timor, Bosnia, Afghanistan and now Iraq, there has been little or no progress in these societies on the economic front. The only economic regeneration that one could pinpoint in all these test cases is the emergence, growth and decay of the service sector.

As Ignatieff succinctly puts it, 'nation-building isn't supposed to be an exercise in colonialism, but the relationship between the locals and the internationals is inherently colonial. The locals do the translating, cleaning and driving while the internationals do the grand imperial planning' (Ignatieff 2002: 5). That there is a discrepancy in terms of the creation of a viable economy can hardly be overemphasised. To quote Ignatieff, again,

> [w]herever the travelling caravan of nation-building settles, it creates an instant boomtown, living on foreign money and hope. But boomtowns inevitably go bust. But the vices left behind by the boomtowns do not dissipate. It pushes the society to new levels of misfortune and despondency. Both in Cambodia and Bosnia the international community created artificial economies and introduced new vices in terms of prostitution, corruption, money laundering and so on.
>
> (Ignatieff 2002)

As a viable method that is removed from the criticism outlined earlier, one could suggest a healthy mixture of both external presence as well as indigenous participation in the transitional state-building undertaking. According to Orr:

> While seeking to build up local governance and participation capacity, the international community must observe the cardinal rule of governance: indigenous ownership of the process is key. Even when local actors are disorganised and disempowered in the wake of conflict, they must be given a leadership role in rebuilding process. Likewise, even when international actors must assume certain functions temporarily, they should always train and empower indigenous counterparts.
>
> (Orr 2002: 140)

Lasting legacy of state-building

Even if the external sponsors of a state-building initiative manage to avoid their mistakes, regrafting the state where the state had been dismantled by years and decades of civil war and social unrest is fraught with other complex internal challenges. For example, how does one create an enduring state structure that is accepted by the entire populace?

As I stressed in Chapter 2 the bedrock of a successful state is a vibrant nation. A homogeneous and consensual national identity serves as the foundation for the smooth workings of a state. In the absence of this sense of nationhood a state may flounder. Some may object to this line of thinking. One could argue that not all successful states have a homogeneous racial, ethnic, cultural, linguistic and religious base – factors that are paramount in building a common national identity. Similarly all homogeneous nations are not successful states.[8]

It is an uphill task to make people appreciate the values associated with civic nationalism in a deeply divided society or in those polarised by long-standing ethno-religious, linguistic and cultural differences. This is true of both economically powerful as well as economically deprived polities. Forging a sense of common identity is just as difficult in Northern Ireland as it is in Nigeria. Another paradox that is worth entertaining in this context is that a strong nation is by no means a guarantor of a strong and successful state (Ottaway 2003: 22). Existence of an all-encompassing primordial identity expressed in terms of homogeneous nationality does not always succeed in making the citizenry work for the smooth functioning of the state. In other words, nationhood, or a sense of common identity, by itself does not guarantee the viability of a state.

In the contemporary period, both Haiti and Nepal fall into this category. Unlike many of their counterparts such as Bosnia, Iraq and the Sudan, the ethno-racial base in these societies is homogeneous. Yet, the state in both Haiti and Nepal has been on a downward spiral for over a decade now. The key questions that crop up in this context are: Why do successful nationalities fail to have a successful state? What explains state failure on those occasions where the nation is strong? What precipitated state failure in these instances?

The goal of nation-building should not be to impose a common nationality or create a uniform identity in a post-conflict setting. Rather it should aim at creating a viable structure that is acceptable to all and is embraced by them to an equal degree. The onus on both the participants and interveners in this setting is to organise the new unit in such a manner that it can administer all the disparate ethnic, linguistic, religious and regional subunits effectively without trampling the latter's autonomy. The role of an external actor overseeing the state-building undertaking is a crucial one. As Anthony Lake cautiously remarks,

> It is a dangerous hubris to believe external actors can build other nations. But where these actors are involved in the process of state-building, either out of altruism or to promote their national interest, they can help nations build themselves and give them time to make a start at it.
>
> (Lake 1996)

But helping these war-torn societies to govern themselves has assumed some form of externally imposed governing structure.

Guided governance

Increasingly the state-building enterprise has come to signify the reconstruction of the political process in fragmented societies. Introduction of a responsible government, it is argued by those involved, is fundamental in holding the state together. For it not only guarantees law and order to a war-weary people but provides a sense of vision and future direction. From a liberal perspective, reintroduction of a central government with a clear command structure provides the main scaffolding on which rests the newly resuscitated state. Forming an indigenous responsible government in the immediate aftermath of conflict, however, is fraught with challenges. First, there still exists a climate of distrust among the former adversaries. Second, the condition of war had denied any possibility of the emergence of civilian leadership. But the need for an interim government is very severe indeed. How was that society to form such a government?

Under these circumstances, very often, the external interveners take the lead role in sponsoring an interim government. This externally imposed transitional post-conflict governance, it is argued, facilitates the emergence of an indigenous political process in due course. Although there is no legal precedence and no such clause exists in the United Nations Charter, the UN itself has been in the forefront of instituting and overseeing an international administration in post-civil war states. In the post-Cold War era such undertakings were first introduced in East Timor (1999–2002). And from 1999 the UN has continued to maintain an international regime in the disputed territory of Kosovo. Taking their cue from the UN, other individual and multinational actors such as the United States and NATO have introduced their own full or part governance structure in Afghanistan and Iraq. But such externally imposed guided governance has provoked plenty of criticism. Letting the international community govern post-civil war states through the UN or some such agency is discredited in both political and policy circles. Some key questions dominate this debate. For example, how can external actors, using benevolent autocracy, help introduce values and ideals such as democracy and good governance? Similarly, if the new post-war condition meant self-rule how could this form of external administration spanning some half a decade (Kosovo) foster ideas about democracy?

Those opposed to such external administration argue that this framework contributes very little in terms of introducing principles of good governance. In fact under the guise of interim administration the US and the UN simply perpetuate their own form of imperialism. Surprisingly many of those critical of the UN and other international bodies have at one time or the other been a part of their administrative structure. According to some of these critics, in recent years UN transitional administration has been responsible for treating the post-war society as a vassal state or fiefdom. They have further argued that the UN transitional authority in many instances has ruled those under their administration with extreme severity while ignoring international standards of human rights, freedom of speech and so on. Given this catalogue of criticisms some have pointed that 'the UN despite of its ability to monopolise the image of legitimacy is ill-suited to administering territories in transition' (Chopra 2000: 35).

Even in those instances where the interim external administration prepared the grounds for an indigenous government to replace it, the criticisms levelled against the former are never far away. It is argued that, instead of creating a shared, confident, legitimate national government, the external actors very often institute a regime of their choice which is far removed from all those the ideals I stated above. Similarly, if the citizenry manages to elect a government of their choice it is hamstrung by the constant interference by the external actor overseeing the state-building enterprise. Such meddling does more harm than good.

Such constant external tutelage, as we have seen in Afghanistan and more recently in Iraq, has denied credibility to the indigenous governments in question. In both these instances the larger populace has described self-rule under the watchful eye of an external intervenor as the 'illusion of self-government'. In Afghanistan, in spite of nearly half a decade of indigenous government a sizeable portion of Afghans consider their leader Hamid Karzai as a stooge of the United States.[9] In Iraq, in spite of a countrywide election and the formation of a national government the new regime failed to gain national legitimacy owing to the constant tutoring of it by the US.

John Kenneth Galbraith, when reflecting on nation-building enterprise in the post–Second World War period, was of the opinion that it was based on the 'shrewd notion that people who are insecure, hungry and without hope are not discriminating in terms of the political system they embrace or the values they are expected to imbibe'. Six decades on it is time to revise and revisit the sentiment expressed in Galbraith's famous remark. In the current context, those in whose name and on whose behalf nation-building enterprises are undertaken have become its greatest critics. Ideals such as democracy, representative government, law and justice and such are not valued enough in the recipient society undergoing a transformation.

The reluctance to embrace these ideals and scepticism over the externally imposed state-building enterprise are based on some genuine anxieties.

According to this constituency, the new mantra of state-building such as 'capacity building', 'civil society empowerment', 'local governance' and such cleverly hides the larger truth. Power of governance in post-conflict states favours the external actors not the local political elite. Although local agents run the day-to-day administration and local potentates exercise some power, in actuality the real decisions are not made in the local setting.[10] In fact, the local political elite are mere functionaries or handmaiden of a faraway leadership that sits in another country. For every decision they take they have to have it approved by their faraway benefactors and their every move is closely inspected and scrutinised.

A long view of state-building

It is now commonly argued that all post-civil war polities are weak states (Fukuyama 2006; Misra 2004b). This particular attribute, one could stress, prevents them from acting and behaving as normal members of the international community. Consequently those involved in their recovery regard long-term intervention and tutoring in their political process as paramount. Although one could detect a certain degree of condescension on the part of external actors in rebuilding the given state, their apprehension about the latter's weakness is not an exaggeration. Such policy undertaking is based on the assumption that these entities are extremely weak and need constant guidance in order to evolve into robust and responsible members of the international community. A comparative assessment of post-war state reconstruction projects around the world vindicates the argument of external actors about 'long-term tutoring' in the governing process.

In May 2006 violence broke out in East Timor which was reminiscent of its turbulent past. The event was so destabilising in its strength that international peacekeepers had to be flown in from Australia as an emergency measure. Although thanks to the presence of peacekeepers the eruption of another round of civil war was averted and the situation was brought under control, the constituency for violence in this newest member of the international community is never far away. As the events there have demonstrated, the internal conflict dynamics in East Timor remained extremely volatile even after six years of constant international involvement. And it had not succeeded in ejecting itself from the weak state category. Given this condition it is hard to undermine those policy-makers who argue that a weak post-civil war state such as East Timor contain enough forces to destabilise the regional peace and security.

Afghanistan retells a similar story. The country was brought back into the fold of global society following the removal of the infamous Taliban regime, and the international community provided billions of dollars in aid and assistance and transplanted the long-disappeared political process of democracy. Nevertheless, the Afghan state remains vulnerable and weak as ever. Pockets of Afghanistan are still under the control of the neo-Taliban forces. Many of these disgruntled rebels have crossed over to neighbouring Pakistan, creating new law and order problems there.

These developments have vindicated the position of actors such as US that there needs to be constant and long-term external involvement in the political process of these weak states. Although affected by 'commitment fatigue' the United States nonetheless recognises a clear link between state weakness and international security or by default the threats to American interests. Thus it intends to strengthen the sovereign capacity of post-civil war weak states in order to combat international threats of terrorism, insurgency (the likes of which we have seen in Afghanistan and East Timor) and organised crime (Patrick 2006: 27–8). It will be instructive therefore to assess the US post-war recovery programme.

Currently, three of Washington's key agencies are pursuing separate and autonomous strategies to prevent the weakness and fragility of states. The Pentagon, for instance, is actively pursuing a tactic whereby it could block the renewal of conflict before it materialises in many of the world's 'ungoverned spaces'. Similarly, the Department of State's Office of the Coordinator for Reconstruction and Stabilisation is involved in identifying states at risk of collapse in order to launch conflict prevention and mitigation efforts. And finally the US Agency for International Development (USAID) has floated its own 'Fragile States Strategy' to provide aid in the capacity-building projects in both weak pre-conflict and post-conflict states. Washington's sponsorship of the Central American Free Trade Area (CAFTA) which includes such post-civil war states such as El Salvador, Guatemala and Nicaragua, it is pointed out, specifically aims at rescuing the weak states (Krasner and Pascual 2005; Patrick 2006).

While it is a key player in brokering peace Washington nonetheless has a rather complicated policy in terms sending an olive branch to the rebels in several conflict zones. Since the events of 11 September 2001 it has treated most rebel groups in civil wars as terrorists. Under this framework, unless that particular group professes complete withdrawal from both the rhetoric and activism of violence the US has threatened to pull back its support from the peace process. A case that clearly demonstrates this approach is Nepal. The decade-old civil war in this Himalayan kingdom, which had claimed an estimated 13,000 lives by 2006, entered a critical phase the same year when the Maoist rebels fighting for the establishment of a republic were invited to join the interim government ahead of a general election in 2007. This overture resulted in a ceasefire. Washington, however, firmly declared that until they gave up arms and underwent complete demilitarisation it would consider the Maoists a terrorist group. In a policy statement the US ambassador to the country James Moriarty emphatically pointed out that 'if the rebels continue to use violence and then enter the government, our law says we cannot supply assistance to those who support terrorism'.[11]

Such hard-line policy undertakings and Washington's loose definition of terrorism even in civil war situations have called into question the traditional approaches to peace. Until now external actors were somewhat ambiguous in their treatment of demobilisation and disarmament in post-conflict situations. In spite of their gory past, very often the rebels in post-civil war societies were allowed to undergo a slow and gradual demobilisation process. In some instances, such as Cambodia, it took almost a decade to see through this process of demilitarisation and demobilisation.

And in Afghanistan, it is still an ongoing process. Washington's insistence on sudden and immediate rebel demilitarisation and demobilisation (as part of the wider state-building programme), over the traditional gradual approach, does raise questions about the efficacy of such policy overtures.

Unsurprisingly, following US ambassador, Mr Moriarty's statement the Maoist rebels of Nepal were quick to accuse the United States of 'trying to undermine the peace processes'. The leader of the rebel group responsible for waging the armed campaign Comrade Prachanda is reported to have argued:

> Even when the Nepalese state and the rebels were prepared to enter into a phase of negotiation and power sharing arrangement the United States was creating an atmosphere of suspicion between both parties. Put simply, was trying to undermine a peaceful atmosphere from building up.[12]

While still on this issue it is worthwhile reflecting on another rebel group that has assumed power through popular mandate but has not renounced its policy of violence. Washington's refusal to recognise the democratically elected government of Hamas in Palestine also raises questions about the efficacy of such policy undertakings. From the perspective of an external actor (involved in brokering peace or responsible for reconstruction initiatives) it is vital that the rebels enter into some form of formal renunciation of violence. This gesture, it is universally recognised, creates an atmosphere of trust between former adversaries and allows for a smooth organisation of the peace process. This, however, is what would happen in an ideal situation.

It is often the case that external actors involved in post-civil war state-building projects have a wider and bigger picture in mind. While entertaining that objective they tend push through their externally imposed reform programme and steamroll many small but vital interim issues associated with the conflict. Such policy undertaking, one could argue, instead of doing good for the host society can be counterproductive. As one critic points out, 'these actors should never forget that they are only temporarily in charge of that people's affairs, territory and sovereignty and one day they have to relinquish that role' (Chesterman 2004: 207–8).

Although aware of their temporary role the external actors, however, can never shy away from their overall responsibility. For the effective long-term positive recovery of weak post-conflict states it is vital that the external actors constantly follow the initiative in all its amplitude. These actors' 'responsibility to rebuild' commitment requires continuous attention to the problems of the given state and demands a generous resource package. Very often these initiatives sit at odds with a sceptical electorate at home, and lack of immediate success makes it impossible to work out a clear exit strategy. Apart from these challenges the involvement and initiative of external actors in mending other people's problems never get the recognition they deserve. Many view this as a thankless task. The question that arises, then, is why do individual actors go to the trouble of taking on such initiatives?

In spite of all the challenges involved and the negative connotations associated with external state-building initiatives there exists an element of altruism in such undertakings. This is clearly the case in those instances where international bodies such as the UN are involved in post-war recovery and post-conflict nation-building undertakings. If one were to assess the role of individual actors such as the United States or the United Kingdom, their post-conflict state reconstruction mission can be linked to a particularised form of liberal thinking. As Amitai Etzioni puts it, these actors 'believe in the possibility of human progress and have a weakness for positive thinking, which leads them to hold that such developments can be brought about relatively easily, especially if one is dedicated to bringing them about' (Etzioni 2004b: 1).

While liberalism-inspired altruism and neo-realist thinking (associated with the security of an interconnected world and the challenges posed by weak post-conflict states) dominate the state reconstruction undertaking not all post-civil war societies elicit commitments from external actors in this regard. Because of the volatile post-war atmosphere, absence of promised funding, impossible logistics and reluctance to see its own personnel in harm's way, the international community often has a selective nation-building approach. For the reasons stated above it has opted to leave some war-torn societies to their fate. As one critic has commented, 'the international community takes a back seat approach to many conflicts whereby it becomes a passive bystander while allowing domestic groups take the lead in restoring the state or in destroying it completely' (Ottaway 2002a: 1021). Nepal following its emergence from a decade-long violent civil war is a case in point. And so is Haiti. Viewed from within the neo-realist perspective Nepal and Haiti pose little threat to wider international security, and thus have not attracted any externally aided nation-building initiative. Although there is plenty of empathy for the plight of the people in these two war-torn societies, lack of concrete external financial commitment has meant there are no takers in the state-rebuilding enterprise.

Notwithstanding the earlier argument about the lack of commitment from the external community or actors in the said enterprise, it needs to be highlighted that the process of nation-building is successful where the post-conflict community is enlightened and capable, where the citizens forgo their previous animosity against one another, make sacrifices for the future well-being of all, and embrace the universal values. In the absence of these fundamental prerequisites, it is hard to attempt any meaningful and reasonable state-building either through indigenous or external mechanisms or through an initiative that is built on a partnership between the two.

Conclusion

State- or nation-building is an extremely slow process. From an external intervener's perspective 'rebuilding institutional structures is a difficult task, particularly in societies torn apart by internal war' (Newman and Schabel 2002: 1). 'Nation' building, as Robert O. Keohane has argued, 'was a bloody 300 year affair in the West' (Keohane 2002: 81). It is worth highlighting here that America's own nation-building experience – reconstructing the South after the Civil War – lasted a full century, until the Civil Rights Act of 1964 (Ignatieff 2002: 2).

It is tough to mend a war-torn state, but not impossible.[13] Introduced at the primary stages of a society's downward slide, a state-building initiative can make the difference between life and death of that particular state. Rebuilding post-civil war states is not only morally binding but also indispensable for the global society. As members of one extended family, the onus is on the better-performing and more able individuals within that family to look into the needs and requirements of those who are less able, lacking, and have failed in their duties and responsibilities for various reasons.

The price to pay for rebuilding these entities, however, is often phenomenally prohibitive.[14] The associated costs and risks are very high and state-building continues to be an expensive affair both in economic and human terms. An effective state-building enterprise both by the United Nations as well as the US has to explore ways of addressing these twin issues if they are to achieve lasting outcomes in their undertakings.

Under the aegis of a post-conflict state-building initiative, one of the key tasks to address is to attend to the state's damaged vital organs – the institutions of governance, judiciary, economic structure, socio-cultural fabric and so on. Given proper care and attention, these institutions can be resuscitated and nursed back to life. However, these are tasks best undertaken by the indigenous community. For it needs to devise a system of administration and governance that is to its liking and accepted by the larger international society. In the next chapter I look at the issue of post-war governance and suggest ways of reconstructing a new political culture that is both robust and visionary in its outlook.

6 Governing the ungovernable

Once the business of war is truly removed from the overall narrative of conflict it becomes pertinent for that given society to take stock of the new situation and devise ways to facilitate the unveiling of a new political process. The end of civil war ushers in an era where there is a visible move from violence into politics. In this new context old 'enmities get played out through more peaceful means'. The spirit of reconciliation and cooperation between former adversaries creates conditions for the introduction of a new narrative of political interaction.

At this juncture it becomes imperative that this society as a whole take on the responsibility of constructing a political framework that will form the basis of all future interaction between its diverse communities. The first prerequisite here is to install a new national government based on consensus. By affirming its faith in such a body, the society as a whole demonstrates that it has openly and consciously embraced the logic of responding to dissent through dialogue rather than violence. Transition from lurid anarchy to tentative institutional reconstruction through the formation of a brand new national government, however, is fraught with challenges. Not only in forming a government where there was none a logistical nightmare, but bringing together former rebels and opponents to form the core of this establishment is an extremely arduous undertaking.

The reflection of Roy Licklider, one of the foremost peace theorists, on this issue is very apt indeed. According to Licklider:

> Ending international war is hard enough, but at least there are opponents who will presumably eventually retreat to their own territories following a clear military settlement. But in civil wars the members of the two sides must live side-by-side and work together in a common government to make their country work. The question, therefore, is how do groups of people who have been killing one another with considerable enthusiasm and success come together to form a common unified government where the underlying norm is cooperation not conflict?

(Licklider 1993: 3–19)

During civil war conditions of anarchy were the norm, as there was a breakdown of communication between those who govern and the governed. Reinstallation or reintroduction of that communication process is one of the first preconditions of transition from conflict to peace. For pre-civil war government was characterised by certain remoteness. Since the system alienated them or they could not relate to it, a significant part of its citizenry had become its natural opponents and detractors.

In the new post-war situation the constituency as a whole needs to feel that it is their government; it is there to help them; and it has to be aware of their needs.[1] A post-civil war society, if it wishes to move forward, has no choice but to make civilian participation into the decision-making process. The onus on the post-war government, therefore, is not only to make the 'tension' disappear but also to make conscious judgment about the exercise of power. As one critic puts it:

> The central need in the aftermath of violent conflict is to rebuild the state's representative function, which should be constructed around an *inclusive* political and civic community. This inclusive community must overcome the fragmentation of society that occurs or is exacerbated during war, and view all members as survivors of conflict.
>
> (Mani 2005: 511)

And as Hartzell and Hoddie suggest 'the more extensive the network of power-sharing institutions the contending parties agree to create, the less likely they are to return to the use of armed violence to settle disputes' (Hartzell and Hoddie 2003: 330). When the erstwhile enemies sit together to draw out maps for a government of post-conflict national unity it confirms the triumph of reason. If they succeed in instituting a government that represents various groups, communal, religious and regional interests and reaches out to the widest possible members of the society then it fulfils one of the key principles of good governance.

The aim of this chapter is to highlight the key factors that contribute to the success of democratisation and power-sharing arrangements and thereby create conditions for sustainable governance in a post-conflict setting. While stressing these points I also tease out the issues that work as irritants in the overall sustainable governance project. My analysis is based on several individual cases such as Afghanistan, Chile, Democratic Republic of Congo, Guatemala, Nepal, Rwanda, among others.

Legitimising the illegitimate

A society that has experienced anarchy and gross unjust violence (as is typical of civil wars) is always suspicious of all forms of authority. This anxiety, to some degrees, is understandable. As Hannah Arendt argued, 'since authority always demands obedience, it is commonly mistaken for some form of power or violence' (Arendt 1983: 92–3). This pejorative reading of authority, then, is mostly due to the illegitimate violence that the authority had imposed during the life cycle of a conflict. The society in question underwent the turmoil, chaos and all the attendant misery as authority itself had become parochial or had disappeared. Although we can appreciate the underlying reasons which made authority a contested issue we simply cannot do away with authority in the post-conflict setting. Authority is paramount if one were to create a normal, peaceful and socially cohesive society which is at ease with itself. How then are we to construct a framework of interaction where authority is present but not contested? Reintroduction of authority in an erstwhile contested setting, to quote Hannah Arendt, again, 'must preclude the use of external means of coercion; where force is used, authority itself has failed' (Arendt 1983: 92–3).

While Arendt's argument makes sense its remits are deeply limiting in a post-conflict setting. For a society recovering from civil war is a volatile place. Although not at war with itself it may contain all those incendiary elements which can trigger violence with the slightest provocation. In order for that authority to be obeyed and not feared, the authority itself should not only have to enjoy popular consent but should also be constrained within a clear legal structure. A post-civil war society ought to have a framework where authority is laced with legitimate power but there is no room for its illegitimate enforcement. It is pertinent that the role the governing body plays in coordinating and in conducting collective affairs should have the character of law only to the extent that it has the accord of the population (Coicaud 2002: 12). A framework made up of popular consent and legal responsibility would act as a 'check and balance' mechanism whereby the authority can only exercise its power legitimately and those who have consented to it can withdraw their support should it use that power unjustly.

As is abundantly clear in those societies where two opposing groups or communities live within one political entity, i.e. a state, the situation is often marked by discrimination against the minority and control of authority by the majority. The institutional discrimination and control in this intra-group conflict is carried out not only for ethnocentric or racial reasons but also as one of the coping strategies created to deal with the threat and danger that the rival group presents (Bar-Tal and Teichman 2005: 90). Very often such discriminatory practices serve as the bedrock of conflict and contribute to the anarchy that follows. If the society is to return to normality and the legitimacy of the state reinstated then there needs to be a clean break in the practice of such institutional discrimination.

Irritants in the governing process

Even when there exist reasonable grounds for cooption there is no guarantee that all former belligerents will enter a shared political domain. Parties to the conflict sometimes have irrational demands and expectations which others find impossible to meet. In such scenarios a return to the earlier conflict dynamics becomes an inevitable prospect. Why do belligerents prefer violence over peace? This peculiarity is best explained within the context of the 'theory of entrapment'. According to James Brockner and Jeffrey, Rubin entrapment is 'a decision making processes in which individuals escalate their commitment to previously chosen, though failing course of action in order to "make good" on prior investments' (Brockner and Jeffrey 1985: 9).

Put simply, entrapment in the context of civil war implies parties to the conflict are trapped in their own previous commitment to violence. This they cannot easily skip, shrug off, abandon or renege on. This is an attitude which manifests itself even when the rebels or the belligerents in the conflict are fully aware that *not* moving forward might not produce the desired goals. Why stick to this illogical logic? As Timothy D. Sisk puts it, within the framework of entrapment actors find themselves in a scenario where they find it hard to move forward in the direction of peacemaking owing to their previous investment in conflict. The 'sunk costs' as he puts it, forces the actors to avoid negotiations and termination of the war (Sisk 2004), for termination of conflict and the setting up of a transparent system of administration undermines their power and authority. This is directly linked to the argument surrounding 'greed theory' of rebellion as business which we discussed in Chapter 1.

The rebels, combatants and their leaders' reluctance to embrace peace settlement through negotiation may be couched in clear, practical and self-interested logic. Very often external actors mediating in a conflict push through a peace plan without ensuring the required groundwork. Under the external guidelines rebels are often asked to disarm, disengage from violence and integrate into public life by the third party while there still exists a prevailing climate of hostility and insecurity. Such manners of engagement do very little in terms of actual conflict reduction.

In their overzealous enthusiasm those responsible for overseeing the peace plan ask the former rebels to embrace peace in spite of the absence of a consensual interim government, clearly recognised legal framework and credible state apparatus. Unsurprisingly, as Barbara Walter suggests,

> Groups fighting civil wars avoid negotiated settlements because they understand that this would require them to relinquish important fallback defenses at a time when no neutral police force and no legitimate government exist to help them enforce the peace.
>
> (Walter 1997: 337–364)

Thus the rebels hold on to their arms. This is a classic situation which is repeated in many post-conflict settings. In Northern Ireland, for example, the IRA kept hold of its arms for almost ten years following the signing of Good Friday Peace Agreements precisely because of the absence of some of the above conditions. It put its stockpile of arms and arsenals beyond use only after it felt that the conditions were ripe for such a move.

The rebels' reluctance to disarm is also heavily influenced by the overall military parity between the parties to the conflict. Negotiated settlements always produce a scenario where one group or party is naturally less powerful than the other. In a scenario where the state and rebel groups enter a peace settlement the latter always end up with a lower position of strength in the overall military balance or equation. Apprehensions about one's own vulnerability and failure to trust the other fully precipitate the demise of any treaty or peace agreement that aims to enforce peace through a negotiated settlement. In such contexts the past always looms large in relation to the future. Inevitably such thinking overshadows the prospect for peace. As Walter argues,

Knowing they will enter a period of intense vulnerability, neither side can convince the other that they will nobly resist a treaty's temptations or naively fulfill its terms. And so, unable to enforce the agreement or survive exploitation, they avoid cooperation and continue to fight.

(Walter 1997: 335–64)

The uneasy peace process in the Democratic Republic of Congo (DRC) following the failure of a national unity government is a case in point, to which I will return later in this chapter.

If by any chance this seige mentality or the condition of entrapment is avoided then there is still the overall role of the intervener which weighs heavily on any post-conflict peace process. In those conflicts where an external third party had intervened to broker peace the final outcome is often hostage to the level of commitment of the intervener. An accountable, responsible and committed third party can critically influence the mood of belligerents in the direction of peace. If the attitude of the intervener or negotiator is haphazard, noncommittal and irregular then the peace process is bound to falter. This is a classic characterisation of weak external mediation. According to some scholars, 'a weak mediation is not effective in creating good faith among the parties and thus, it is more likely that the parties will continue to war and not admit to a peace process' (Sisk 2004: 15–16). Adversaries in a civil war, as a rule of thumb, require some form of guarantee in order to affirm their faith in the peace process. They remain edgy and jittery if they realise that there is no credible guarantor to the undertaking. The role of Norway in the Sri Lankan civil war is a case in point. The Norwegians who have been involved in the negotiations between the Sri Lankan government and the rebel Liberation Tigers of Tamil Eelam (LTTE) to end twenty-five years of civil war have been accused of such an attitude by the adversaries. Although Oslo managed to broker a ceasefire of sorts between the Sri Lankan government and LTTE the ceasefire was constantly being violated by one or other of the parties partly because of the weak position of the mediator.

Enfranchise / power play

Disenfranchisement often lies at the heart of rebel behaviour and insurgency. As we noticed earlier, a civil war typically starts with the ejection of the concerned group from mainstream politics and power play. This uprooting not only creates a condition of alienation among those ejected from the overall process, but also provides a solid ground outside from which to fight against this ejection. This not only provides them with a cause to fight against the central authorities and the state concerned but also helps them garner the support of civilian members of the group. Evidently both the discourse and activism relating to civil war usually point in the direction of the absence of a shared governing space.

Bringing these disaffected constituencies back into the mainstream has the potential advantage of calming rebel insurgency and their violent activism. There is, of course, no set rule for such manoeuvre. As Terrence Lyons puts it:

One of the most important aspects of successful cases of demilitarised politics is the institutional transformation of that most characteristic institution of civil war, the insurgency or military government, into that distinctive organisation of electoral competition, the civilian political party.

(Lyons 2005: 125)

One of the key objectives in this situation is to provide a political framework which would allow these former combatants to organise themselves. Once these actors are organised into civilian political parties it becomes relatively easier to negotiate their grievances. And it also paves the way for democratisation and power-sharing. Facilitating the provision of self-government to the disaffected group by the central authority often holds the key to the reduction of violence and prepares the groundwork for eventual conflict resolution.

In cases of negotiated settlement of civil wars elections occupy a central position. Elections help create a democratic consensus and in turn contribute to the reduction of hostilities among former adversaries. As a crucial part of the peace process, elections aim to terminate the civil war and contribute to sustainable peace building (Lyons 2002: 215). Post-war elections fulfil a wide variety of requirements. On a political level, election implies the process of enabling the citizenry to participate in the shaping of government policies through representative participation (Schwarz 2005: 441). For the belligerents it provides an opportunity to share power through democracy. And for the 'international community, post-war elections serve as a symbolic endpoints for the high-profile intervention in the realm of peacekeeping or peace implementation' (Lyons 2002: 215).

Building a new governing structure that is deemed representative by all the citizenry is a very complex, drawn-out and arduous process, particularly so when it is undertaken in a setting where questions about complicity, guilt, violence, responsibility abound (Misra 2004b; Schwarz 2005). However, as an exhausted rebel group puts down its arms and an elected government settles down to rule, both militancy and state repression which were the norms during the civil war years retreat into the background. This ideal situation, however, is only possible in some specific situations. It is most likely to occur when the civil war dynamics involves one particular group and the state. Self-rule or some form of autonomy is easy to introduce in those instances where the conflict is primarily bipartisan in nature. For instance, following ten years of civil war in Punjab the central government in New Delhi was able to stem the increasing tide of separatism by introducing limited autonomy and facilitating self-rule in the province (Kohli 1997; Misra 2001). The Spanish government too was able to cap the quarter of a century old violent Basque separatist movement by granting them limited autonomy and self-rule (Alonso 2004: 695–713).

However, this approach is hard to choreograph when there are more than two parties involved in the overall conflict dynamics. The promise and offer of self-rule and elected government in the post-war setting, instead of creating an atmosphere of tranquillity, paradoxically contributes to the opening-up of new avenues of dissent. There is, of course, no surprise as to why this happens. Anyone who has tried to find his or her way out of a conflict situation in everyday life would testify that it is relatively easy to negotiate in a conflict involving just two disagreeing individuals or parties as opposed to a conflict situation that involves a multitude of actors. When there are more than two parties to the conflict the normal strategy of negotiation becomes redundant. This new situation often demands tailor-made conflict resolution strategies.

In spite of the challenges and complexities, the protagonists in those conflicts involving more than two actors do sometimes manage to abandon the status quo and agree to be a part of the new civilian governing process. But even after these rebels have gone through a changeover – into what might be called conscientious political actors – there is no guarantee that they will fulfil their duties and obligations professionally. After a generation-long conflict, as part of the Good Friday Agreement of 1997 the British government finally made provisions for the introduction of self-rule in the troubled province of Northern Ireland through a power-sharing arrangement between the nationalists and the republicans. However, unlike the Punjab and the Basque Country where both New Delhi and Madrid were dealing respectively with one set of actors, in the case of Northern Ireland London was in the midst of a tripartite conflict and worked hard to build a modicum of cooperation between Sinn Féin and the Democratic Unionist Party (DUP). But owing to the squabbles between these two adversaries the self-rule provisions could be implemented for long four years since after the initial agreement.[2]

Civil wars are products of the failure of democratic leadership. Sometimes, it is the incapacity of professional politicians to find solutions to the grievance of the people they represent which facilitates the rise of militant leadership. It is true that the civilian masses become converts to the incendiary discourse of the rebels and are mobilised occasionally out of fear. But they also affirm their trust and faith in the violent logic of the rebels when they realise that the latter are their only hope in relation to a change in the status quo. In other words, the political indecisiveness and impotency of civilian politicians to respond to changing demands facilitates the intervention by the militants. Once a section of the masses are mobilised professional politicians lose control and the militants take over. This was the classic scenario in the Tamil uprising in Sri Lanka. The failure of various Tamil political parties to win concession from the Sinhalese central government in Sri Lanka for over three decades made a desperate population finally inch towards the violent discourse of the LTTE. Once it had a sympathetic audience the LTTE pushed the professional politicians out of the equation through both intimidation and killing.

Even when a community affirms its faith in the militancy for a viable solution to its problems and grievances it has no option but to retreat from its dependency on the rebel militancy and make way for civilian politics in the post-war phase. Ironic as it may seem the rebels who had earlier rejected the narrative of negotiation and consensual politics ultimately find themselves in a situation where they have no alternative but to reorient themselves into the civilian political process if they wish to be effective forces in the post-conflict political process. If one were to make a quick assessment of the above argument we come across contemporary examples which prove that to be the case. The changeover from Basque separatist ETA rebels to civilian politics in Spain, the Nepalese Maoist insurgents' adoption of a civilian political role in the post-civil war phase, and that of the Sikh militants in the separatist civil war in the Punjab all point in that direction.

Of course, there will be situations where the militant leadership may reject such a changeover. The role of the state in this situation becomes very crucial indeed. In those instances where the rebels are hesitant to embrace civilian politics or the political process the state can nurture alternative leaders and make available to them the required space to step into the shoes of the militant leadership, and thereby facilitate peace. Take the Sikh civil war in the Punjab, India in the 1980s. New Delhi which was fighting a fierce battle against the separatist Sikh militants in the troubled province when chanced with limited victory allowed for the return of civilian Sikh politicians and moderate leaders to populate the political space hitherto controlled and occupied by the militants. Once nurtured, the civilian professional politicians gradually pushed the discourse of militancy out from the overall political process. A tired and terrified population, which had once accepted militancy as the only way out of the conflict, soon reaffirmed its faith in the civilian government (Misra 2001; Singh 2000).

Although the whole process may appear easy, for the civilian political force to take control of a previously violent society some other necessary preconditions need to be met. These preconditions are (a) the state must have secured a clear and decisive military victory; (b) the civilian populace must have reached a state of battle fatigue; (c) the professional politicians must come from within that community; (d) the demilitarisation of politics must pay adequate attention to the grievances of the community concerned; (e) a long-term viable economic package is necessary to revive the battle-scarred economy of the concerned area; and (f) most importantly the re-adoption of militants into civilian ways must be achieved. Such a multi-pronged approach has the benefit of not only winning over the disaffected constituency but also eliminating all those factors that aided the militancy and rebellion in the first place.

Politics of post-war governance

The catalogue of preconditions I highlighted above, although noble in sentiment and character, is very hard to adopt in all post-civil war societies. In this section, in examining the politics of post-war governance in two contemporary societies, I show that to be the case.

Iraq

The conflict in Iraq is a special case. Here was a functioning state that was forced to undergo regime change through unilateral intervention by the United States and its allies. The regime change was followed by the complete breakdown of law and order, leading to a million civilian deaths over five years (2003–2008). These deaths mostly occurred within the dynamics of sectarian violence, militancy, rebel insurgency, fighting against the foreign occupation force and so on.[3] In addition the sectarian killing during this period caused massive internal displacement. Over 300,000 Sunni and Shia Muslims fled from one part of the country to another (*The Economist*, 14 October 2006: 72). On the third anniversary of the invasion of the country there were three different civil wars raging in Iraq. The first involved the fight against U.S.-led coalition forces and anti-government insurgents, the second between the Kurds and other communities in northern Iraq, and the third between Sunni Arabs and Shi'ite Arabs in the centre of the country (Kaufmann 2006: 156–7).

Within the framework of post-conflict governance, 'power sharing', it is argued, can ease the transition to participatory politics, reduce uncertainty between former adversaries and produce the broadest possible coalition in the government (Jeong 2005: 95). However, in spite of the formation of a government of national unity and reconciliation and deep international involvement in Iraq's state-building undertaking there was no prospect of conflict reduction in the country until the end of 2007. How does one interpret the complex politics of post-conflict governance in Iraq?

The problem of governability in Iraq can be interpreted as a product of communal and sectarian politics, the dominance of which in the governing process could not have been avoided as its roots go back to the origin of the Iraqi state. Iraq was an artificial state that was created at a time when European colonialism was entering its final stages. It was formed following the collapse of the Ottoman Turkish Empire (of which the region was a part). The peace settlements that followed allowed the victorious British in the region to bring together Baghdad, Basra and Mosul under one unified authority of a Sunni monarch. This new bureaucratic state, however, did not enjoy legitimacy in the eyes of of all the constituent communities. Thus conflict over issues of identity and over distribution of resources remained an abiding concern of those who came to live in this new polity. These questions, although important, were kept tightly under control by successive Iraqi governments and especially during Saddam Hussein's twenty-five years rule.

The Allied intervention in Iraq, however, created a hitherto unavailable space within which communities could afford to express their grievances and reassess questions about their identity. As Vali Nasr put it, 'rather than viewing the fall of Saddam Hussein and the regime change as an occasion to create liberal democracy, many Iraqis viewed it as an opportunity to redress injustices in the distribution of power and resources among the country's majority communities' (Nasr 2006: 58). The unravelling of the once unitary Iraqi identity was very sudden. As many observers have pointed out, before 2003 virtually all Iraqi Arabs identified themselves as Arabs, in opposition to Kurds and others. Three years on, in 2006, the whole country was divided along communal lines with the previous 'Iraqi Arabs' expressing their allegiance to various sectarian identities. The ensuing violence was a product of the complex multidimensional nature of the conflict.

Given the complexities of the conflict in Iraq, the traditional practice of imposing of a civilian government and backing it up with superior firepower to curb violence had little merit. Since the United States and its allies created the condition that Iraqis found themselves in, it was but natural for the international community to expect the former to explore and implement a viable approach that could bring society back from the prevailing anarchy. This has led some scholars to suggest that rather than a slash and burn strategy one could have a gradual and determined approach to contain civil war. According to Kenneth Pollack of the Brooking Institution a 'step-by-step pacification approach' works best where the society is extremely divided. The external intervener could concentrate on 'securing a gradually expanding swath of territory and on protecting the local population therein, giving it better government and thereby winning its cooperation in marginalizing violent rebels, extremists and insurgents' (quoted in Dobbins 2006: 154).

Stemming adversarial sectarian politics in Iraq necessitated satisfying Shi'ite demands for power and autonomy while placating Sunni anger and alleviating Sunni anxiety (Nasr 2006: 60). Similarly the Kurds in the north, with a long history of domination and torture at the hands of Sunnis, required some form of federal autonomy. With that aim in mind the Iraqis adopted a new constitution, which made provisions for the election of a government of national unity and devolution of power through federalism. Paradoxically, instead of consolidating peace this new federal structure alienated the minority Sunnis and strengthened sectarian divisions. And as one critic put it, 'elections in Iraq had the most wondrous aspects, but they also divided the country into three hostile communities and hardened these splits' (Zakaria 2007: 5). If the lessons of Iraq are anything to go by, it would be right to argue that sometimes the best-intentioned governing structure may run aground. The constitutional arrangements based on accommodation and harmony through power-sharing and federal autonomy may allow federal boundaries to coincide with ethnic and sectarian divisions (Jeong 2005: 102).

Democratic Republic of Congo

One of the fundamental challenges to ensuring peace in society that has just emerged out of civil war is the establishment of a consensual democratic government that contains leaders who are known pacifists with a deep commitment to peace. Elections, it is argued, allow the opportunity for this changeover. Elections in a post-civil war setting, however, do not necessarily allow the option of getting the peacemakers to take charge.[4] It is often the former warlords, rebel leaders or dictators who simply decide to come back to power through another means, under a new guise.

When the Democratic Republic of Congo (DRC) went to elect a new president after ten years of a torturous civil war the electorates themselves were not overtly enthusiastic about this new-found option or the prospect of seeing a democratically elected leader. To sceptics, choosing the president in the 2006 elections was like 'having to choose between cholera and the plague'. When the results were finally declared it proved far too contentious. The election, though conclusive with 58 per cent votes going to Joseph Kabila and 42 per cent to his opponent Jean-Pierre Bemba, was nonetheless contested by the losing side. The former warlord Bemba's supporters fired machine gun shots at the Supreme Court in the capital Kinshasa while their defeated leader vowed to fight on. And in the months following its victory Kabila's government happily pursued a policy of intimidation against the losing side. In early February 2007 with the aid of police and soldiers his government killed at least a hundred opposition protesters who were disputing the results of the provincial election. Unfortunately, the new army, which was revamped by the UN Peacekeeping mission MONUC to protect the civilian population, was busy killing civilians – a development which led many Congolese to argue that the army in the post-conflict Congo was the main human rights abuser (*The Economist,* 2007: 62). This trend continued throughout 2007 and resulted in thousands of opposition members being killed by the army for opposing the demilitarisation of ex-militants campaign.

Although one cannot undermine the process of disarmament, demobilisation, reinsertion and reintegration (DDRR) of former insurgents and combatants in transitions from war to peace in post-civil war societies, the manner in which their demobilisation takes place is crucial to the overall peace. In the ultimate analysis the choice of strategy for dealing with this aspect is greatly determined by the nature of leadership. If the regime in power is assured of its position it is likely to favour democratisation and approach the issues by non-military means. By contrast those whose powerbase is contested and who lack complete consensus as to their rule can resort to military option to find a solution to the DDRR programme. The government of Kabila in DR Congo lacked such a clear mandate for its rule. Thus it gave in to the temptation of using violence in the post-conflict setting in order to steamroll a particular agenda.

In addition, as the DRC example shows, the government of Kabila was able to resort to arms to silence the opposition in a post-conflict setting owing to the crucial support of the military. In this particular instance both the civilian and the military leadership appear to be working in unison. Why such a symbiotic relationship exists within the framework of post-conflict governance is not hard to gauge. This is based on simple practical thinking. Very often the new civilian government finds its powers compromised by the army. And since the government lacks the power to end the army's stranglehold on everyday politics it sometimes ignores its complicity in previous crimes and worse still enters into a partnership with it.

Accountability and governance

Permitting the armed forces to make themselves immune to prosecution for dreadful crimes seems intolerable; yet it also seems irrational to insist that an elected civilian government should commit suicide by provoking its armed forces (Neier 1998). This dilemma illustrates the fragility of most of the elected governments that have taken over from dictatorship or assumed power after years of civil war. As a rule of thumb on a matter that is crucial to the military, the commanding officers still wield decisive power in the post-conflict setting. Yet, if the new civilian governments are to evolve into genuine democracies, it is essential that the rule of law should prevail and that the armed forces should be subordinated to democratic rule (Neier 1998).

Following its transition from military to civilian rule Chile took almost twenty years to confront its military for its excesses during the civil war years. Furthermore, it dragged its feet when it was faced with demands for prosecution of the chief violator of human rights during this period, General Augusto Pinochet, and heaved a sigh of relief when he died without having to face the judiciary in 2006. Similarly, after it emerged from a civil war lasting for almost half a century, the civilian government in Guatemala found it impossible to confront its military (the key actor responsible for most of the human rights violations and killings).

While administering justice in cases of war crimes continues to be problematic, the international community, it appears, is facing up to the challenge. A global body the International War Crimes Tribunal, pursues and prosecutes the military leadership responsible for their actions during the chaos and carnage of civil war. In addition, the United Nations has openly called for the newly appointed non-military democratic governments in states freshly out of their violent past to bring to justice everyone guilty of their crimes.

In recent years, the UN High Commissioner for Human Rights Louise Arbour has made it amply clear on various occasions that 'the UN totally rejects any amnesties for very serious offences – genocide, war crimes and crimes against humanity'. While visiting Nepal in 2007, following the end of the Maoist-led civil war, she urged the newly formed government not to ignore the vital issue of addressing the grievances of victims of civil war. This, she argued, should be done by prosecuting both the government troops and former Maoist rebels for their human rights abuses. However, just like its counterparts in Chile and Guatemala the fragile post-civil war transitional government in Nepal was hamstrung by practical challenges. It could not engage in such a 'witch hunt' for fears of jeopardising its own political survival and also for fears of renewed fighting. In addition, since many ex-Maoist rebels and military personnel who fought against one another during the civil war were members of the new government it made the demand for accountability all the more difficult.

On another front, paradoxical as it may seem, the end of civil war often gives birth to new grievances and aspirations. Those who had silently suffered during the conflict and had given up hopes of any transformation of their lives suddenly assume a position of strength when faced with the new post-war situation. Groups and communities who had previously been ignored and had always had a marginal presence in the overall socio-economic and political structure suddenly expect a major share in the new decision-making process. Given the fact that the new post-civil war government aims to have a consensual basis to its legitimacy it finds such demands hard to ignore. But meeting such demands immediately – as these groups often insist – usually proves daunting. Under these circumstances while, on the one hand, the country or state manages to put an end to the main conflict, at another level it confronts various small and low-level insurgencies – often products of its inability to respond to these immediate demands. Let me return to the example of civil war in Nepal in order to put this argument in context.

Soon after it emerged from an eleven-year old bloody civil war that claimed nearly 13,0000 lives, Nepal was faced with a new bout of insurgency in early 2007. During this period demonstrations and violence became commonplace in the southern part of the country: a reminiscence of the earlier civil war era. In the centre of this insurgency were a previously unknown group called Madheshis (inhabitants of southern Nepal). The Madheshis' participation in this new uprising was based on a rather simple line of argument. They claimed that although they formed one-third of the total population of the country their presence in the economic and political arena was rather marginal. To support their claim they stressed that while they constituted a third of the country's citizenry they occupied only one-tenth of the government work force. And in the army they had virtually no presence. Owing to this long-running institutional discrimination and exclusion, they argued, they were no longer ready to accept their marginal position in a post-war society that claimed to provide equality for all.

Under the banner of reformation Madheshi demands for equality ranged from complete independence to limited autonomy and better representation at the centre. Their medium of protest against this unjust system was primarily violent. An oddity one might say on the part of a group that had no previous experience of violence – even during the civil war era. On closer inspection such violent activism would appear to be both opportunistic as well as ascriptive. The decade-long Maoist insurgency had caused many hitherto unconsolidated and unassertive groups to replicate the former's strategy of confrontation, which meant following a more aggressive and assertive path. Those who undertook it were convinced that political violence was likely to yield greater results than silent protests.

This hard-line attitude of the Madheshis not only plunged the country into chaos, its violent activism also became a blueprint and instant source of inspiration for some other groups. Soon after the Madheshis' violent activism in the south of the country there appeared a new countrywide political front that wanted to highlight the grievances of the indigenous people in Nepal. The Nepal Federation of Indigenous Nationalities (NEFIN) initiated a general strike in the capital Kathmandu on 15 February 2007, which coincided with the continuing violence in the south. The strike paralysed the capital, leading to further apprehension about the survival of the new peace process. As the above two cases illustrate such new post-civil war activism (violent or otherwise) bring to the fore the unrecognised gaps existing in the socio-economic and political structure and consequently the need to devise new approaches in the process of governance to address such maladies.

Government beyond prejudice

Discrimination in its various forms when institutionalised leads to grievances becoming organised. As we know, if these grievances remain unaddressed over a long period of time they provide the basis for conflict. It is vital that communities that aim to move in the direction of post-conflict positive peace get rid of their past animosities and prejudicial thinking towards one another, for the absence of commitment to new thinking is bound to be an obstacle to successful post-conflict cohabitation. While a post-war society can eliminate institutional discrimination and prejudice by means of a good transparent system of governance based on equality, it is slightly more difficult to tackle the discriminatory practices perpetuated at the individual or group level.

As many contemporary examples of post-war societies affirm, even when individuals and groups enter into a consensual peace process they are not necessarily free from their inherited prejudices against one another. In the post-war phase, while the erstwhile adversaries may publicly acknowledge their decision to bury differences, nonetheless they keep it alive in their private domain. If forced to display a sense of unity under the new system of governance they soon find other groups or minorities on whom to vent their anger and insecurity.

Northern Ireland provides an interesting example in this regard. This troubled province entered into a formal peace process in 1994 after almost a quarter of century of intense violence. The peace process known as the Good Friday Agreement effectively put an end to the civil war. However a decade later it was found that some of the main signatories to the agreement had hardly abandoned their prejudice and hatred against those who were not like them and in fact they had since learned to invent and identify new targets. The 2005 Northern Ireland Life and Times survey made the startling discovery that the percentage of Northern Irish natives admitting they are prejudiced on the grounds of racism, or are xenophobic, had doubled from 11 to 25 per cent since the paramilitary ceasefires of 1994 (McDonald 2006: 15).

The most startling aspect of the survey was that the prejudice cut across all social classes. It stressed that when it came to entertaining rabid prejudice against another individual or group there was no significant difference between those who lived at the bottom end of the society and those who were better-off. A manager who admitted to being prejudiced against a particular section of the society, the survey pointed out, might not be the one torching an immigrant's house but he or she might not give that immigrant a job (McDonald 2006: 15). The new racism and public display of prejudice and violence by both Catholics and Protestants (against all those who did not belong to the two majority communities) contributed to Belfast being dubbed the 'race hate capital of Europe'. Such a public upsurge of negative activism in the post-war phase is not specific to Northern Ireland alone. South Africa, which emerged from almost a century of segregation and a quarter of a century of civil war also threw up similar levels of prejudice and violence against others. As the new multiracial South Africa became a magnet for many immigrants from neighbouring Mozambique and Lesotho it created tension within the country. These immigrants, in spite of their racial affinity with majority South Africans, found themselves as targets of hate and race attacks.

The question that one needs to ask in this context, however, is why do societies that resolve to move forward give in to a fresh new bout of prejudice and enemy profiling? In an underdeveloped or developing context prejudice can be argued to have its basis in competition over resources. What is the basis for perpetuation of such prejudice and low-level violence against new communities in supposedly developed societies? Let us return to the case of Northern Ireland to find some answers to this question. Asked why racism and xenophobia was commonest among the DUP (Democratic Unionist Party, the main Protestant party, in the province), one of the authors of the 2005 Northern Ireland Life and Times Survey is reported to have stressed that those who harbored such feelings felt that they have lost out since the cease-fires. For them the whole world is against them, the Catholics, the British Government and finally the minority non-whites and many white non-whites from Eastern Europe and the Baltic republics.

(McDonald 2006: 15)

As I have emphasised on in several occasions, the transition from conflict to peace is a long and arduous process especially for those whose lives were circumscribed by the politics of difference. Belligerents in a civil conflict often are psychologically damaged owing to their years, decades and sometimes centuries-old mistrust, hatred, prejudices. Hence in the intermediate phase, they find it almost impossible to develop a new narrative of interaction that facilitates confrontation over cooperation towards one and all. Yet, over time, some groups may display an attitude which is a step away from their habitual confrontational framework of interaction.

A demonstration of that change of heart or alternative thinking was seen in the case of the arguments within the Orange Order about changing the Protestant Orange Parades to something of a carnival. In June 2006 Drew Nelson, the Grand Secretary of the Orange Order, made public his wish to step away from this traditional 'war-like parade' and turn it into something of a cultural event. This long-standing tradition that celebrates the commemoration of William III's 1690 victory at the battle of the Boyne is a constant reminder to the Catholics of the superiority of the Protestants. For almost a quarter of a century the Orange Parades on 12 July have been the focal point for sectarian clashes between Catholics and Protestants and an important factor in perpetuating the civil war dynamics. Drew Nelson's conscious attempt to dispel the confrontational posture and replace it with an attitude of cooperation certainly held the key to 'ease tensions between communities venting anger over disputed marching routes' (Bowcott 2006: 7), offering the potential to reconfigure the relationship between Catholics and Protestants.

A successful post-conflict government is one which not only embraces liberal democratic values but also works towards the betterment of all the constituencies within that polity. It needs to constantly remind itself that every individual in the post-war setting is a survivor and therefore has a natural stake in the society and deserves respect, compassion and equality. Occasionally some governments rise to these challenges and become an example to others. South Africa is a case in point here.[5] Here was a majoritarian government that had the option of using the past atrocities to prepare a case against the minority responsible for excesses of violence against the majority. However, it chose to move forward and instead of exacting revenge it facilitated true reconciliation among its diverse groups and made forgiveness a part of the philosophy of governance.

Some post-conflict governments, by contrast, are known to draw upon the memory of past division, animosity and violence between groups in order to consolidate their authority. This is at best a short-term strategy. While it whips up passion for indigenous state- and nation-building initiatives it nonetheless sets a dangerous precedent. Such strategy is known to generate extreme xenophobia and isolate minorities or worse still make them targets of the majority community. Following the 1988–91 civil war the Armenian majority government in Nagorno-Karabakh engaged in ethnic cleansing against virtually its entire Azeri population. Similarly, although the disputed region of Kosovo is yet to gain full international recognition as an independent state (at the time of this book going to press) the governing regime is known to have been engaged in a form of story-telling that vilifies the minority Serbs. While such government-mediated narrative has succeeded in uniting the Kosovo Albanians and infused in them a sense of commitment towards their war-torn, land it has at the same time undermined the position of various traditional minorities (most importantly Serbs), within the disputed region.

Such developments in post-civil war societies have created a deep sense of unease and anxiety in policy circles. Thus now it is suggested that should a post-civil war society succeed in achieving independence or enter into a peace pact it should treat sovereignty as a responsibility. As the International Commission on Intervention and State Sovereignty (ICISS) argued, in the changed post-conflict context those in charge of governance should realise that they are responsible for maintaining international standards of democracy and human rights. They need to recognise that on a scale of values the sovereignty of a state does not stand higher than the human rights of its inhabitants (ICISS 2001: 11). This, in effect, implies that the legitimacy of the new government at the international level is largely dependent on the policy measures it adopts internally.

Slow pluralism

Our assessment of the process of governance, so far, has produced a narrative, which suggests that all post-conflict governments need to have an inclusive political framework. The key constituents of this framework, among others, should include multi-party democracy, protection of minority and group rights, an independent judiciary, rule of law and freedom of speech (press) and so on. Making it possible for former adversaries to join a government of national unity is based on the argument that being in power will make all the participants act more responsibly. Those who embrace this framework, it would appear, have a greater degree of success in terms of preventing future conflict and are less likely to fall in with rebel demands and insurrections. But there is a sticking point here. What if the government in charge feels that too much of these recommended guiding principles might actually hinder the effective functioning of the government, inhibit developmental initiatives and push the state back to the earlier mode of contest and conflict?

In the end, the theory of inclusive governance is often ignored in many post-conflict societies. If the direction of conflict was *even,* where both the majority and the minority exchanged regular violence and there were no clear winners, then the process of governance creates a condition of inclusivity where both get an equal share in the process and structure of governance. However, in the event of the conflict having been perpetrated by the majority community and the minority being the principal victims, the survivors get the upper hand in the key decision-making process in the post-conflict governance. Exclusion of the majority in these instances operates along a simple logic, i.e. the majority behaved irresponsibly and could do so again, thus they need to be absorbed into the power structure gradually but *not* immediately. Therefore, we encounter scenarios where the post-conflict government is led by a government that allows a preferential treatment to its minorities.

After the civil war, Afghanistan had an initial governing structure that allowed the state-forming ethnos, i.e. the majority Pashtuns, a decidedly second-tier position in the key government positions (Misra 2004b). The minorities, by contrast, were at the top of the decision-making hierarchy.[6] Turning to Rwanda we find a similar policy mechanism at work. Although constitutionally committed to a pluralist governing structure in the post-genocide phase the Rwandan Patriotic Front (RPF) government of Paul Kagame put stealth barriers against the Hutu majorities to prevent them from occupying key government positions. Kagame's government made it extremely difficult for other parties to operate in the same political arena, which thereby successfully eliminated the possibility of the emergence of multiparty politics. Consequently this move effectively killed any potential opposition.[7]

In addition, pluralist ideals such as absolute equality among the masses, transparency in the activities of the government, and decentralisation of authority were never fully taken on board by the Kagame government. Although controversial, especially in the context of a post-conflict society, where the aim is to create a unitary spirit among the citizenry with a divided a bitter past, such policy measures were nonetheless supported by many. While some groaned against this 'soft authoritarianism', the international community remained fairly supportive of the whole enterprise. Responding to the critics Kagame's supporters argued 'too much democracy too soon will split Rwanda apart again' (Kinzer 2007: 26). Thus it was fully justified to have a period of benevolent authoritarianism under the watchful eye of the international community.

The reason why some post-conflict societies are allowed to continue the practice of partisan governance by the international community is based on pragmatism. One could argue the promotion of multi-party democracy can be deeply problematic, as it would let the perpetrators of violence return to power through a democratic mandate. Thus, in some scenarios, one is forced to support a government that is not totally committed to the narrow definition of 'good governance'. As Kagame himself has stressed, 'defining these aspirations too narrowly or by the book can be counterproductive and undermine the overall stability of the country' (Kinzer 2007: 26). Thus while the logic of co-option through democracy is the most attractive of options its application in a post-conflict society depends on the political self-confidence of both the politicians as well as electorate.

Conclusion

Alexander Hamilton was not exaggerating when he suggested, 'a nation without a national government is an awful spectacle' (Hamilton 1987: 487). The question of governability following civil war is a testament to the resilience of the state itself. If it succeeds in creating a spirit where the citizenry do not see themselves as 'victims' or constantly refer to the past 'injustices' but consider themselves as wise men and women who could remove themselves from narrowness and treat every other individual as an equal, the process of governability becomes an easy endeavour. In the end,

> it is the forging of an inclusive political community out of the shards of war that will be the touchstone of a peaceful future. By the same token, the failure to rebuild such an inclusive political entity could spark the embers for a future relapse into violence.
>
> (Mani 2005: 512)

Successful conflict resolution requires the new governing structure to make the system transparent, equitable and most importantly a great deal more flexible in terms of granting autonomous space and rights to various groups and communities. In this regard the government and civil society partnership is fundamental to the creation of lasting peace. The process of sustainable governance need not be limited to the clearly defined power-sharing arrangements at the central, regional and local levels. Creating a viable socio-political arrangement where there is respect for authority and general involvement in the workings of various aspects of government is to a great extent dependent on formal power and civil society interaction.[8]

As we have seen in our interrogation of various cases, post-civil war society is marked by intense power struggles between various actors. Conflict-ridden societies have a good prospect of recovering from war's overpowering shadows if they built up social capital in the form of practices of cooperation, norms of participation and institutions of civil society (Keohane 2002: 75). The role of civil society is crucial in the sense that it can act as a pressure group and effective balancer. As some argue, 'a flourishing civil society can substantially influence the balance of power among the power elites, especially those who are at the helm of authority' (Sulistiyanto 2007: 76). The moment that post-civil war society commits itself not only to a legitimate government but also to civil society organisations the process of governance becomes smooth, easy and fulfilling, for 'civil society is strong enough to counterbalance the state and, while not preventing the state from fulfilling its role of keeper of the peace and arbitrator between major interests, can nevertheless prevent it from dominating and atomising the rest of society' (Gellner 1994: 5).

The establishment of a new government following the end of civil war is both an opportunity and a challenge. It is an opportunity because the society finally has the chance to redress its grievances after years, decades and generations of misfortune. It is a challenge because working on its grievances requires a great deal of insight, which means that those responsible for allocating opportunities and rights to the constituency do it equitably and do not ignore the needs of the voiceless. Very often such clear thinking is absent in most post-civil war society. Usually in the euphoria of victory or termination of the conflict those in charge of restructuring the governing structure conveniently ignore the defeated or forget the needs of those groups that are less powerful. Hence most of the post-conflict governing process in the non-western context is marked by what one might call the 'winner takes all attitude'. This, in fact, is a major impediment to post-conflict peace.

7 Realms of reconciliation

There is something perverse about most civil wars. The liberal notion that all groups and communities belong to one great political family and therefore should be bound together through a common fraternity is grossly undermined in most civil war-affected societies. Where there had been violence there is scope for revenge. Liberating the disrupted society from the equation of a continuous war depends to a large degree on the introduction of a framework of reconciliation that eliminates the possibilities of revenge. Reconciliation, in this context, presumes the formation of a common arena where both the perpetrators of violence and their victims come face to face with each other in order to reassess the impact of conflict on their lives. This exercise is not aimed at seeking revenge but is intended to explore ways of moving forward. Such an interaction in the post-conflict phase, it is argued, provides the perfect ground for the cancellation of estrangement via a morally grounded forgiveness, achievable only when perpetrators and beneficiaries of past injustice acknowledge collective responsibility for wrong-doing and shed their prejudices, and when victims, through the same process, regain their self-respect (Bhargava 2000: 60–3).

No post-conflict society can afford to move forward unless it engages in some form of judicial procedure to make perpetrator of crimes accountable for their wrongs. Without this soul-searching exercise within a transparent judicial framework reconciliation cannot take root.[1] But this raises a whole host of questions. What is the correct procedure for enacting the judicial process? How should war-torn societies go about upholding justice? Is 'crime and punishment' the only acceptable form of reconciliation? Can there be a universal principle of justice? Although this chapter wrestles with these questions of law it also concentrates on non-judicial aspects of reconciliation.

All civil wars, as pointed out earlier, operate within a specific set of dynamics. Hence at the outset I would like to emphasise that although civil war invariably results in the loss of life and property, each affected society or community is qualitatively and quantitatively different from one another in terms of the level and impact of the conflict. Therefore, the process of reconciliation in a post-conflict setting should not only have to take into account those specific dynamics but also needs to be tailored to fit that particular situation.

Forms of reconciliation

Just as there is no single cause of civil war, there is no unitary method of dealing with the irregularities or crimes committed during the years of civil strife. The model that works in a given environment or society may be completely untenable in another. A particular state may adopt a certain method in order to confront its past based on the specific needs of the larger society. Put simply, the make-up of justice is ultimately coloured by the needs, the overall character and the capacity of that given society to see through that particular approach.

In the following section I will use Lyn S. Graybill's taxonomy of post-conflict reconciliation methods to represent a divergent approach to conflict resolution. Graybill developed this framework to assess post-conflict peace in Africa (Graybill 2004: 1117). However, I believe this particular framework also has a universal applicability. Approaches such as 'pardon', 'punishment' and 'amnesia' as remedial measures for crimes committed during the years of civil strife have been practised by various societies in the past and contemporary period in both African as well as non-African settings. Therefore I am transposing that regional framework into a larger setting. I will use a cross-section of empirical evidences to underscore this point.

Punishment

While civil wars are distinctly chaotic in nature there is a certain orderliness when it comes to the perpetration of violence. The intensity of the conflict, to a large degree, is determined by the command structure of the belligerents. That society is more prone to violence where there is a clearly defined organisational framework binding the groups in a clearly defined chain of command. Both elites and masses in this framework interact in a perverse harmony. In the absence of such synchronisation violence could only be sporadic as well as short-lived. Our assessment of many contemporary conflicts provides us with a clear indication of elite and mass complicity in such violence. In these instances, where the identity of the perpetrator of violence is known and verifiable, an open judicial trial and sentencing of the guilty assumes an inescapable urgency. In the opinion of jurists the adoption of such judicial measures is one of the most effective methods of setting the standard of personal culpability and ensuring justice. This mode of imparting justice, which often amounts to carrying out some form of punishment, is probably the easiest of ways to deal with crimes committed during civil war.

Punishment amounts to the restoration of justice, rule of law and affirms the post-conflict society's resolve to uphold the rights of the victims. A post-conflict society, if it has to take a clear stand on justice and fairness and establish a modicum of normality, is expected to consciously embrace the logic of punishment. For such an undertaking not only aims at redressing the grievances of the survivors but it legitimates the authority of the state or the regime overseeing the workings of the state in equal measures. Punishment, it is widely believed, has a deterrent effect. It reduces the likelihood that similar crimes will be repeated in the future. This approach often symbolises the clear break with the past. It has both local and universal implications.

Punishment seeks out the truth. It establishes the moral position of the victims and denounces the actions of the perpetrators of violence. While engaging in a legally recognised framework of punitive measures a society enters into a period of reconciliation. Such measures reinstate the confidence of the citizenry in the state. Since there is an aspect of visibility associated with punishment the victims feel genuinely compensated for their suffering. On these grounds alone reconciliation becomes an immediate possibility. Yet, punishment through trials is an extremely sensitive undertaking. It can only be adopted in circumstances where the new regime is stronger both politically and morally than its predecessor, a situation which enables it to impose a new set of rules upon the old (Sulistiyanto 2007: 74).

Although it is an effective tool, punishment as a method facilitating justice and paving the way for future reconciliation has practical limitations. How does a state or regime, for example, alot punishment where there was mass participation in violence? Similarly, what happens when a post-conflict society resorts to selective high-profile punishment? How just and fair it is when society metes out capital punishment to sectarian leaders, rebel commanders, warlords, heads of the former regime and so on who were major catalysts in perpetrating the conflict but now happen to be on the losing side? Was the sanctity of law upheld in these instances, or was the judiciary used as a convenient tool to exact revenge?

While punishment may be an effective means of creating grounds for reconciliation in some contexts where the 'victims are crying out for justice', at the same time, however, it may exacerbate group hatreds and even set the country back on the path toward apocalypse (Kinzer 2007: 26). In addition, adopting and exercising a just legal procedure to redress the rights of those who were wronged is not only extremely expensive but also often unviable, as it contains the danger of opening up old wounds. Now let me concentrate on Rwanda and the former Yugoslavia, where punishment has been heavily used as a method of disposing justice. I select these in order to explore the validity of the argument that punishment can be a problematic procedure.

In Rwanda the Hutu-led genocide of Tutsis was 'not a spontaneous outburst of ancient hatred'. To all intents and purposes it was 'meticulously planned and executed' by the Hutu regime, which had been preparing for such a mission for years. Since the country gained independence from Belgium in 1962 Hutu rulers had used all available constitutional and non-constitutional methods to isolate and deprive the minority Tutsis (who constituted around 9 per cent of the population) of a share in the country's overall socio-economic and political space. Put simply there was concerted institutional bias against the Tutsis cultivated by Hutu leadership over decades. As one critic puts it, 'the violence from below could not have spread without cultivation and direction from above, it is equally true that the conspiracy of the tiny fragment of *genocidaires* could not have succeeded had it not found resonance from below' (Mamdani 2001: 7). This would suggest a wider countrywide participation in genocide. How was one to decide who should be punished? The post-conflict regime in this situation punished some prominent leaders and released their less prominent counterparts. The reason why it chose a selective punishment was because it could not put the entire Hutu population behind bars. Selective punishment also served a symbolic purpose, suggesting the supremacy of the rule of law and justice. And it did go some way towards upholding the rights of the victims.

If we shift our focus to another equally unfortunate event, i.e. the Yugoslav civil war, we detect a similar pattern of elite-orchestrated conspiracy intended to whip up the passion of the masses. According to Bogdan Dentich 'the civil war in Yugoslavia was the result of policy decisions from the top combined with an all-too-effective use of mass media, especially television, which in turn united the masses (read Serbian militias) to engage in genocide against the Muslims' (Denitch 1994: 62).

Considering the level of mass complicity in extreme acts of violence in Rwanda and in the former Yugoslavia, it is hard to determine whether selective punishment is the right method of dealing with past injustices. Similarly, given the fact that the conflict was one-sided, with one community bearing all the brunt of the atrocity, it is hard to know whether the victims themselves could live alongside their perpetrators in a true spirit of reconciliation. The demand for justice and retribution is always high in a conflict-ridden society. From a disputants' perspective, viable peace is possible only after 'justice has been done' (Galtung 1996).

This argument can clearly be seen in the context of the aftermath of Argentina's 'dirty war' (1973–82), which claimed 30,000 civilian victims. The National Commission on Disappeared People argued that:

> The wish to torture the torturer and to kill the murderer was overwhelming, but stronger was the sense that such acts of revenge would become indistinguishable from the acts that caused them and would become, in some abominable way, a victory for the abusers.
>
> (Manguel 1996: 128)

Hence it recommended that the guilty ones stand trial, in front of the society that had been wronged and according to the laws of that society. The strongest opposition to the idea of reconciliation came from the Mothers of the Disappeared victims of this civil war. The position of the Madres de Plaza Mayo, as the group that seeks justice is popularly known, has always been that 'We're not going to forgive. We're not going to forget. We're going to carry on with our fight'; this makes for a hard case in the search of reconciliation.

Even if the post-conflict government widens the scope of justice by moving from being selective to fishing in a much bigger pool, there is no guarantee that the social cohesion of the pre-civil war years in societies such as Rwanda or the former Yugoslavia can be fully restored. Even with aggressive use of punishment as a conflict reduction tool, sometimes it may take generations and often centuries for a community that had experienced inhuman violence to develop a level of trust against its erstwhile persecutors and accept them unreservedly. If this is so it is indeed impossible to know if the Tutsis will ever be able to trust their Hutu counterparts in Rwanda. In these scenarios, the most effective way forward may be to work out a strategy that allows the disputants to put their past behind and move forward (Enright and North 1998; Rothstein 1999).

Popular pardon

Punishing those who had committed crimes and atrocities against their fellow citizens during civil war 'removes their influence and example from the political scene and makes it easier for voices of reconciliation to be acknowledged'. This attractive and plausible idea, however, has grave limitations. As Anthony Dworkin asks, how we are to impose a system of justice where the participation in atrocities was widespread, and pervasive? (Dworkin 1996: 140). This dilemma at times forces some societies to look for alternatives and other ways of imposing a system of justice, which is not predicated upon the framework of retributive justice.

The Truth and Reconciliation Commission established in South Africa soon after the end of the apartheid era was unlike many other truth commissions that had made their appearance in several Latin American countries earlier. The model that was adopted in South Africa had a mechanism that had little do with upholding retributive justice: rather it was geared towards establishing a forum where those who had committed crimes could enter into an arena of public confession of their past crimes and it was up to the victims and their families to decide whether to forgive them. Unlike punishment this method of truth-seeking and admission of guilt was not premised on seeking vengeance or judicial retribution, being a mechanism which aimed to serve as a nation-building and reconciliatory function. As Nelson Mandela put it, in order for the majority of South Africans to 'to forgive and forget the atrocities and violence of the apartheid era and the excesses of civil war they must know what actually happened'. Thus within the remits of the Truth and Reconciliation Commission the new government made provisions whereby perpetrators of violence during apartheid were required to testify before a truth commission about any crimes they may have committed under the previous regime. If they told the truth and asked for forgiveness, they were eligible for an amnesty.

As a framework of true reconciliation the role of truth commissions can hardly be underestimated. The truth commission allows an arena for 'participatory engagement' between the victim and the victor. If anything, this form of non-judicial strategy of dealing with the past complements the judicial procedure of retributive justice. In fact, in societies where

> judicial institutions are unable to deal with the past atrocities (owing simply to the sheer number of crimes where a significant portion of the citizenry is complicit in some form of violence or the other) the non-judicial Truth Commission provides an excellent informal communication of public opprobrium, the protection of direct and indirect victims and the repentance of some perpetrators.
>
> (Biggar 2003: 17)

The strategy of providing amnesties through such commissions is based on the idea that for the sake of protecting the political stability of new fragile democracy, its new leaders may choose not to prosecute the perpetrators and instead grant amnesties. Many post-civil war societies find it attractive to adopt this framework when they realise the high political cost of prosecuting the perpetrators and its eventual effect on the very survival of the new regime.

(Sulistiyanto 2007: 74)

Amnesty, following the admission of guilt within the framework of a truth commission, therefore, is a pragmatic strategy. It has relevance in dealing with some conflicts. But it cannot be used in all post-conflict societies as a universal framework.

Amnesia

Both retributive justice in the form of punishment and popular pardon through truth commissions are extremely time-consuming and expensive affairs. In order to adopt these two methods a post-conflict society is often required to have considerable economic capital. In those instances where there is an absence of indigenous economic base to deal with such issues the international community sponsors such undertakings. Some post-conflict societies, however, may not be in a position to attract this level of international support and may lack an indigenous economic pool. How are they to respond to the questions of justice and reconciliation? Which framework should they adopt?

Mozambique stands out from other societies for the unique way in which it has come to terms with a past marred by extreme violence. This African country experienced two decades of uninterrupted civil war following its independence from the Portuguese rule in 1974. Peace finally came to Mozambique in 1994 through the signing of a General Peace Accord that prepared the way for multi-party elections. Although almost one million civilians perished in the civil war and thousands were tortured, and some of the most horrendous acts of barbarism were committed, surprisingly there were no calls for retributive justice. The question of accountability that usually features prominently in many post-conflict societies was largely absent in Mozambique. There were no truth commissions, no investigations into the past and no attempt at finding a constituency to whom to attribute the blame. And neither have there been any individuals held to account for human rights violations (Graybill 2004: 1125).

This mode of reacting with complete silence to the past belongs to the category of reconciliation through amnesia. While this is not an uncommon practice, what is curious, however, is the rationale behind the adoption of such a strategy. In this context it is imperative to inquire: Why did the people of Mozambique prefer to embrace collective amnesia as a method of reconciliation? If one were to examine it up close one would realise that the conscious 'public silence' over the past had its basis in the cultural trappings of the society. The notion of 'speaking out' which appears to be the foundational element behind many reconciliation processes was less appreciated and was alien to most Mozambicans.

To talk about the 'past atrocities' and 'recall' the gory events was not viewed as a necessary precondition or prelude to a healing process. To open those floodgates of emotion and the attendant grief, it was believed, only creates 'space for the malevolent forces to intervene' (Green and Honwana 1999: 10). This particular cultural thinking on the part of the masses could prevail when it was aided by clear government guidelines. Amnesia as reconciliation method was firmly anchored in the pragmatic vision of Mozambique's post-civil war government. The regime like its citizenry did not wish to rake up the past for fears of jeopardising the future. As a result of this partnership Mozambique shifted a page in its history without bothering to examine what was in that page.

As a neutral observer if one were to identify the actors responsible for Mozambique's tryst with two decades of civil war the compass of blame would point in the direction of its soldiers. Put simply, had there been any attempt at exercising retributive justice the constituency that was most likely to have faced legal persecution was its soldiers. True, it was the soldiers who had been at the forefront of perpetuating the conflict that saw the complete devastation of the society and the loss of over a million civilian lives. Yet it was the civilian populace that was first to recognise that the soldiers came from civilian backgrounds. Thus from the very outset of the peace process the Mozambican society came to appreciate the futility of seeking justice or vengeance against its soldiers. The dominant narrative that Mozambicans held in the post-conflict period was that it was the situation and circumstances which transformed ordinary citizens into violent soldiers. Therefore if the society were to persecute these soldiers and prevent their return to civilian life, these soldiers would simply go back to their earlier ways and use violence and destabilise the peace (Graybill 2004: 1126).

Mozambique showed a form of maturity in its treatment of ex-soldiers which many liberal societies cannot even comprehend let alone embrace. In the best African tradition the dominant narrative in the post-Peace Accord period was that it was the situation and circumstances which transformed ordinary citizens into violent soldiers.

Yet, no matter how forgiving a society and its culture, there will always be individuals and groups who will find it hard to reconcile themselves with past injustice. Seeking justice or revenge against a wrongful action is after all an acceptable universal human character. The question therefore is: Surely there must be some individuals or groups in Mozambique who were resentful of reconciliation without having a process to oversee some form of retributive justice. And there were plenty of these individuals. Yet, whenever a Mozambican expressed his or her wish to seek retributive justice or revenge for the injustice done to him or her the larger society inculcated into that individual the futility of such an enterprise. The dominant narrative in this context was a fairly simple one. It stressed that it was this very 'dynamics of revenge' that had kept Mozambique in the throes of continuous civil war for over two decades. Therefore wanting to avenge violence would only lead to counter-violence and so forth (Nordstrom 1997: 232). The release or liberation from that perpetual cycle of violence depended on individuals, groups and the larger society adopting a total forgiving attitude and embracing collective amnesia over remembrance.

The Mozambican experiment with amnesia as a reconciliation strategy, although unique, was not the first of its kind. Cambodians had to engage in this form of reconciliation following the end of their civil war in the late 1970s. When the infamous Khmer Rouge regime seized power after a brief civil war in 17 April 1975 it started a campaign that abolished schools, hospitals, factories, banking, money, religion and private property. It marked the beginning of its four-year reign of terror by declaring it Year Zero, which literally unveiled the return of the society to primeval savagery. As part of its macabre ideological campaign children were ordered to kill their parents and whole communities were murdered in the name of 'restructuring the society'. At the end of this four-year period of violence nearly half of the Cambodians had perished. Once this genocidal regime had been removed the Cambodians had to undergo a kind of soul-searching unparalleled in modern times. Here was a post-conflict society where every surviving Cambodian had lost a family member or a loved one to this mindless violence brought upon them by an insane ideology and its equally insane leaders.

Reconciling to these extremely painful memories and the attendant loss was very exacting indeed. But Cambodia did not engage in unveiling any organised judicial process to oversee retributive justice. Those Khmer Rouge leaders who had given themselves up were guaranteed immunity by the new post-war government. As for identifying those responsible for the atrocity the country's Prime Minister urged that Cambodia and his countrymen should 'bury the past'. Just like Mozambique there were two overarching factors which led Cambodians on the path of amnesia. These were based on pragmatism and the nature of the Cambodian culture. Even though they were not directly involved in the killing of their fellow citizens those who survived the killing fields recognised some kind of moral failing. Since nearly half of the population perished in this intramural struggle the other surviving half acknowledged some kind of complicity in this conflict. Owing to this collective complicity Cambodians could not put themselves on trial. Hence in the best Buddhist tradition, they decided to forgive their erstwhile enemies and made a pact with themselves to move forward.[2]

Sierra Leone is yet another example of a contemporary post-war society that chose to follow the 'collective amnesia' route. There are probably more people who have suffered amputation of limbs in this country than anywhere else in the world. The civil war that erupted here during the mid-1900s and continued until early 2001 spawned hundreds of thousands of armed militias (often child soldiers) who went on a rampage: chopping off their victims' hands and legs and on occasion eating their victims – often their own relatives (Dowden 2007). The country achieved an uneasy peace of sorts when the main rebel leader Foday Sankoh was arrested. With the end of the civil war, however, arose the question of retribution. While sifting through the past, Sierra Leoneans acknowledged that most of those who committed this gory violence were youngsters who were brainwashed by the 'evil' leadership. Moreover many of these war criminals had perpetrated violence against their own family members. The challenge before this battle-scarred community was how to bring to justice your own brothers, sons or friends.

The enormity of this undertaking ultimately led the community to engage in a form of forgiveness bordering on 'collective amnesia'. This act of forgiveness was not forced upon the victims. Neither were they coaxed into it following the introduction of some sort of compensation package. The victims, in this particular instance, simply realised the futility of demanding justice for the crimes committed against them by their own friends, neighbours and even family members.

On balance, a group, a community, or the larger society adopts and embraces 'collective amnesia' in a post-conflict setting for a whole host of reasons. The primary motive, however, is the resolve to see the termination of the conflict even if that demands forfeiting the right to some form of retributive justice. Here one needs to remember that this mode of reconciliation is not specific to poor and underdeveloped societies alone. Amnesia as a reconciliation mechanism is equally attractive to a developed society. The decision by the British government to provide general amnesty to paramilitaries involved in countless sectarian killings in Northern Ireland between 1970s and the unveiling of the peace process under the Good Friday Agreement in 1997 is a case in point.

Unsurprisingly in countries such as Afghanistan there is not even talk of putting the leaders of its long civil war on trial. In a fractured clan- and tribe- dominated culture such as Afghanistan, it is thought that trials will only alienate the perpetrators by putting them on the defensive. Given their easy resolve to embrace violence such trials would at best be counterproductive.[3] Thus after undergoing unspeakable misery spanning more than a quarter of century the Afghans have found themselves at a juncture where they neither have the resources nor the will power to pursue those who put them through this misery. Little wonder the country has sleepwalked into amnesia in so far as seeking justice for past crimes is concerned. If one were to prepare a balance sheet on the appeal and attraction of amnesia as a reconciliation strategy it would be fair to suggest that in the end it is the bare practicalities and the demands placed on the society which force it to embrace this particular attitude over all other available frameworks of reconciliation.

Does it work?

Although 'collective amnesia' as a post-conflict peace strategy appears to have struck roots in Cambodia, Mozambique and Sierra Leone, and been adopted to a limited degree in East Timor, there are plenty of people and societies who have found it hard to embrace the logic of 'forgiving and forgetting'. According to critics such as Vamik Volkan a society that does not engage in some form of retributive justice or avoids talking about the pains and memories associated with violence committed during civil strife and unrest only stores up that trauma for the future generations (Volkan 2000).

Accordingly it would seem, one generation's decision to 'forgive and forget' does not necessarily lead to a complete termination of all the conflict dynamics. Equally importantly 'just because one generation might want to forget the past does not mean that subsequent generations will remain satisfied with leaving it covered up' (Rigby 2001: 3). In fact, if anything, an unaddressed trauma 'may lie dormant for years and decades, ready to be rekindled by elites and leaders of a particular group or society to consolidate their strength and group solidarity' (Volkan 2000: 177–94). Should that community chose to remember trauma at any given time it is bound to affect the status quo.

Volkan's argument appears to have some basis when we focus our attention on those post-war societies which had initially entered into a collective 'forget and forgive' pact only to realise that it is impossible not to exorcise the ghosts of the past. In Argentina, Chile and Guatemala where the general population had once decided to forget some of the atrocities committed during the military dictatorship and civil war years (between the 1960s and the 1980s) those populations are now reassessing their decision. There is now a renewed insistence on judicial process to bring the culprits to book in all these societies. Some critics such as Lyn S. Graybill sympathise with such demands. She, for instance, argues that 'the pact to "let time heal all wounds" may overestimate the affected people's capacity to let bygones be bygones' (Graybill 2004: 1127).

A society's decision to 'forget and forgive' a particular part of its history at one given time and seek retributive measures in future poses some challenges to the overall reconciliation process. How does one reclaim the past without undermining the current peace? One way of confronting this issue would be perhaps to employ a form of remembrance where the past is told for the consumption of all communities concerned from an absolutely neutral perspective. This form of public acknowledgement allows for the perpetrators to feel ashamed of their past crimes. And the victims and their families get a chance for their grief to be acknowledged and shared by the wider community.

Very often in a post-conflict setting the past is retold either from the victim or the victor's perspective. Exploring the narrative of conflict from an objective perspective in a deeply divided society allows for the restoration of the 'forget' clause that Volkan and some other scholars had found problematic. Therefore, I would argue that immediate punishment as part of retributive justice is not the only way to uphold the law in a post-conflict setting. One can still fulfil the objectives of justice by making 'truth' part of the public knowledge. If there is such an exercise involving universal and unanimous acknowledgement of the crimes committed, the future generations, from a victim's viewpoint, would not feel 'let down'. Equally importantly, those responsible for perpetrating this trauma would remain hostage to their crimes and learn not to go down that path again. Owning up to history as if future mattered is currently gaining rapid recognition in the Balkans. Thanks to the pioneering work of the Centre for Democracy and Reconciliation in South East Europe, a Salonika-based think-tank, the history of the Balkans over the past few centuries is now presented to the people across the region as it is. This, it is hoped, would allow for every community to face up to the past and bear some degree of responsibility and learn not to commit the earlier mistakes.

In Rwanda a similar effort is well underway. The post-war ruling Rwandan Patriotic Front (RPF) encouraged Rwandans to avoid and abandon the spurious history of the colonial period that was responsible for creating the divide between the Hutus and Tutsis. Instead it insisted that Rwandans should seek their pre-colonial non-divisive narrative. As a true measure of reconciliation the regime, which had both Tutsi and Hutu members, 'encouraged the Rwandans to think of themselves as one happy family' (*The Economist* 2004: 26). Furthermore, in its attempt to create 'good patriotic citizens', the RPF encouraged people to develop a fresh, new, and objective-neutral view of Rwanda's past. As a practical policy measure in this direction, the RPF, for instance, emphasised that 'ethnicity was unimportant' in Rwanda before their tryst with Belgian colonialism.[4]

Similarly, in its revisionist approach to history it disseminated the idea that all the communal killings that took place under Belgian rule and during the post-independence period were results of bad governance (*The Economist* 2004: 27). In addition, the RPF regime abolished ethnic identity cards (the chief identity marker) and forbade the breakdown of official statistics by tribe or ethnicity. As a further measure to eradicate the traces of communal division young Rwandans were obliged to attend 'solidarity camps', where they were taught 'lessons in equality' and encouraged to respect and express love for one another. Although it is too early to predict what results these reconciliatory efforts will produce one cannot help but appreciate the overall approach to the problem.

The above analyses take us one step closer to the argument that facing up to the past is a fundamental need in all post-conflict societies. However unpleasant and difficult the truth may be, unless there is an honest and objective admission about the role of individuals, groups or communities in any wrongdoings during the civil war it is impossible to prepare the ground for any future reconciliation in that society. Whenever and wherever a post-war society avoids dealing with the past and fails to engage meaningfully in the reassessment of its history the past is bound to haunt that society until it finally does address it objectively.

I would like to cite the case of the Armenian genocide here. In Turkey this is a very sensitive topic. In the 1915 civil war in Turkey there was a purge against ethnic Armenians by the Ottoman Turks. According to Armenians some 1.5 million of them perished in this purge. This, they have always insisted, was a form of genocide against their community. The Turks, however, have a very different view of the events. They have always maintained it was a conflict instigated by the Armenians when they allied with the invading Russian troops and what ensued was a national liberation struggle which claimed some 300,000 Armenian lives. The Turks also insist, lest one forget, that the civil war also claimed an equal number from their side of the ethnic divide.

The 'Armenian Question' and the failure to own up to their past honestly by the Turks is not the only one of its kind. The Spanish civil war that ended nearly seventy years ago has thrown up many unsettling questions about 'responsibility', 'guilt', and 'justice' in much more recent times. The conflict between communist partisans and fascists claimed tens of thousands of lives on both sides. These excesses were ignored and remained unaddressed by the fascist dictatorship of Francisco Franco who assumed power following the civil war. When Franco died and Spain embraced democracy the country had a chance to reexamine its past. But there were no truth commissions or attempts to seek out the truth. Officials responsible for these crimes were not tried for their role in the past. The reinstated King Juan Carlos issued a royal amnesty for many convicted of political crimes during the period. And police files detailing the conduct of officials during the civil war and dictatorship years remained sealed. The newly appointed democratic government of Adolfo Suárez Gonzáles argued that 'the question before the state was not to ask people where they are coming from, but where they are going to'. As an exercise in pragmatism the government 'opted not to investigate the atrocities committed during the civil war, mostly as a way of maintaining national unity (Sulistiyanto 2007: 74).

Put simply, 'Spain chose simply to turn the page of history. An unwritten agreement, known as the pact of forgetting, meant that mere mention of the civil war was kept out of everything from politics to dinner party conversation' (*The Economist* 2006b: 66). However, when in 2006 the socialist government of Jose Luis Rodriguez Zapatero decided to delve into the past and allow 'public recognition' of victims of both the civil war and the 36-year fascist dictatorship, emotions were high.[5] While a section of society lauded such an effort others accused him of 'indulging in "moth ball" politics, and of trying to revise history and revive old hatreds' (*The Economist* 2006b: 66).

Both the Armenian and Spanish examples tell us that it is impossible for a community to move forward without properly addressing the questions surrounding its civil war past. Therefore the contemporary trend seems to be to respond to the unexamined cases of violence as soon as there is an available opportunity. Within this framework some post-civil war societies have adopted a mix of punishment, popular pardon and amnesia to deal with 'old wounds'.

Like many other societies gripped by the chaos and violence of civil war, Northern Ireland had its own share of 'missing dead'. During the thirty years of bitter feuding between Catholics and Protestants some 3,268 people in the province had encountered 'unnatural deaths'. As part of the resolve to institute retributive justice under the Good Friday Agreement all persons convicted of a 'terrorist-type crime' before 1998 were incarcerated for no more than two years. For some, a short sentence of two years may appear to be a travesty of justice. However, this mode of punishment, while upholding the principles of retributive justice, also had an element of popular pardon built into it. This limited exercise in punishment, it was thought, would facilitate adequate reconciliation. Thus there was no provision for a truth-seeking initiative in the original peace plan. However, a decade on from the formalisation of the peace process there was a fresh demand from the people affected to find out the truth behind the deaths.

In an effort to 'drain the reservoir of mistrust' and facilitate 'true reconciliation' among the people, Northern Ireland was forced to establish its own Truth and Reconciliation Commission in the form of the Historical Enquiries Team (HET) in 2006. The task of this independent body is to produce before the public the circumstances and reality behind the causes of those casualties. HET's six-year task and £31m budget is geared towards investigating the truth surrounding those deaths. The findings, it is hoped, will allow the affected families, friends and the larger society to formally become reconcile with the past and move forward.

Such belated attempts to address grievances (hastily pushed aside at the onset of the peace process) go on to suggest that a civil war-affected society is never fully reconciled to the violence of the past. The insistence on justice is a continual process in such settings and the society concerned may have to adopt various mechanisms and methods to deal with it as and when these demands appear.

... the way forward

The primary goal of reconciliation is to 'address, integrate and embrace painful past and the necessary shared future as a means of dealing with the present' (Lederach 1997: 35).

'Reconciliation is politically expedient during a transition when the new government or regime is committed to democratization and due process of law' (Jeong 2005: 162). Reconciliation, in order to be possible, needs to have an interim phase. Many societies deliberately establish that interregnum while others merely sleepwalk into it.

Societies that succeed in achieving complete reconciliation manage to do so owing to their conscious commitment to let the past be their epilogue rather than their prologue. Commitment to this new thinking, however, needs to be wrapped in a language that binds rather than divides. For the continuation of the old language and symbolism of 'victim' and 'victor', 'us' and 'them', 'justice' and 'vengeance' are bound to perpetuate the earlier conflict dynamics. The task for the post-war society, therefore, is to redefine itself. As Long and Brecke argue 'redefinition of parties to a conflict whereby narrow identities of victim and perpetrator or repressor and insurgent are replaced with a new sense of self and other makes a new relationship devoid of the earlier fractured past possible' (Long and Brecke 2003: 69).

Introducing and making people embrace this new language of reconciliation, however, is not an easy enterprise. For example, how could a person or group of persons become reconciled with generations of oppression forced upon them by a given group or community? How could an individual forget the horrors of death and destruction at the hands of another fellow citizen? Switching off that part of the brain that clings to such horrific memories is not always easy. We, as human beings, are sometimes incapable of completely forgetting such events. In addition neither are we able to fully forgive those who did wrong to us. If forgetting and forgiving were so easy we would not still be observing Holocaust Day and other such events linked to the remembrance of victims of such war crimes.

Another interrelated argument that crops up in this context is that if we were to expect the victims of a certain tragedy not to seek some form of justice, then whatever happens to the very concept of justice and rule of law in modern society? Is not justice itself on trial if the system were to allow complete impunity to those who committed the crimes in the first place? What message would those who perpetrated the crimes receive if justice were to be abandoned? Some scholars argue that seeking complete retributive justice in such situations is neither possible nor appropriate (Ignatieff 2002; Long and Brecke 2003; Mani 2005). There are three points to highlight in this context. First, the quest to impose the full force of justice on those responsible for gross violence during civil war is likely to rake up an unpleasant past that cannot be easily dealt with. Second, it is impossible to bring to book every single crime committed. Third, in those societies where a significant portion of the populace was complicit in this 'collective crime', for instance having been involved in the practice of slavery, racism or genocide, seeking complete justice for the above lapses would make the society unable to function. As Long and Brecke argue:

> Limiting retribution for wrongs may be valuable for the society as a whole when so many share guilt for their actions or inaction at wartime. To prosecute fully all the sins of omission and commission committed during a civil conflict could destroy the society it seeks to restore.
>
> (Long and Brecke 2003: 149–50)

The favoured method, in this context, should be a half-way house between complete justice and forgiving. Although it may be intensely frustrating to the victims, a post-conflict society must consciously embrace some form of limited justice in lieu of full retribution. This mode of response to past crimes not only asserts society's or the system's commitment to justice as a universal humanistic value but also allows for the discontinuation of the cycle of violence and retribution that a full imposition of justice might have spawned (Long and Brecke 2003: 149). Such a framework of interaction with the past then is not only morally defensible but also has fundamental value owing to its pragmatism.

Similarly, while one cannot underestimate the role of the central authorities in setting the broad rules, aims and objectives, the ultimate task to oversee the process of reconciliation is dependent on the masses. For it is hard to reconcile the emotions, traumas and grievances of a multitude of people – scarred by memories of a prolonged war of oppression – through a simple 'top-down design'. That society has the ability to move forward where the people themselves choose to do so. The reconciliation process in South Africa that put an end to generations of racism and bigotry became a success owing primarily to the majority of the Black Africans' resolve to put their past behind them and embrace the future. The Xhosa concept of *Ubuntu* was a catalyst here.

> *Ubuntu* posits I am a human only because you are a human. If I undermine your humanity I dehumanise myself. You must do what you can do to maintain that great harmony, which is perpetually undermined by resentment, anger, desire for vengeance.
>
> (Graybill 2002: 47)

The above interpretation makes it abundantly clear that *Ubuntu* is a framework that embodies the best of liberal humanistic principle. *Ubuntu* definitely allowed a dehumanised majority to show empathy with its former minority oppressors. Had there been no such thinking within the cultural fabric of the Blacks in South Africa, no externally mediated reconciliation effort could have taken root in this intensely divided society. Turning to another African example, Rwanda, one comes across a similar resolve among the country's Hutus and Tutsis.

Similarly, the upper house of the Afghan Parliament passed a bill in February 2007 which provided amnesty to people accused of war crimes during the country's quarter of a century of civil war. Although the amnesty was controversial and opposed by the President of the Republic Hamid Karzai, supporters of the amnesty nonetheless were of the opinion that it was the 'right' move towards reconciliation. Unsurprisingly, prior to the bill becoming law many Afghans openly declared that without a blanket amnesty for those implicated in the civil war they would return to their guns.

South Africa, Rwanda and Afghanistan represent cases where popular pardon would appear to have played a crucial role in reconciliation. Some other post-war societies might have an entirely different approach to this issue. Iraq, for instance, has a much more reticent attitude to reprieve. Of the three approaches to reconciliation, i.e. punishment, amnesty and amnesia, its chosen path was to uphold punishment and offer limited amnesty. While unveiling the reconciliation plan in December 2006, the Iraqi Prime Minister Nouri al-Maliki made abundantly clear his government's commitment to limited amnesty and to pursuing punishment as the best way forward. Nouri al-Maliki's subsequent insistence that 'there can be no agreement with the ex-rebels or insurgents unless they face the justice' (Steele 2006: 14), although non-reconciliatory, had nonetheless certain merits. Anthony Dworkin, for example, argues, 'punishing those who have committed atrocities removes their influence and example from the political scene and makes it easier for voices of reconciliation to be acknowledged' (Dworkin 1996: 140). Maliki's argument that his government's 'reconciliation initiative should not be read as a reward for killers and criminals or acceptance of their actions', would appear to have been couched in the overall needs of that society and the projection of its future.

On balance

The idea of reconciliation through forgiveness and in some instance through the introduction of forms of restorative justice can create conditions for a stable future. Its success, however, is never easy. The transition from war to peace, from totalitarianism to democracy, from genocidal regimes to accountable government, is fraught with practical, moral and political dilemmas (Index on Censorship 1996: 3). Truth commissions do play an important role in trying to create conditions for forgiveness through accountability, amnesty and reparation. Yet, as some critics ask, 'can a nation be reconciled to its past as individuals can, by replacing myth with fact, lies with truth?' (Ignatieff 1996: 123). A similar question is raised over the role of war crime tribunals, which establish and enforce criminal accountability. The inquiry here is, 'can trials of a few individuals be justice enough when thousands have been implicated in horrific human rights abuses?' (Index on Censorship 1996: 3). In spite of these obvious shortcomings, in the end, with neither justice nor any belief that justice is possible there can be no trust in either legal protection or in a nation based upon acknowledged rights (Smith 2001: 67). Equally importantly, true reconciliation can only be possible where there is a form of justice that is inclusive and uniting rather than exclusive and dividing (Mani 2005: 521).

In the end the very process of reconciliation and affirming one's faith in it is an individual choice. The framework often elicits a diametrically opposite response from the same group of individuals or leaders. Some come forward and for the greater good of the society embrace its fundamental precepts, while others denounce it as they find it hard to go through a conversion of heart or give up the ideology in which they had originally affirmed their faith. Take for instance the manner in which two of South Africa's apartheid government leaders reacted to the Truth and Reconciliation Commission that probed the evils done during the years of conflict. While one of the former presidents P.W. Botha refused to appear in front of what he called the 'circus' of the Truth and Reconciliation Commission there was a complete and opposite reaction from his successor F.W. De Klerk. He was recorded to have commented:

> I stand before you today neither in shame nor in arrogance, but deeply conscious of my responsibility . . . to be open, frank and helpful . . . to stand by those who served under me . . . to admit that which was wrong, to defend that which was right and to continue to build bridges in our quest for reconciliation . . .
>
> (F.W. De Klerk, National Party leader, Cape Town, 21 August 1996)

Reconciliation is impossible to introduce let alone formalise between victims and perpetrators if the latter refuse to acknowledge their past role. In places such as former Yugoslavia where the parties to the civil war have murdered and tortured each other for years, the prospects for truth, reconciliation and justice are much bleaker (Ignatieff 1996: 113). For example, almost a decade after the civil war in the Serbian-run entity of Bosnia-Herzegovina many Serbs did not believe that the genocide of Muslims ever took place, and they have had no incentive to believe otherwise.[6] The knowledge they held is, 'if any Muslims were killed they were killed in combat or attacking Serbs' (Bringa 2002: 219). 'Even if the truth could be considered to be crucial, cathartic and reconciliatory, this would depend on the extent to which both the process of accumulating and distilling the truth and the process of dissemination and consumption of the truth is undertaken' (Mani 2005: 519). In the absence of a wider constituency that agrees to participate in the recognition of truth any talk of reconciliation would remain a distant prospect.

Trying to see violence through external eyes often provides a critical insight into peace and reconciliation. In recent years, some human rights organisations have been vocal in their assessment of peace plans in many post-conflict societies. In direct opposition to some societies who have preferred to let the brutality of conflict years be best forgotten, the human rights organisations have argued to the contrary. Human Rights Watch, for example, argues that, 'Without justice peace is illusory'. Thus it takes a very critical approach to post-conflict reconciliation. Following the signing of the peace agreement between the Nepalese Army and the Maoists (who were locked in a decade-long civil war that led to some 13,000 deaths), Human Rights Watch was quick to highlight the absence of a responsibility clause in the peace deal. It argued that both sides must own up to their actions and cooperate with the investigations and initiate prosecutions of those responsible for the atrocities. The absence of 'judicial or penal measures to enforce accountability during the civil war', it reiterated, would keep the conflict simmering for years to come.[7]

Conclusion

A growing body of work has put forward the argument that the truth about the past must become public knowledge. A post-conflict society 'could not reaffirm itself and built a new self as long as the fate of those who fell victim to the civil war is unaccounted for or remains shrouded in lies or hidden in sealed records' (McCaughey 2001: 259). Thus, 'truth, justice and reconciliation are not esoteric academic debates: they lie at the heart of what happens next in countries like South Africa, former Yugoslavia, Rwanda and Iraq' (Index on Censorship 1996: 3). However, there is no 'universal' reconciliatory way of addressing mass crimes. What works best in one context may be completely out of place in another. Therefore various societies follow different patterns of reconciliation based according to context and on specific individual needs.

Scholars have often wondered what has to happen before a nation can look honestly at the darkest chapters in its own past. In the end,

> [r]emembrance, acknowledgement, and admission of collective responsibility are just not enough. Other strategies and institutions, say public trials of the most notorious of perpetrators or policies designed to restore political self-confidence among former victims, will be necessary to bring about a stable, minimally decent order.
>
> (Bhargava 2000: 59)

Moments of truth can occur when a society finds itself in the midst of an international intervention to defeat and neutralise the actors responsible for the carnage, as in former Yugoslavia, East Timor or Rwanda. At the other extreme 'such moments are also possible when a nation feels so secure that it can discuss past misdeeds without fearing for its future existence' (*The Economist*, 21 October 2006), like South Africa, Mozambique or Sierra Leone. Still in another mode the new rulers in a post-civil war context can mirror to their constituency the 'moral turpitude of their predecessors' and let the past bury itself as was the case in post-Khmer Rouge Cambodia. But as I stressed earlier, 'burying the hatchet' may not be the solution in all scenarios.

One of the primary conditions of reconciliation is the introduction of a framework within which the atrocities of the past can be freely discussed. Equally importantly attempts must be made to establish a workable unity among the erstwhile adversaries. In the absence of an overarching framework that allows these two groups to operate within the same socio-political structure, the perpetuation of hostility and animosity of the past is likely. It was the breakdown of trust between various groups within a single political unit that had resulted in civil war. Therefore, it is imperative that the society as a whole take up the responsibility of reinstating that trust. The post-conflict reconciliation framework, in this context, must endeavour to see the return of both the civilian and the military populace to a common arena where they 'coexist as neighbours if not friends'.

No individual or group can easily forget the traumas incurred during the savage violence of civil war. If a post-war society is to move forward there is an intense need to address how those affected by the conflict view their past. If they perpetually carry the memory of suffering and injustice then it is hard to build a stable society. The task here is for the entire society to enter into some form of soul-searching. This, in itself, has the potential to allow the victims and perpetrators to come face to face and engage in a process of forgive and forget for the greater good of the community. This non-political reconciliation is crucial, as the state cannot always bring to book all those who committed the crimes during the conflict. Also, seeking absolute justice in a post-war phase can be counterproductive and put the communities at opposite camps and help renew the earlier conflict dynamics.

8   Closing the conflict cycle

As the old adage goes 'it is easier to get into a conflict than to get out of one'. Yet conflict is not a permanent condition. States and societies ill-fated enough to find themselves in the midst of such situations do get out of it eventually. Unfortunately the exit option from such conflicts is usually long and arduous. Very often these conflicts follow their own course and leave the society in complete ruin. It is imperative, therefore, to inquire if it is possible to cobble together a general theory of conflict termination that can be applied in all civil war situations. Or can we develop a universal framework of conflict resolution? It is necessary to bear in mind – at the outset – that civil wars are products of a myriad of factors. Hence it is not possible to have one overarching formula or method to counter them all. Put simply, we can neither develop a comprehensive theory to address this problem nor can we suggest a single strategy to bring about an end to such conflicts. What is imperative in this situation is to examine various ways and methods and use that inquiry to build up a range of approaches.

Thus within the context of civil war one can introduce methods such as conflict management, conflict resolution or conflict termination in order to bring about a qualitative change in the status quo. It is useful, however, to have a broad understanding of what these terms mean. Let me briefly attend to these fundamental concepts. In those situations where the severity of the conflict is protracted in nature the state may embark upon a strategy of conflict management focused on the long-term redressal of the grievances of those concerned. This formula, however, does not guarantee a successful end to the conflict. There may arise an occasion in the life of a particular conflict when those involved in it realise that the way forward is conflict resolution: meaning the need to find acceptable ways of resolving the dispute with the approval of all the parties concerned.

Conflict resolution is a long process. If the fundamental agreements within the conflict resolution framework are recognised and respected by the previous enemies over a long period of time without any hiatus, then one arrives at a juncture at which one could state that the conflict has been terminated. Conflict termination, however, can occur in intra-state conflicts where there is a decisive end to conflict either through the break-up of the existing unit or the complete annihilation of the rebels or belligerents. These, however, are rare outcomes.

By and large most civil war-affected states manage to maintain their territorial unity. Similarly, the rebel or insurgent constituency continues to live within that state. This would imply some prearranged solution to the problem. In this chapter I look at some broad strategies that aim to make conflict completely redundant in a given society or situation. With this goal in mind I examine the relevance of some broad approaches including negotiation, military solution and peace accords. Furthermore I also interrogate the relationship between aid and conflict termination, arms embargo and conflict management, disarmament and ceasefire, and evaluate their relevance in securing long-term peace.

Two ways to peace

As intra-state conflicts have become frequent they have come under intense scrutiny by scholars and practitioners of peace studies. Traditionally one school has argued that the best way to end civil wars is through a negotiated settlement. Within this framework 'conflicting parties enter into an agreement that resolves their central incompatibilities, accept each other's continued existence as parties and cease all violent action against each other' (Wallensteen 2007: 8). This approach, which is known as 'conflict resolution', has focused primarily on strategies such as federalism, peace pacts, elite incorporation and imposition of a strategy of conflict management from the top (Licklider 1995; Zartman 1989). This top-down approach, which emphasises formal negotiations between the key actors in the conflict, has its weakness and does not necessarily produce lasting peace.

Parties to the conflict often enter into this kind of negotiated settlement discussion when both sides realise that an outright military victory is unlikely. Yet neither side entrusts its faith to the outcome of such negotiations. Given that belligerents by this time have encountered a heavy loss of personnel, both fear that the other side would use the talks to build up military strength while pushing for reductions in the size of their opponent's defence capability. The fear of a decisive military edge for the opponent prompts both to actually engage in increasing their firepower during the negotiations. The rebels' commitment to the negotiations is often lacklustre, as they are perpetually afraid of exposing too much of their organisation and that would enable the government forces to launch a massive surprise attack in a 'dirty war' – capable of eliminating the bargaining position of the rebels once and for all. Unsurprisingly the peace accords which appear as the result of such negotiated settlements have a very short life.

Thus there have been many instances where societies that had committed themselves to peace accords and agreements at the top level were soon back in the earlier conflict mode. For instance, (as I highlighted in Chapter 3) in spite of a peace plan that was claimed as a success Rwanda relapsed into genocidal violence soon after the signing of the Arusha Peace Accords. Similarly, Angola, Mozambique and Somalia during various phases of their civil war continued fighting while there were formal peace agreements in place. Why such paradox?

If the parties to the conflict are fearful that a negotiated peace settlement will undermine their long-term political survival they are likely to express less of a commitment to any effort to reach such conclusion. Perverse as it may seem actors in some protracted civil wars have often resorted to such measures. For instance,

> both the LTTE and successive governments in Colombo, in Sri Lanka, have come to depend on war as a means to political survival. Throughout this conflict both sides have professed peace as their immediate goal but neither was willing to risk their gains in opting for lasting peace. Fear of power and position, and control of their distinct constituency to their rivals have been instrumental in preventing both the LTTE and the government from taking a bold step that could ensure a permanent settlement to the decades long conflict.
>
> (Chadda 1996: 109–10)

The second school of thought that has been prominent in suggesting ways and means through which civil war-affected societies can draw back from the abyss recommends a bottom-up approach to the problem. While the 'conflict transformation' school (as it is called) recognises the importance of formal peacemaking through mechanisms such as elite negotiation and institutional restructuring, nonetheless it considers them inadequate (Galtung 1996; Kriesberg 1992; Lederach 1997). The process of resuscitating the affected state or society, its proponents argue, cannot be accomplished effectively through changes at the top level. A genuine transformation from conflict to peace would require changes at all level of the society and particularly in the bottom strata. Long-term peace-building, they suggest, is possible only when there is wider participation by the affected constituency or citizenry. Although it has its merits the 'conflict transformation' approach suffers from a range of problems. For instance,

> [w]hile it is acknowledged that transitions to peace should be conceptualised broadly, there is a danger that the notions of the conflict transformation and peace-building may end up being too vague and all-inclusive to guide analysis or policy towards peace.
>
> (Stokke 2006: 1024)

In spite of their shortcomings, both the 'conflict resolution' as well as the 'conflict transformation' school provide important pointers in tackling the problem of grafting peace on to an erstwhile violent landscape. Although they suggest two different approaches it is not easy to simply discount one and embrace the logic of the other. In fact, a viable peace strategy that would yield success would require that we combine both approaches. As one study suggests, 'resolution of a conflict requires a fundamental transformation of the structures as well as the dynamics of the conflict. Thus action towards resolution constitutes transformative politics and praxis' (Uyangoda 2005: 14–15). To put it simply, while a peace pact or agreement can provide a modicum of legality to the new thinking, that thinking can only be transformed into concrete results when there is a simultaneous initiative across the society that looks at addressing various issues from a holistic perspective. A society visited by civil war, to quote Johan Galtung, has within it deep seated 'structural violence'. Such structural violence can only be addressed when there is a coming together of both 'conflict resolution' and 'conflict transformation' approaches.

A holistic approach

As I have already mentioned, a significant number of civil wars that end in some kind of conflict resolution tend to return to the earlier conflict mode after a brief thaw in violence and fighting. An audit of civil wars in the twentieth century provides us with some very perplexing statistics. A study produced in the early 1990s concluded that only about 15 per cent of civil wars over the previous ninety years were terminated by some form of peace negotiations (Stedman 1991). In her study Barbara Walter has consistently highlighted the fact that of all civil wars that took place between 1945 and 1996 only about 20 per cent ended in some form of negotiated settlement (Walter 1997). In yet another of her recent assessments she has shown that about one-third of these civil wars had restarted after some form of resolution (Walter 2004: 371). In other words, civil wars are notoriously had to cap. They simply reappear. Does their reappearance highlight the inadequacy of both conflict resolution and conflict transformation approaches?

There are several underlying causes that explain such an anomaly. The most important of these is the structural inequalities model – developed by peace theorist Johan Galtung. According to Galtung the end of conflict through a peace deal, peace accord or peace resolution does not necessarily unveil an era of perpetual peace. Formalisation of peace through any of those above processes merely terminates the constituency for direct violence (Galtung 1996). He describes this condition as an indication of the prevalence of 'negative peace'. Negative peace is a situation characterised quite simply by the absence of war. Thus if one turns to the question of the peace dividend for those affected by the conflict, Galtung's framework would suggest that they have not necessarily received the fruits of the peace process.

In a similar vein Galtung's theory of negative peace would propose that many post-conflict societies are marked by the presence of structural and cultural violence. Inequalities in life chances, differences over group rights and similar problems remain even after the signing of formal peace accords and the formation of a pluralist government. A post-conflict society can truly say that it is in the throes of 'positive peace' when these forms of structural and cultural violence are eliminated from the overall framework. Therefore, if negative peace marks the absence of explicit conflict, its other constituent part, i.e. positive peace, aims to create a viable egalitarian order. Positive peace is primarily concerned with transforming structural violence. Taken together they form the basis for the true return of the war-torn society to normality. Viable peace, then, has a maximalist agenda.

If one uses the framework of 'negative' and 'positive' peace in a post-conflict setting it becomes easier to comprehend the reasons behind the persistence of recurring violence. There is a simple explanation as to why some war-torn societies return to peace and prosperity within a very short period while others find it hard to achieve those objectives. Societies vary in terms of their economic and social capital. Those with a high level of social capital – in terms of an educated population, strong entrepreneurial capacity and a fairly acceptable level of economic development prior to the civil war – pick up their broken lives much faster than those who have never had these resources.

Although civil war impoverishes all, the resolve to put the scars and sufferings visited by that conflict behind them is much more profound in those societies with a higher level of social capital. To pitch this argument in an empirical context, while the citizenry of both Rwanda and former Yugoslavia experienced the breakdown of their society and were sucked into a macabre world of violence by the raging civil war, those living in former Yugoslavia were to make a quick return to normal conditions compared to their Rwandan counterparts. Peace-building, therefore, is more successful in countries with relatively high development levels (Doyle and Sambanis 2000: 795).

Similarly there exists a mistaken belief in some quarters that all civil war-torn societies are equal and face more or less the same kind of problems in the post-conflict phase. To assume that there can be one overarching framework of peace which can be used in all contexts is a grave policy error. Some societies may just need the termination of the conflict in order to pick up the fragmented pieces of their lives and move forward. Others may need comprehensive capacity-building packages. And yet some others may require long-term all-round assistance at all levels in the form of state-rebuilding and national consolidation. From a policy perspective, there needs to be a full-scale assessment of the social conditions during the conflict stage in order to prepare a framework of reconstruction in the post-conflict phase. Put simply, the greater the social and economic devastation the greater the need for assisting that society to return to the folds of normality. Progression towards sustainable peace is possible when the social capital aspect is paid adequate attention.

While arguing about the reconstruction of the society one also needs to pay close attention to retaining the social capital during and after the conflict. Many war-torn societies find it hard to prevent the migration of the best and ablest members of society. The prevailing conflict is a major push factor which forces this constituency to flee the country in search of better pastures. Out-migration is an irreparable double loss for the country concerned. First, losing this social capital seriously hinders the everyday working of society. Secondly, absence of this social capital in the post-conflict phase gravely undermines the rebuilding of civil society. Following the regime change and war in Iraq, the Iraqi society encountered a massive out-migration of the middle class, the white-collared professionals and the intelligentsia from the country. Suffice to say the out-migration was a major hindrance to the nation-building undertaking there. The breakdown of the Somali state created a similar situation. To begin with, many of these societies normally had a very small pool of social capital, and the long civil wars almost dissipated it altogether. This loss and the continuing conflict create a vicious circle which prevent the society concerned from rebuilding itself effectively.

In other words, 'diminished social capital is both the cause and the result of conflict. Its absence can impede the ability of groups and states to recover once hostilities have ended' (Brinkerhoff 2006: 30). Therefore nurturing a degree of normality following a protracted civil war depends on refilling the dried-up social capital pool. Regeneration of a society is facilitated when the able, conscientious and motivated citizenry of the erstwhile battle-scarred state decide to affirm their faith in the new society. With that aim in mind most post-conflict initiatives in recent years have taken on board the task of rejuvenating the social capital pool by asking the ex-patriates of that affected society to return to their country and take part in its rebuilding.

Establishing positive peace, in this context, would imply facilitating conditions for retaining as well as bringing back the key members of the society. This, it would appear, is an indigenous undertaking. But it is as much an indigenous responsibility as an external one. There may be occasions when, taking advantage of the chaos of civil war, an external actor or state might engage in exploiting the social capital. For instance, in order to increase its own social capital, Canada was engaged in providing lucrative contracts to Serbians who wished to migrate to Canada during the civil war in former Yugoslavia. According to Tin Judah 'the Canadians operated a shameless and highly profitable policy of creaming off the best of Serbia's up-and-coming scientists, engineers and others. Canada's gain was obviously Serbia's loss' (Judah 1997: 276–7).

In addition, as already highlighted, the recurrence of civil war in many developing and underdeveloped societies is solidly grounded in the failure of the peace process to deliver tangible benefits to its members. A war-ravaged community's capacity to recover from the depredation of war and embrace peace is largely determined by the chances of future material gains. If there are reasonable grounds for optimism, communities and societies that had once committed the worst crimes against each other can work towards settling their differences. Belief in a secure future can be a powerful inducement for the populace in putting the residues of the conflict behind them. Such thinking is acutely felt in post-conflict Balkans.

Although the civil war in the Balkans is formally over, people remain hostage to their fears and anxieties. Given their bitter, violent and incendiary experiences, people have not really come to terms with their past. The constituency for another round of violence, therefore, is never far away. Yet that deep anxiety that threatens to surface is steamrollered by the aspirations of a good life within an enlarged European Union. As one long-time observer of the Balkan conflict observes, most of the inhabitants in former Yugoslavia–now living within the frontiers of half a dozen odd new nation-states–feel they need the security of membership in the EU to keep them from slipping back into violence and hatred (Judah 2005: 46). Aspiration to membership in the European Union is the most powerful incentive behind the continuation of that truce. If the hope of future membership is dashed, it is argued, in some parts of the Balkans conflict may well flare up again (Judah 2005: 46).

Capacity-building and conflict-capping

Internal violence or civil war, as I argued in Chapter I, gains sustenance in states with wide economic disparities. That there is an intimate link between prevailing unequal economic growth and persistent civil war condition is widely recognised.

Polarisation of economic conditions leads to what is generally seen as 'micro-level motives' of participation in rebel activities (Collier and Hoeffler 2000; Fearon and Laitin 2003; Walter 2004). More importantly it is suggested that such forms of disorder and violence are likely to persist in those regions that fail to advance in economic development commensurate with the overall global economic growth (Lacina 2004: 201).[1]

In the light of the nexus between poverty and violence several theorists have suggested attending to economic development as the primary objective in all post-conflict situations. Edward Azar's observation is particularly relevant in this context. According to Azar:

> Reducing overt conflict requires reduction in levels of underdevelopment. Groups which seek to satisfy their identity and security needs through conflict are in effect seeking change in the structure of their society. Conflict resolution can truly occur and last if satisfactory amelioration of underdevelopment occurs as well. Studying protracted conflict leads one to conclude that peace is development in the broadest sense of the term.
>
> (Azar 1990: 155)

Elimination of economic backwardness and establishing some form of parity in the developmental sector among various constituent communities within a state is fundamental to preventing civil war and its recurrence.

Within the broad framework of development and underdevelopment Barbara F. Walter has proposed two key arguments on civil war termination. First, she postulates that 'countries whose citizens enjoy high levels of economic well-being are less likely to remain trapped in civil war dynamics'. Second, she argues that an autocratic political system fosters civil war recurrence while a democratic one significantly reduces the chances of that society relapsing into violence (Walter 2004: 372). Civil wars, she goes on to suggest, are dependent on the mobilisation of dissenting individuals and a constant recruitment drive. In the absence of a healthy scepticism over the economic and political condition there would be very little individual incentive to participate in the conflict. As Walter puts it:

> Civil wars will have little chance to get off the ground unless individual farmers, shopkeepers, and workers voluntarily choose to enlist in the armies that are necessary to pursue war, and it is the underlying political and economic conditions that make enlistment attractive that are likely to drive a second or third civil war (as well as the initial war).
>
> (Walter 2004: 372)

Put simply, economic deprivation causes people and communities to become predatory, which eventually leads to the breakdown of the social and political fabric. Our earlier reference to unemployment, lack of purchasing power, chronic material shortage, continual decline in the GNP and GDP confirmed the symbiosis between economic hardship and conflict. Taking this particular dimension into account the conventional argument posits that massive doses of external aid and other forms of financial assistance can be a useful deterrent against the recurrence of civil war. Pumping in significant amounts of international or external aid into the hitherto malfunctioning economy, it is argued, swamps the feelings of rivalry and curtails the need for competition over limited resources between the warring communities.

As Keen (2000) argues, 'external aid to civil war affected societies may reduce the need for civilians to turn to violence in pursuit of sustenance. More significantly, such aids can increase the economic benefits of peaceful activities'. This theory is echoed by other observers as well. According to Anderson, 'aid saves lives, reduces human suffering and supports the pursuit of greater economic and social security in conflict settings' (Anderson 1999). Roland Paris goes a step further by proposing 'pacification through political and economic liberalisation', which would imply transplanting western models of social, political and economic organisation into these war-torn states in order to control recurring civil conflicts (Paris 1997: 56). Fortunately such academic propositions have found their way into the policy undertakings of various international bodies. As the United Nations Sustainable Growth (UNSG) report makes clear, conflict prevention, sustainable economic growth and equitable development are mutually reinforcing activities (UNSG 2000). This report also pays high regard to economic growth and institution-building in post-civil war societies.

In recent years, states and societies that have experienced internal disorder and violence as a result of civil war have become the centre of focus for various external financial bodies such as the World Bank and the International Monetary Fund. A favoured method of these institutions in their attempt to rehabilitate the war-torn societies has been to introduce and impose Structural Adjustment Programs (SAPs) on these. SAPS are a form of shock therapy that, while providing aid and investment to boost economic growth and allow a sense of economic worth within a given society, also require very many reforms from within that community or state. Yet such measures have their limitations. While the general spirit of SAPs is a noble one (in the manner in which it is implemented), instead of rescuing the civil war-affected state occasionally it pushes it back into violence.

According to Caroline Hartzell, SAPs, owing to their strict codes of conduct, have a potential negative impact on reforms. In fact, in some instances SAPs create greater inequality between communities and groups, facilitate greater hardships for various constituencies within the state and open the question of distribution of resources. In some instances SAPs, instead of capping violence, clear the path to renewed violence (Hartzell 1999). However, the contestation of external aid in post-civil war recovery endeavour does not necessarily discount the relationship between development and conflict prevention. Some scholars point out that underdevelopment can only be brought to an end, as it ended in many dysfunctional societies, by homegrown political economic and social reforms and entrepreneurs that unleash the power of democracy and free markets (Easterly 2006). But for a resource-starved economy this can only be done in partnership with the external economic bodies. And in these instances SAPs prove enduring and indispensable.

Disarmament and arms control

Conditions of civil wars persist not only because parties to the conflict have irreconcilable differences or are governed by a particular ideology which makes it difficult for them to accept and adopt a new framework of interaction, but also in some instances its prevalence can be attributed to what I call negative intervention by external actors. In this section I am going to look at the issue of arms supply and arms embargo and how these twin issues contribute to both the perpetuation and the termination of civil war.

The primary purpose of an arms embargo is to deny access to weapons, thereby inducing military stalemates and preventing conflicts from escalating. Imposing arms embargoes when conflicts are active is often seen as logical first step towards halting violence (Oudraat 2000: 114). Yet, imposing an arms embargo to bring an end to civil war has its limitations. Arms embargoes work best in situations of military parity between conflicting parties or in situations where neither of the parties has access to external military hardware. By denying the source it becomes easier to cap the conflict and bring it to a reasoned resolution.

However, in the event of one of the parties being weaker than the other an embargo ensures a one-sided military victory. As Oudraat points out, 'embargoes tend to favor the warring factions that have access to government military ordnance and industries while making it very difficult for those on the other side to organise and defend themselves (Oudraat 2000: 114–15). For instance while the blanket arms embargo imposed on the former republics of Yugoslavia by the UN Security Council in 1991 had a limiting effect on the nature of the civil war, it nonetheless proved catastrophic for the Bosnian Muslims. They found themselves particularly disadvantaged *vis-à-vis* their Serb aggressors, who, owing to their already existing stockpile of arsenals, were able to ignore the effects of the embargo.

Having realised its grave errors in former Yugoslavia and the costs the Bosnian Muslims had to pay for its misjudged arms embargo, the international community (i.e. the UN Security Council) has since been more reluctant to deploy this particular method. Following on from this mistake it has resisted the temptation to impose a military sanction in other civil war-affected states such as Burundi, Sudan, Afghanistan, Sri Lanka and Nepal. Although they may be considered as an effective method of conflict-capping, arms embargoes have their limitations.

Thus, although it is an important diffuser of conflict, an arms embargo has limited applicability. In those situations where the conflict is dependent on homegrown or indigenous weaponry an externally sanctioned embargo has little or no relevance. Some studies have noted the fact that many contemporary civil wars are largely conducted with small and light weapons (Goose and Smyth 1994; Lumpe 2000). They are often fought with locally available indigenous light weapons such as rifles, knives, machetes and other improvised weaponry.

The correlation between small arms and civil conflict is a simple one. Small arms are easy to procure and are economically viable weapons. As a rule small arms are portable and therefore make the rebels extremely mobile and able to shift the locale of the conflict with comparative ease. Unlike heavy weaponry which is hard to shift and can be brought under control if the state succeeds in winning the battle, it is almost impossible to bring small weapons under control even if a state victory is assured. In some extreme situations even if the state manages to put a substantial cache of small arms out of commission the relative low cost of such weaponry means that the rebels can procure a fresh supply should they wish. The worst genocide of our times, i.e. in Rwanda, was performed not with heavy weaponry but with agricultural tools such as machetes. The decade-long Himalayan people's war in Nepal rarely relied on heavy external weaponry. According to Control Arms Campaign some 1 million people were killed by small arms between the years 2003 and 2005. Even when there is an arms embargo on the supply of small arms it is hard to enforce.

The illegal international trade in small and light weapons is big business. Light weapon-producing countries that publicly profess their commitment to peace are often major suppliers of arms to conflict-ridden states. The hypocrisy surrounding the sales of small arms to volatile third world countries where they spawn civil conflict was made clear when some twenty British bishops wrote an open letter to the *Guardian* newspaper on 23 June 2006. In their letter they said that up to 1,000 people are killed every day by armed violence. They pointed out that while there were tight regulations on the sale of postage stamps and dinosaur bones there was no such law against the sale of small arms (Norton Taylor 2006: 11). This unregulated aspect of the small arms trade in the end is a primary factor in fuelling the conflict. The responsibility to end conflict lies with the arms suppliers. While they tend to claim a neutral status and follow a benign and benevolent foreign policy, these supplies states are often the key indirect actors in such conflicts. Reflecting on the viciousness of small arms combat in civil wars some scholars have argued for the adoption of a 'wildfire approach' whereby external actors or interveners in a conflict should oversee an end to the supply of these weapons that make violence so easy (Woodward 1995: 290).

Neutering the irritants

In Chapter 1 I pointed out that civil wars often attract an irregular stream of actors who participate in it for profit motives. Very often war provides the only means of survival to these people. War is like a vital skill to these participants. Without war they have little or no use of their skills and consequently no basis to their existence. The absence of a chaotic and violent state of affairs in a post-conflict setting denies these actors the basis to their existence.

Paradoxical as it may seem, to those who have been brought up in a state of war and have known no other life the very talk of peace can be a threat in itself. The termination of the conflict, therefore, may not be to their liking. While the economic or material advantage that war offers is partly responsible for their continuance with this 'profession', the culture of war also provides some combatants with a kind of spiritual succour (Misra 2004b). As one critic puts it, it is the mid-level combatants such as child soldiers, foot combatants and non-commissioned officers who are most afraid of any change in the status quo. The fear of unemployment, homelessness, loss of social status and a highly insecure political future in an uncertain post-war era all contribute to their resolute embrace of war (Sisk 2004: 256).

Although this whole constituency of ex-soldiers and rebels are responsible for hindering the move towards peace, another issue that calls for closer attention is the demobilisation of child soldiers. Odd as it may seem, children are the catalysts in most contemporary civil wars. They form the backbone of most insurgent movements in the underdeveloped and the developing world. According to one study, child soldiers as young as six years of age can be found in three-quarters of the world's fifty or so civil war affected zones (Singer 2005). They are often the worst perpetrators of crimes against their fellow countrymen or citizens and are ardent followers of the central ideology of the movement that catapults them into the front lines of war. As one critic put it 'not only have conflicts fought by children become easier to start, hard to end, messier, and with greater loss of life, but they are creating a brutalised and disaffected generation who are growing up knowing nothing but violence' (Moorehead 2005: 46).

Terminating civil wars, then, is linked to disengaging children from war duties. Scholars have argued that states that engage in recruiting children into war efforts must be made accountable for their actions under international humanitarian law (Halsan Hoiskar 2001: 352). Although this is a fine proposition, it is extremely hard to enforce any such legal rulings. As our analyses have illustrated it is mostly in failed, failing or collapsed states with unaccountable governments that civil war often assumes a reality. To bring these entities to international judicial norms during civil war is an almost impossible undertaking. Similarly, imposing international legal rulings in those cases where a specific group (e.g. LTTE in Sri Lanka, the Lord's Resistance Army in Uganda or Hamas in Palestine) is involved in recruiting children for political/war efforts is harder still. Put simply, when the rebel or insurgent leadership is not accountable under the domestic laws, to uphold and implement international law in these situations is quite simply impossible.

Finding viable alternatives to neutralise these groups of irritants is a Herculean undertaking. However, it is crucial to do this in order to terminate the conflict. One of the primary reasons why these irritants remain active has to do with the availability of alternative opportunities in the post-conflict stage. According to Barbara Walter, in a post-civil war society that constituency whose quality of life remains at a critically low level and who are given little or no additional access to central decision-making are much more likely to re-enlist in a rebel organisation than those participants whose welfare has improved or who have the ability to participate in a competitive political process (Walter 2004: 371). My own intimate study of rebels in three civil wars, i.e. Afghanistan, Northern Ireland and Nepal, confirms this line of argument.

In Afghanistan the neo-Taliban rebels who constantly fought against the government and international forces following the end of civil war in 2002 were untouched by any developmental initiative and were far removed from the political process. In Northern Ireland the paramilitaries simply did not have the skills or were incapable of being a part of the new peace process.[2] Although it was not a widespread movement, a good number of Maoist rebels remained active in the period following the unveiling of peace process in Nepal in 2007. In an extremely poor, backward and poverty-stricken country the new government that emerged after the end of the civil war, although committed to the spirit of rehabilitating the former war participants, was unable to cater for the requirements of all. Consequently a good number of these rebels continued to engage in low-level conflict in spite of the peace deal signed by their leaders.

Courting the diaspora

Organised diasporas have always played a significant role in inciting violence and promoting regime change in their home territories (Brinkerhoff 2006: 27). A large dissatisfied diaspora from a weak or failed state considerably increases the risk of civil war in their country of origin (Collier and Hoeffler 2002: 17). Some recent studies have suggested that 'the greater the span of an ethnic or religious diaspora across international boundaries, the higher the potential for external support for insurgencies and the higher the risk that a country will experience a civil war' (Gleditsch 2007: 298).

The participation of the diaspora in a given conflict often produces long-lasting outcomes. It is well known that diasporas often provide a whole range of support to their community in the conflict zone.[3] Their contribution, however, is particularly crucial in the civil war economies (Duffield 1998: 84). Many insurgency movement and civil wars appear to owe their existence to the economic contribution made by the diaspora community. Sikh separatism in India in the 1980s, the Kurdish war of independence, the Eritrean self-determination struggle, sectarian war in Northern Ireland and the Tamil liberation movement have depended and some of them are still dependent on the vital financial support of the diaspora. As one critic put it 'foreign remittances by the diaspora have not only supported families in need of assistance, but also provided money to purchase weapons and salaries to sustain fighters in conflict zones' (Forman 2002: 137).

Although the diaspora by its very nature is often far away from the location of the conflict their loyalty to the homeland can be very profound indeed. The diaspora's commitment to its homeland can often be emotional as well as determined. For those displaced by the conflict a sovereign 'homeland' has a great appeal and attraction. The first-generation diaspora, owing to its own experience of persecution and subsequent uprooting from its place of birth, sees the conflict through a prism of extreme violence and intolerance. Later this vision is passed on to successive generations, who may not have a direct experience of the conflict itself, but nonetheless harbour this image. As Terrence Lyons says:

> The trauma of violent displacement is vivid in the first generations' minds and is often kept alive in subsequent generations through commemorations and symbols. In fact, one function of conflict-generated diaspora networks is to ensure that displacement's original cause is remembered and the grievance passed on to the next generation.
>
> (Lyons 2006: 4)

The danger with this form of remembrance is that it is fixed, uncompromising and challenging in its outlook. But more importantly the diaspora's conception of the conflict may be far removed from reality. For instance, while the diaspora is locked in a particular period of history, the community or the inhabitants living in the conflict zone may have fostered new ideas and conceptions and would have an entirely different method of confronting the challenges and realities present within that situation. The emotional and clouded vision which I earlier talked about is often a major catalyst in the perpetuation of the conflict. This argument gains strength if read alongside Benedict Anderson's interpretation of diaspora and the members contribution to the homeland from which he/she is now physically separated.

> While technically a citizen of the state in which he comfortably lives, but to which he may feel little attachment, he finds it tempting to play identity politics by participating (via propaganda, money, weapons, any way but voting) in the conflicts of his imagined *Heimat* (homeland) – now only fax time away.
>
> (Anderson 1992: 13)

There is no denying the fact that the position the member of a diaspora occupies is a unique one. It allows him/her to influence and alter events within the given state from a faraway place without directly feeling the consequences of his/her actions. Take for example, the role of the Irish Northern Aid Committee (NORAID, the Irish diaspora organisation in the United States) in the conflict in Northern Ireland. For decades NORAID was instrumental in keeping the momentum of insurgency and resistance from the Catholic side alive by providing the IRA with much-needed funds. There was, of course, a general grassroots approval of IRA from among the Catholic population. But had NORAID not been bankrolling the IRA the latter's campaign perhaps would have been much less dramatic. A similar story can be found in the Tamil diaspora's contribution to the civil war in Sri Lanka.

The civil war in Sri Lanka displaced some 1 million Tamils, half of whom remained in the country and the other half went abroad as refugees.[4] Tamils displaced by the ethnic war can now be found on every continent.[5] This diasporic community over the years has been the main financier to the liberation struggle. Thanks to their 'economic muscle and international influence, they have been successful in waging an ideological separatist battle for LTTE from overseas'[6] and through their financial contribution they have aided the insurgency war within Sri Lanka. The LTTE in the past was instrumental in sending some of its sympathisers overseas to eke out a living and simultaneously generate income for the 'liberation struggle'. Once the LTTE was banned as a terrorist organisation (by the United Kingdom in 2000 and the European Union in 2006) and there were greater restrictions on diaspora remittance, there was a significant decrease in rebel violence in Sri Lanka.

True, member of the diaspora often work as agents of 'war', aiding, abetting and fuelling the conflict from a distance. But the diaspora can also make a crucial contribution in terms of the peace dividend. Diasporas offer potential to deflect conflict escalation and re-emergence (Brinkerhoff 2006: 27). Diasporas are agents of both 'war' and 'peace'. They impact upon both peace and violence in a civil war situation. While on one hand they could be chastised as architects of conflict, on the other they can be seen as agents responsible for rebuilding a shattered society and contributing to the termination of the conflict.

Let me reintroduce the Irish diaspora and its role in the enforcement of peace in Northern Ireland. The role of Americans for a New Irish Agenda (ANIA) is a case in point. Instead of fanning rebel sentiments ANIA exerted pressure on those actors and powers that were responsible for taking decisions that would be instrumental in Northern Ireland's return to peace. ANIA developed an integrative power strategy that combined such elements as trust, loyalty and admiration with the influence of Clinton Presidency that in turn pushed hard for a successful conflict resolution to the Northern Irish conflict which materialised in the signing of the Good Friday Agreement. This constructive engagement facilitated Northern Ireland's speedy return to normality. Another high-profile case in point is the role of the Armenian diaspora in putting an end to the civil war in Nagorno Karabakh. Thanks to their assistance there is not only peace in this disputed region but they (the diaspora) have assisted this unrecognised state to engage with such liberal political ideals like the rule of law and democracy.

A diaspora's participation in unveiling the peace process and rebuilding the post-conflict society is very vital, indeed. If the diaspora continues to nurse historical grievances in this phase it can all too easily be exploited by the rebel organisations. Similarly a rebel organisation can carry on with its armed offensive after the unveiling of a peace process if it continues to receive financial support from the diaspora (Collier and Hoeffler 2002: 18). Thus in the post-conflict phase, a diaspora has a moral responsibility to see that its remittance is invested in nurturing peace and directed at post-conflict reconstruction efforts. By turning off their economic assistance to war and investing in peace the diaspora can deter and discourage any splinter group from launching any new offensive. In fact as some studies have stressed rebel leaders who find themselves without any diaspora financing are unlikely to grow large enough to engage in civil war or puncture the fragile peace process (Weinstein 2002: 2). Most important of all, diaspora participation in post-conflict peace provides the much-needed psychological boost to a war-fatigued society. They feel motivated and inspired by the presence of member of the diaspora amidst them. This, in the end, helps that society to move away from the conflict for ever.

Post-war depression

Civil war is never an easy experience. It leaves its participants or those whose lives it has touched permanently affected. While civil war degrades, the time after the war, which we call post-war, commits people to a state of collective depression. There is something paradoxical about peace that comes after war. One would like to believe that the end of war creates dividends for collective and communal jubilation and euphoria. Nothing could be farther from the truth.

Civil wars scar those who live through it. Those who escape direct physical violence often end up with deep psychological problems. Post-traumatic Stress Disorder (PTSD) is now found to be the most common ailment among civilians as well as combatants in the aftermath of civil war. It is a debilitating anxiety-inflict-ing psychological condition of the victims. According to one report the level of anti-depressant consumption in Iraq following the outbreak of sectarian violence and civil war between 2003 and 2006 rose to almost half the population. The afflic-tion was so severe that even children as young as five were prescribed this drug. In another location, Kashmir, according to some estimates, four-fifths of the five mil-lion people in the valley were suffering from PTSD in one form or another. The problem with PTSD is that it is not a short-term condition. Sometimes an entire generation grows up in the shadow of fear and entertains deep psychological stresses. Thus even when there is a constituency of peace, which is established after a long-drawn-out violence, those affected by PTSD carry the psychological and mental scars. As a result, they come to have a long-term impact on the recovery of that society.

While for a civilian PTSD could mean lack of enthusiasm in the new rebuilding initiative, for a rebel or former combatant this implies disillusionment with the whole post-war project. Consequently while the civilian remains inactive, disinterested and uncommitted to any form of positive developmental mission taking place within the society the rebel returns to the spell of violence. PTSD and resumption of rebel vio-lence are often closely interlinked. The reason why former combatants return to their guns is partly due to their untreated psychological traumas. This constituency remains uncommitted to the peace dividend not only because of the absence of opportunities for their successful integration into the society as I highlighted earlier, but also because of their prevailing debilitating psychological condition.

One way of combating this affliction is to provide sustained socio-psychological counseling to victims and, in the worst cases, to offer qualitative medical inter-vention. The importance of such medical aid is acknowledged to be of primary importance by those working in the post-conflict recovery sector. In some instances the donor community makes provision to invest in this sector. The Balkans under the post-conflict recovery programme received adequate resources from the donors to oversee the needs of those affected by PTSD. Ten years on, the effectiveness of such measures is now widely felt and appreciated. Not all post-civil war societies, however, receive the required attention or funding to engage in a large-scale PTSD combat exercise. Afghans who lived through twenty-five years of civil war were less fortunate on this front. Neither the government nor the donor community pro-vided the required assistance in this regard (Misra 2004b). An extremely poor peo-ple, those affected could not even afford anti-depressants, while their counterparts in Iraq could. As a result, there was a steep rise in the female suicide rate in the country in the five-year period following the international intervention. The return of many male Afghans to warmongering during this period in the form of resurgent Taliban forces could also be attributed to the persistence of the PTSD condition.

Conclusion

Why belligerents or protagonists prefer 'fighting to talking' is one of the enduring puzzles in the literature on civil war. As our earlier study showed there can be far too many reasons for groups going to war. Similarly there can be as many reasons why parties to the conflict prevent a peaceful outcome. The meaning and logic of war often overtakes the desirability and logic of peace (Sisk 2004: 253). The termination or successful outcome of a civil war settlement can be situated within two diametrically opposite approaches. These can be summed up as (a) the end justifies the means principle; and (b) the means justifies the end principle. According to the first principle, if one of the parties in a civil war uses force until the very end against its adversary that eventually leads to a successful conclusion of the conflict. Since achievement of a lasting resolution is the primary goal in this conflict the belligerents are never reluctant to use any means to reach that outcome. The second line of argument, that is, the means justifies the end principle, totally contradicts the first one. It argues that the means that were used in moving towards the resolution are crucial in terms of determining the ultimate nature and duration of the resolution. It posits, for instance, that the greater the use of violence in terms of introducing a resolution, the less likely is that resolution to last.

The discourse on civil war has always been state-centric. It tries to favour the state instead of the affected groups in the event of a conflict between the two. Thus it is not surprising that when one turns to conflict termination the emphasis is heavily biased towards good behaviour from the rebel side. However, one ought to ask in this context what possible role the state or central authorities should have in post-conflict situations. Many of the multinational states fighting civil wars within their frontiers often find themselves in this situation owing to misconceived and misguided policies. Ending divisions that lead to war and imposing a viable conflict resolution strategy requires that there is a greater degree of consensus-building between the affected groups and the state. In the end, as various scholars have consistently suggested, termination of civil war is fundamentally linked to the manner in which the original grievance which created the condition of war is addressed. In those instances the government that is willing to address and settle key rebel or insurgent grievances has a higher chance of avoiding renewed conflict than the government that leave important issues unattended and unanswered (Gurr 1971; Tilly 1978; Walter 2004).

If anything, this study has shown that every civil war has its origin within a particular historical context. It develops around a specific set of variables. It has its own dynamics and operates along a given logic. Put simply, no two civil wars are alike. Therefore, there cannot be any standard universal blueprint for war-torn societies engaged in their search for peace (Lundin and Gaspar 2003: 305). What works in one particular context may be inapplicable and completely irrelevant in another. Yet, most civil war-affected societies exhibit a certain common need. While we cannot use a universal primer we can certainly improvise our techniques to suit the needs of a particular case.

Conclusion

The key consensus to emerge from our study is that civil wars are typical of weak states, a problem of underdevelopment as well as spurious politics (Lacina 2004: 191). A large majority of the contemporary civil war-affected societies happen to be in the underdeveloped or developing part of the world. Why civil wars are a persistent feature of non-western underdeveloped societies has a controversial explanation. Uncharitable as it may appear there is some basis to the argument that peaceful cohabitation and sharing of national wealth in an equitable manner is a product of political maturity; that individuals and communities take centuries to learn about and then appreciate 'the other' not as an enemy but an equal.

Most modern states in the non-European context began their political career as multinational entities. This heterogeneous profile was more of an inheritance than the product of a conscious choice. In more ways than one, Europe itself was a stranger to ethnic pluralism and it took centuries to protect the rights of minorities and then adopt and appreciate the multicultural ethos. For Europe, to succeed meant burying centuries of prejudice. Seen in this trajectory developing societies lacking a robust democratic political culture and accompanying economic malaise can hardly be expected to display the same degree of ethnic reconciliation as their developed counterparts.

The allure and attraction of bonding with one's own kind, based on such markers as race, religion or ethnicity, is very deep even within the so-called developed and industrialised societies. A survey published in the *Economist* magazine in 2004 highlighted the fact that the 'Levels of trust and cooperation are highest in the most homogeneous neighbourhoods. People living in diverse areas, it turns out, are more suspicious of people who don't look like them; because of that, they suffer socially, economically and politically' (*The Economist* 2004: 33). If such a mindset is so prevalent in societies which have always paraded themselves as modern, outward-looking and cosmopolitan one can hardly blame the traditional, culture-bound economically deprived communities in Asia, Africa or Latin America for not being accommodating to their neighbours who have a different skin colour, speak another language or worship an alien god. So long as individuals entertain this 'narcissism of small differences' conflict will prevail.

My attempt, in the second half of this study, was primarily concerned with the exploration of various conflict resolution strategies. As a strategy, conflict resolution serves a useful purpose in terms of both putting a cap on the potential conflict and finding a viable solution to the problem once conflict has occurred. Methods such as intervention, peace-keeping, reconstruction, reconciliation and pluralist governance are all parts of the overall conflict resolution strategy. As I demonstrated in the previous chapters, in order for these methods to produce the desired outcome, there has to be an active partnership between both indigenous and external actors. Given the right kind of commitment from all the actors involved a society can truly consign the experience of civil war to history.

Yet, as I mentioned in the previous chapter, unfortunately many civil wars that appear to have ended often reappear.[1] There are a variety of reasons why this happens. Reoccurrence of civil war is a result of multiple contributing factors. Given the limitations of conflict resolution in capping the conflict permanently, one is tempted to wonder if we can look for other ways of bringing it to an end. It must be stressed here that, as a method, conflict resolution aims at resolving the conflict. If we are to find a lasting or permanent solution to the problem, we need to devise ways of 'terminating' the conflict. Conflict termination requires the community to go a step further. It needs to use some unconventional approaches to peace. These are human-centred approaches and dependent on individual initiative. If our discussion of the politics of civil wars has suggested anything it is that people have fought with each other over small differences and will continue to do so. The solution to the resulting conflicts, therefore, must come from people themselves. But that is the hardest part.

While institutions, frameworks and brand new ideals are critical as regulatory mechanisms they may lack the power to bring about a complete transformation in human behaviour that was the main catalyst in violence. Appealing to that individual self, therefore, is crucial. And this is best done by an individually mediated transformation process. The vision of a landscape of open borders and shared pluralist values has the best chance of striking root among the whole citizenry in a post-war society if this message comes from individuals with a cross-cultural appeal. In a war-torn society, where an individual becomes an activist for peace – while successfully resisting the logic of a divisive ideology – the chances of conflict termination are very high indeed. When widely respected members of that society take on the task of introducing the message of unity across groups, communities and boundaries, conflict termination becomes a reality. Such is the power of these leaders that sometimes they orchestrate ways of making people think the unthinkable, helping them rise to gestures of reconciliation that the society could not perceive in earlier (Ignatieff 1999: 188).

Individuals or leaders pursuing these strategies are often blessed with what one might call 'moral capital'. These are people accepted by a hitherto divided community as natural moral leaders untarnished and untainted by any form of narrowness. And, when they deploy their moral authority strategically, it leads to a significant peace dividend (Kane 2001). Thus when they speak of reconciliation, peace and individual responsibility it has wider resonance. Such a humanistic individual-centred approach by a person or persons blessed with moral capital is not altogether a rarity.

Such humanistic individual-centred approaches to end the conflict forever have been practised in various cultures and contexts. When approached by deeply angry parents who had lost their home and child to the violence perpetrated by the civil war following the partition of India in 1947 M.K. Gandhi, the apostle of peace and non-violence, is reported to have asked that bereaved couple to adopt an orphan from the community that they thought was responsible for killing their own child. Such a level of self-sacrifice and empathy with the erstwhile enemy brings about a total transformation in the individual and thereby prepares that person and subsequently the community to abandon hate, prejudice, distrust and all other negative emotions associated with the conflict.

Preah Maha Ghosananda, a Buddhist monk in Cambodia, undertook several *Dhamayietra* or 'Pilgrimages of Truth' in the country to put an end to the psychosis of violence of the civil war era. In his long pilgrimages Ghosananda made Cambodians appreciate the futility of violence. He preached, 'Hate can never be appeased by hate; hate can only be appeased by love'. Following his message rebels laid down their arms and groups previously divided by hatred embraced each other while committing to a united future. In South Africa similar a transformation of heart took place under the leadership of Nelson Mandela.

Away from these high-profile cases there are also instances where local actors at the grassroots level undertake the task of slow transformation of the conflict dialectics. In Mozambique and Sierra Leone traditional healers have consistently engaged in purification rituals involving the whole community in post-civil war settings. While using concepts such as 'pollution' and 'purification', these traditional healers often created an awareness that stressed the period of violence as 'abnormal' and thus 'unacceptable' (Pouligny 2005: 502). Even more importantly by engaging in such a discourse they created cross-community awareness that rejected the overall logic of violence. Unsurprisingly this mode of intervention has helped facilitate conflict termination – at least at the local level. Although it may appear unscientific, these rituals are often the best defence against negative propaganda (the root cause of inspiration behind various conflicts). Given their uncontested traditional authority the discourse of these healers[2] often assumes a level of legitimacy which no incendiary divisive rhetoric can counter.

Some societies, in spite of their horrendous experiences of ethnocide, genocide and the like, commit themselves to such an ethos. The acceptance of the other, without harping back to the past, through reconciliation as we saw in the case of Rwanda, South Africa and to some degrees Mozambique are important pointers in post-civil war peace-building. Such a resolve, of course, requires enormous courage and foresight among not only the politicians or leadership at the top but needs to be equally shared by all constituencies with the society. And should any one of the participating constituents, say a group or party, decides to withdraw from this project or operate outside it then the chances of that society finding itself on the brink of another round of conflict is very high, indeed.

Notes

Introduction

1 The first recorded civil war in human history dates back to 636 BC when Elamites revolted against the rule of Asshur-bani-pal. Another notable event is the first to Jewish Revolt against Imperial Rome between 66–70 AD, with a second one in 132–135 AD. In the non-western context the first major civil war took place during the final days of the reign of Moghul Emperor Shah Jehan in mid-sixteenth century.

2 As Stathis N. Kalyvas puts it, 'contrary to conventional war, civil war displays a "triangular" character. It involves not just two (or more) competing actors, but also civilians. Civilian support matters for the outcome of the conflict. Typically, civil war involves little fighting between combatants and much action in which civilians play a prominent role'. Kalyvas, 'The Logic of Violence in Civil War', *Working Paper 1*, Universidad Autonoma de Madrid, www.uam.es/centros/derecho/cpolitica/wpapers.html, p. 6, accessed 15 April 2007.

3 Warlordism, banditry, looting and hostage-taking are some of the commonest forms of activism in many contemporary civil war zones stretching from Afghanistan to Angola and Chechnya to Congo.

1 Theorising civil war

1 As Håvard Hegre and Nicholas Sambanis have put it, 'there is no theoretical agreement on what is the "right" set of variables to include in the sensitivity analysis of empirical results of civil war onset model, and there is also mixed empirical support for many variables'. Håvard Hegre & Nicholas Sambanis, 'Sensitivity Analysis of Empirical Results on Civil War Onset', *Journal of Conflict Resolution*, vol. 50, no. 4, p. 515.

2 The story of the Colombian civil war is captured succinctly in the paragraph below by its most celebrated novelist and commentator Gabriel Garcia Marquez. According to Marquez: 'In the 1960s, the guerilla arm of the Communist Party, the Revolutionary Armed Forces of Colombia (FARC), had set themselves up to defend the unarmed peasants against the rapacious landowners. This original idea swiftly degenerated, and to finance their war the guerrillas raised money from the cattlemen through kidnapping, blackmail, and extortion. The landowners responded by recruiting private armies, some of which were even given legitimacy by the government on the grounds that they were "self-defence" groups. At first, everything was directed towards the physical elimination of communism. But then they started on cattle rustlers, then criminals in the towns, and even began killing beggars and homosexuals. The cattlemen who survived not only lost much of their fortunes, but found themselves threatened by gangs of outlaws whom they themselves had first given arms to'. Gabriel Garcia Marquez, 'The Future of Colombia', *Granta 31*, p. 91.

3 Some might argue that other identity markers such as language and regional divide are important contributing factors in civil wars. I am of the opinion, however, that these two issues, while they divide communities, do not necessarily lead to a conflict that would merit being put into the category of civil war as I defined it in the Introduction.
4 The scholarly literature on this is far too extensive to mention here.
5 Representation of this mode of interaction was very much present in the Balkans when the Serbs rallied around the leadership of Slobodan Milosovic at a time of deep national crisis. Iraqis who had lived a secular existence for over several generations under the Ba'ath Party rule underwent a conversion into narrow religious identities in the uncertain socio-economic and political world of post-Saddam Hussein Iraq.
6 As Blimes puts it: 'an ethnically diverse society is no more likely than an ethnically homogeneous society to experience civil war given the absence of factors that increase the probability of civil war such as low per capita income'. Randall J. Blimes, 'The Indirect Effect of Ethnic Heterogeneity on the Likelihood of Civil War Onset', *Journal of Peace Research*, vol. 50, no. 4, p. 539.
7 There are, of course, exceptions. ETA in Spain, which is fighting for an independent homeland, does not fully appreciate the democratic dividend.

2 Poverty of nationalism

1 As Ramón Maiz argues, 'nationalism generates collective identity by means of mechanisms that involve the aggregation and selection of differential traits (language, religion, race, history, etc.) and that produce stereotypes of the distinction between "us" and "them" by exaggerating differences from things foreign and minimizing internal differences within the community'. Ramón Maiz, 'Framing the Nation: Three Rival Versions of Contemporary Nationalist Ideology', *Journal of Political Ideologies*, vol. 8, no. 3, pp. 252–67.
2 In most instances, as Charles Tilly reminds us, the post-colonial state could maintain its statehood by following coercion-intensive methods. Charles Tilly, *Coercion, Capital, and European States, AD 900–1992*, Oxford: Blackwell, 1992.
3 This phase is marked by the dominance of 'territorial integrative nationalism', a temporary spiritual solidarity among diverse communities who for the first time identify themselves freely with the notion of a common nationality.
4 Adoption of neo-liberal economic reforms in general, and the increasing marketisation of primary resources in particular in the context of globalisation is a key factor in sparking armed conflict in many vulnerable states. Paul D. Williams, 'International Peacekeeping: The Challenges of State-building and Regionalization', *International Affairs*, vol. 81, no. 1, p. 170.
5 The African island republic of Mauritius is a case in point. It is one of the continent's most successful economies. It was one of the first states in Africa to integrate into the economic globalisation process and thus has been enjoying the fruits of this process for well over two decades. By contrast those African states who were late arrivals on the scene or became a part of the economic globalisation process only recently have had all forms of challenges. One can mention Zimbabwe as a contrasting case in point.
6 This vision could be very profound and articulated in clear ethnic, religious and geographical terms as was the case with the Bosnian Muslims aspiration of self hood. Or as banal as that of the Lord's Resistance Army in northern Uganda which lacked any cogency and coherence in its insurgency.
7 Multinational states such as India, Russia and Turkey all exhibit a tendency to impose the majoritarian culture on the entire population.
8 Where a group has achieved an independent separate state following a prolonged civil war, the newly formed government adopts policies that consolidate the power of the national ethnic majority often at the cost of the newly emerged minority.

9 I have paraphrased Robert O. Keohane's interpretation of democracy (Keohane 2002: 233–4) and have used some of the sentiments produced in that context in order to build up my own argument on the slow decline of nationalism.

3 Erotics of violence

1 The prejudice against another fellow community may run so deep among some groups that the elders in that group would use every opportunity to initiate its younger members into its savagery. During the Rwandan genocide many Hutu fathers taught their boys how to butcher a Tutsi. 'They made them imitate the machete blows. They displayed their skill on dead people, or on living people they had captured during the day. The boys usually tried it out on children, because of their similar size'. Jean Hatzfeld, *A Time for Machetes*, London: Serpent's Tail, 2005, pp. 34–5.

2 As Martha C. Nussbaum, documents in her meticulous study on one of the worst cases of Hindu–Muslim riot in contemporary India (in Gujrat, March–April 2002) most of the women victims 'were first raped, and tortured before being killed and burned. Children were killed with their parents; foetuses were ripped from the bellies of pregnant women to be tossed into the fire'. Martha C. Nussbaum, *The Clash Within: Religious Violence, and India's Future*, Cambridge, MA: Harvard University Press, 2007.

3 The prejudice and stereotyping, therefore, is very often couched in what one might call spurious fabricated history. One of the most fundamental aspects of violence in many contemporary deeply divided societies is the appreciation and misappropriation of their own past. A certain way of memorising history has been the key factor in pitting communities against each other. The distorted debate about the past is at the root of various intra-state conflicts in Africa and Asia.

4 For instance, following one of the worst cases of religious riots between Hindus and Muslims in the western Indian province of Gujrat in March 2002 in which some 2,000 innocent Muslims were killed by Hindu fanatics and mobs, the Prime Minister of the country Atal Bihari Vajpayee is said to have condoned the killing while declaring that 'wherever Muslims are, they don't want to live in peace' (Nussbaum 2007), which led to another bout of fresh violence.

5 For a detailed discussion, see Tim Judah, *The Serbs: History, Myth and the Destruction of Yugoslavia*, New Haven, CT: Yale University Press, 1997.

6 According to Milos Vasic the Serb paramilitaries who engaged in mass murder and ethnic cleansing during the Yugoslav civil war of the 1990s consisted on average of '80 percent common criminals and 20 percent fanatical nationalists'. For details, see Milos Vasic, 'The Yugoslav Army and the Post-Yugoslav Armies', in D.A. Dyker and I. Vejovda (eds.) *Yugoslavia and After: A Study in Fragmentation, Despair and Rebirth*, London: Longman, 1996.

7 Especially relevant is Ivo Andric's controversial literary narrative *The Bridge on the Drina*, where the author introduces the reader to a climate of ancient hatreds and suggests that it was responsible for breeding generations of people who were susceptible to violence in the Balkans.

8 As Carl Gustav Jacobsen put it, 'Rape is integral to war and other depravity; it is the rogue soldier's unholy price for death's threat'. Carl Gustav Jacobsen, 'Bosnian War Crimes: Problems of Definition and Prosecution', *Security Dialogue*, vol. 25, no. 2, June 1994, p. 239.

9 The irony, however, is that both Serbs and Bosnian Muslims belonged to the same ethnic category – the South Slavs.

10 The Hutu authorities reinforced their genocidal campaign of Tutsis at the grassroots level by rewarding those Hutus who killed their Tutsi neighbours with the latters' cows, land and other worldly possessions.

4 Impasse in intervention

1   At its core, humanitarian intervention is decidedly western in origin. Its roots go back to the colonial period. Every major colonial intervention on behalf of the colonised was defined as a humanitarian civilising mission from the time of Christopher Columbus onwards. As a rule many of the idiosyncrasies and violent practices among the colonised, be it the practice of child sacrifice in the pre-Columbian civilisations in the Americas, widow-burning in India or female genital mutilation in parts of Africa all 'provided a moral pretext' for the external colonial powers to intervene in their affairs. As Neta Crawford argues, 'debates about humanitarian intervention are in many ways a continuation of arguments about colonialism and imperial responsibility', Neta Crawford, *Argument and Change in World Politics: Ethics, Decolonisation and Humanitarian Intervention*, Cambridge: Cambridge University Press, 2002, p. 400.

2   As an extension of the argument one could stress that a state loses its moral standing and consequently its legal rights to self-defence if it fails to protect those under its protection.

3   A. McSmith and J. Dillon, 'Blair Seeks New Powers to Attack Rogue States', *The Independent*, 13 July 2003.

4   Under the UN Charter the Security Council determines the existence of threats to peace. Article 2(4) of the UN Charter prohibits the use of force by states (except in self-defence), and Article 24(1) gives the Security Council the primary responsibility for the maintenance of international peace and security. However, the UN Charter gives the Security Council the power under Article 42 and Chapter VII to take any measures necessary to 'restore international peace and security'.

5   When a military coup took place in the Pacific Island of Fiji and threatened peace and stability in the country in 2006 the neighbouring superpower Australia dissociated itself completely from any talk of intervention. As the Australian Prime Minister of the time John Howard put it, 'it was not in Australia's national interest to intervene in the Fijian coup'.

6   It has now emerged that the Liberation Tigers of Tamil Eelam (LTTE) chief Vellupillai Prabhakaran was not serious about peace negotiations with the government in Colombo in 2002. According to Colonel Karuna Amman one of the breakaway leaders of LTTE the rebel supremo Prabhakaran had a different agenda when it entered into a short-lived ceasefire deal with the Sri Lankan government. Prabhakaran is alleged to have instructed his negotiators to 'drag the peace talks out for about five years, somehow let the time pass by, meanwhile let the organization build up its depleting arms stock and then resume the next stage of fighting'.

7   As Richard Dowden's powerful argument asks, 'If the ICC cannot bring peace and reconciliation to the victims of war, what is the point of justice? Who is it for? I suspect it is for us, watching these wars on television. We demand an end to immunity for terrible crimes and need to see the baddies go to jail. The court may be a salve for our consciences for doing nothing about the wars in the first place'. Richard Dowden, 'ICC in the Dock', *Prospect*, Issue 134, May 2007, p. 13.

8   One ought to be aware that intervention violates most interpretations of customary as well as codified international law.

9   As David Holloway and Stephen John Steadman have argued in most cases of Africa's tryst with civil wars 'artificial borders, quasi-states, low human capital, underdeveloped economies, a statist model of political and economic development have all contributed to the constant presence of violence'. David Holloway and Stephen John Steadman, 'Civil Wars and State-Building in Africa and Eurasia', in Mark R. Beissinger and Crawford Young (eds.) *Beyond State Crisis? Post-colonial Africa and Post-Soviet Eurasia in Comparative Perspective*, Washington, DC: Woodrow Wilson Centre Press, 2002.

10 The African Union (AU), while successful in some peacekeeping missions (in West Africa), has been largely ineffective.

11 While the African Union's peacekeeping efforts in Darfur largely failed owing to economic, strategic and legal constraints, there was no immediate effort to replace AU
forces with some form of UN or other international interventionist force. The absence of
external non-intervention was also shaped to a large extent by a regional Arab view that
the civil war in Darfur was an exaggerated issue and an age-old tribal and resource-based
conflict and, simultaneously a western/US/Jewish/Christian plot to discredit an Islamic
Arab government. Owing to this interpretation, in October 2004 some members of the
AU such as Chad, Egypt, Libya and Nigeria condemned the idea of external intervention,
describing the civil war as an 'African question'.

5 Responsibility to rebuild: tasks for Sisyphus

1 A nation, according to Anthony Smith, can be defined as 'a named population, sharing
an historic territory, common myths and historical memories, a mass public culture, a
common economy and common legal rights and duties for all members', Anthony D.
Smith, *National Identity*, London: Penguin, 1991, p. 14.
2 One could cite the example of East Timor here.
3 Although the US involvement in all these conflicts has followed a uniform pattern, i.e.
military intervention and subsequent efforts at bringing that state and society back into
the fold of the international system, it has been accustomed to describing these operations under various terms such as occupation, peacekeeping, peace enforcement, stabilisation, reconstruction and nation-building.
4 With hindsight, one could argue that the US as well as the UN stumbled into Somalia
without a plan. Consequently what began as a humanitarian mission to feed the starving
Somalis was transformed into a misguided attempt at ad hoc nation-building.
5 Of the eight American-led missions only four of the nations involved (Germany, Japan,
Bosnia and Kosovo) were at peace, while the other four (Somalia, Haiti, Afghanistan and
Iraq) were not. *The Economist*, 5 March 2005, p. 60.
6 For a detailed and exhaustive study, see James Dobbins *et al.*, *The UN's Role in Nation-
Building: From the Congo to Iraq*, Santa Monica, CA: Rand Corporation, 2005.
7 See the introduction of Gary Dempsey and Roger Fontaine's *Fools Errands: America's
Recent Encounters with Nation Building*, Washington: Cato Institute, 2001.
8 How some of these units operate as successful entities is a valid line of enquiry. In situations such as these, the state creates a common national identity by inculcating in its citizenry a sense of civic nationalism and multicultural citizenship. States such as the
United States, France and the United Kingdom, while greatly diverse, have nonetheless
succeeded in forging a sense of unity. To a large extent their success as multicultural
polities is partly based on their affirmation of civic nationalism.
9 Hamid Karzai is often described by his critics as a puppet who cannot trust his own
people for his personal safety and security and has to be protected by US bodyguards.
10 For details, see Michael Ignatieff, *Empire Lite: Nation-Building in Bosnia, Kosovo and
Afghanistan*, London: Vintage, 2003. p. 6.
11 For a complete version of the story, see 'US aid threat angers Nepal rebel',
http://news.bbc.co.uk/1/hi/world/south_asia/5138238.stm accessed 3 July 2006.
12 Ibid.
13 *The Economist*, 5 March 2005, p. 59.
14 The UN mission in Liberia costs $800m a year.

6 Governing the ungovernable

1 I am paraphrasing Ryszard Kapuscinski's observations on post-colonial government in
Ghana. For details, see Ryszard Kapuscinski, *The Cobra's Heart*, Harmondsworth:
Penguin, p. 8.

2 A decade after the introduction of the Good Friday Agreement the peace process culminated in a power-sharing deal between the two previous archrivals, Gerry Adams of Sinn Féin and Ian Paisley of the Democratic Unionist Party (DUP) in late March 2007. In his statement Gerry Adams said it was 'a time to be mindful of the common good and of the future of all our people'. A similar sentiment was expressed by Ian Paisley, who stressed 'We must not allow our justified loathing of the horrors and tragedies of the past to become a barrier to creating a better and more stable future'. For details, see 'Northern Ireland: The Impossible Becomes Reality', *The Economist*, vol. 382, no. 8522, 31 March 2007, pp. 35-6.

3 While the external interveners have vehemently opposed the interpretation of the conflict as a civil war the conflict cannot be described in any other manner. According to some scholars the escalating violence in Iraq is not a nationalist insurgency, as was common in many newly independent countries in a post-colonial world, but a 'communal civil war' (Biddle 2006; Diamond *et al.* 2006).

4 Those peace brokers involved in the Dayton Accords which oversaw the end of civil war in Bosnia have often argued that 'the heavy schedule of elections in the peace process served to legitimise criminal leaders rather than facilitate political stability' (Quoted in Pascual and Pollack 2007: 16).

5 The reflection of Desmond Tutu is vital in this context. 'Sometimes when I have felt a little depressed I would go to Parliament to sit in the public gallery and look down at all those "terrorists" now occupying the government benches. It is something to lift the heaviest heart to behold those who were regarded by previous apartheid government as the most dangerous terrorists, and who now, in the new democratic dispensation, are the Hon Minister of this or that. I would recall that some of them were fellow marchers in rallies against the awfulness of apartheid, and with some we were targets for teargassing, and now here they are, members of a democratically elected National Assembly' (Quoted in Sachs 2000: vii–ix).

6 President Hamid Karzai came from the Pashtun background. But his post, it was argued, was symbolic in the sense that, while it allowed for the Pashtuns to have their representation in the overall power architecture, at the same time it excluded them from exercising power in other domains, which was extremely favourable to other minorities.

7 The judiciary banned some opposition parties in Rwanda, using the argument that they stirred up group hatred, but not because they posed an legitimate political threat.

8 Such an arrangement would involve autonomous and independent non-state actors from various backgrounds and affiliations, i.e., members of civil society such as professionals, activists, teachers, lawyers, doctors, social workers, clergymen and women, students, public intellectuals and so on.

7 Realms of reconciliation

1 Generally there are two principal judicial methods of unveiling the process of reconciliation. Depending on the nature and character of the perpetrators and their victims, either open or closed judicial trials are undertaken. Couching reconciliation within such trials is based on the idea that it would help uphold the principle of 'rule of law' and deliver 'justice', both concepts conspicuously absent during the period of civil war. And for the citizenry, upholding these judicial practices legitimises the process of democratic transition.

2 In 2006 following considerable international pressure Cambodia oversaw the appointment of an international team of judges who were sworn in in order to bring to trial the Khmer Rouge leaders 'crimes against humanity'. The UN tribunal, however, is unlikely to make much progress, as most of the top leaders including Pol Pot, Khieu Samphan and Ta Mok all died natural deaths prior to the opening of the trials.

3 According to one observer, 'if trials were to become norm it will further sharpen the divide between perpetrators and victims', Rama Mani, 'Rebuilding an Inclusive Political Community After War', *Security Dialogue*, vol. 36, no. 4, p. 521.

4 As Stephen Kinzer, points out 'Ignorant of the complex web of mutual obligation that had bound Tutsi and Hutu together for generations, the colonizers placed one group in direct control of the other', Stephen Kinzer, 'Big Gamble in Rwanda', *New York Review of Books*, vol. LIV, no. 5, 29 March 2007, p. 25.
5 For many Spaniards the legacy of the civil war years poses an uncomfortable dilemma, for it invariably puts some of them in the category of perpetrators of violence even though indirectly. As Giles Tremlett suggests, because of this fear many Spaniards prefer to erase the civil war years from public memory; recognising it would imply that their parents and grandparents had supported or collaborated with the fascist regime of Franco for nearly four decades. For details, see Giles Tremlett, *Ghosts of Spain*, London: Faber & Faber 2006, especially Ch. 3. 'Amnistia and Amnesia: The Pact of Forgetting'.
6 The ruled International Court of Justice (ICJ) in the Hague ruled on 26 February 2007 that Serbia was not directly responsible for genocide in Bosnia during the 1992-5 civil war. The ICJ, however, stressed that the massacre of nearly 8,000 Bosniaks at Srebrenica in 1995 by Bosnian Serb soldiers did constitute genocide and denounced Serbia for failing to prevent it. The elimination of Serbia's responsibility from the genocide, many critics in the immediate aftermath of the verdict argued, was politically motivated, for allowing the separation of Kosovo from Serbia. The Bosniaks who have all along high-lighted the Serb denial of genocide reacted to this verdict by calling it 'a "fraud", an "insult", and a "disgrace"'. 'Bosnia: Where the Past is Another Country', *The Economist*, 3 March 2007, pp. 6 and 42.
7 http://news.bbc.co.uk/1/hi/world/south_asia/6198974.stm/ accessed 1 December 2006.

8 Closing the conflict cycle

1 As Collier highlights, 'eighty percent of the world's 20 poorest countries have suffered major civil war in the past 15 years'. For detailed discussion, see Paul Collier, *Breaking the Conflict Trap: Civil War and Development Policy*, Oxford: Oxford University Press.
2 'A peace process includes one or more peace agreements. It can be defined as a formal process in which the warring parties either have decided to settle the incompatibility in a process in which one issue at a time is regulated by an agreement, or where an agreement that builds on a previous peace agreement is signed'. Lotta Harbom, Stina Högbladh and Peter Wallensteen, 'Armed Conflict and Peace Agreements', *Journal of Peace Research*, vol. 43, no. 5, p. 623.
3 In situations of conflict diaspora communities may create awareness about their grievance and influence international public opinion in favour of their cause. They may facilitate an international intervention in the conflict and may also act as 'spoilers' when their compatriots in the conflict zone are prepared to negotiate. Jennifer M. Brinkerhoff, 'Digital Diasporas and Conflict Prevention: The Case of Somalinet.com', *Review of International Studies*, vol. 32, no.1, p. 27.
4 It is estimated that there are over 250,000 Tamil expatriates living in Europe and 220,000 in North America. Elsewhere their number is slightly less – with 90,000 in India and 40,000 in Australia.
5 While the 'largest settlements are located in Canada, England, Germany and Switzerland, there are Tamil communities in most countries of the world from Japan, Botswana and Lithuania to Malaysia, Panama and Finland', Oivind Fuglerud, *Life on the Outside: Tamil Diaspora and Long Distance Nationalism*, London: Pluto, 1999, p. 2.
6 Jehan Perera, 'Expatriate Power: To End War or Prolong it?' www.geocities.com/CapitolHill/4708/it/junart1.htm accessed 21 September 2007.

Conclusion

1 'Of the two hundred-odd wars, civil wars and other violent conflicts that have taken place since the end of Second World War, all but twelve occurred in parts of the world that, until recently, were called the Third World'. Walter Lacquer, *New Terrorism*, London: Phoenix Press, 2000, p. 247.
2 These healers may be known as Kimbanda in Mozambique, Kruu and Ruup in Cambodia, or Faqir in Kashmir.

Bibliography

Addi, Lahouari (1997) 'The Failure of Third World Nationalism', *Journal of Democracy*, 8, 4: 110–24.

Addison, Tony and Murshed, S. Mansoob (2006) 'The Social Contract and Violent Conflict', in Helen Yanacopulos and Joseph Hanlon (eds) *Civil War, Civil Peace*, Milton Keynes: Open University.

Adorno, Theodor W., Levinson, Daniel, Sanford, R. Nevitt and Frenkel-Brunswick, Else (1950) *The Authoritarian Personality*, New York: Harper.

Akçam, Taner (2006) *A Shameful Act: The Armenian Genocide and the Question of Turkish Responsibility*, New York: Metropolitan Books.

Ali, Tariq (2007) 'The General in His Labyrinth', *London Review of Books*, 29, 1, January.

Alison, Miranda (2007) 'Wartime Sexual Violence: Women's Human Rights and Questions of Masculinity', *Review of International Studies*, 3, 1: 75–90.

Allen, Beverley (1997) *Rape Warfare: The Hidden Genocide in Bosnia-Herzegovina and Croatia*, Minneapolis: University of Minnesota Press.

Allen, Tim (1999) 'Perceiving Contemporary Wars', in Tim Allen and Jean Seaton (eds) *The Media of Conflict: War Reporting and Representations of Ethnic Violence*, London: Zed.

Alonso, Rogelio (2004) 'Pathways Out of Terrorism in Northern Ireland and the Basque Country: The Misrepresentation of the Irish Model', *Terrorism and Political Violence*, 16, 4: 695–713.

Amnesty International (2004) *Darfur: Too Many People Killed for No Reason*, London: Amnesty International.

Anderson, Benedict (1992) 'The New World Disorder', *New Left Review*, 193: 1–22.

Anderson, M.B. (1999) *Do No Harm: How Aid Can Support Peace – Or War*, Boulder, CO: Lynne Rienner.

Andric, Ivo (1959) *The Bridge on the Drina*, London: Unwin Hyman.

Arendt, Hannah (1983) *Between Past and Future: Eight Exercises in Political Thought*, 4th rev. edn, New York: Penguin.

Ascherson, Neal (2004) '"Better off without them?" Politics and Ethnicity in the Twenty-First Century', *International Affairs*, 80, 1: 99–106.

Azam, Jean-Paul and Hoeffler, Anke (2001) *Violence against Civilians in Civil Wars: Looting or Terror?* Helsinki: UNU World Institute for Development Economics Research.

Azam, Jean-Paul and Hoeffler, Anke (2002) 'Violence Against Civilians in Civil Wars: Looting or Terror?' *Journal of Peace Research*, 39, 4, July: 461–85.

Azar, Edward (1990) *The Management of Protracted Social Conflict: Theory and Cases*, Aldershot: Dartmouth.

Balibar, Etienne (2001) 'Outlines of a Topography of Cruelty: Citizenship and Civility in the Era of Global Violence', *Constellations*, 8, 1: 15–29.

Ballentine, Karen (2003) 'Reconsidering the Economic Dynamics of Armed Conflict', in Karen Ballentine and Jake Sherman (eds) *The Political Economy of Armed Conflict: Beyond Greed and Grievance*, Boulder, CO: Lynne Rienner.

Ballentine, Karen and Nitzschke, Heiko (2004) *The Political Economy of Civil War and Conflict Transformation*, Wiesbaden: Berghof Research Centre for Constructive Conflict Management.

Bandura, A. (1999) 'Moral Disengagement in the Perpetration of Inhumanities', *Personality and Social Psychological Review*, 3, 3: 193–209.

Bar-Tal, Daniel and Teichman, Yona (2005) *Stereotypes and Prejudice in Conflict: Representation of Arabs in Israeli Jewish Society*, Cambridge: Cambridge University Press.

Bartos, Ottomar and Wehr, Paul (2002) *Using Conflict Theory*, Cambridge: Cambridge University Press.

Bauman, Zygmunt (1991) *Modernity and the Holocaust*, Ithaca, NY: Cornell University Press.

Beah, Ishmael (2007) *A Long Way Gone: Memoirs of a Boy Soldier*, New York: Sarah Crichton Books / Farrar Straus and Giroux.

Beck, Ulrich (2005) 'War Is Peace: On Post-National War', *Security Dialogue*, 36, 1: 5–26.

Beinart, Peter (2006) *The Good Fight: Why Liberals – and Only Liberals – Can Win the War on Terror and Make America Great Again*, New York: Harper Collins.

Bell, Wendell and Freeman, Walter E. (eds) (1974) *Ethnicity and Nation-Building: Comparative, International, and Historical Perspectives*, Thousand Oaks, CA: Sage.

Bell-Fialkoff, Andrew (1996) *Ethnic Cleansing*, Basingstoke: Macmillan.

Berdal, Mats (2005) 'Beyond greed and grievance – and not too soon . . .', *Review of International Studies*, 31, 3: 687–98.

Berdal, Mats and Malone, David. M. (eds) (2000) *Greed and Grievance: Economic Agendas in Civil Wars*, Boulder, CO: Lynne Rienner.

Beveridge, W.H. (1967) *Full Employment in a Free Society*, London: Allen and Unwin.

Bhargava, Rajeev (2000) 'Restoring Decency to Barbaric Societies', in Robert I. Rotberg and Denis Thompson (eds) *Truth v. Justice*, Princeton, NJ: Princeton University Press.

Bhavanani, Ravi (2006) 'Ethnic Norms and Interethnic Violence: Accounting for Mass Participation in the Rwandan Genocide', *Journal of Peace Research*, 43, 6: 651–69.

Biddle, Stephen (2006) 'Seeing Baghdad, Thinking Saigon', *Foreign Affairs*, 85, 2: 2–14.

Biggar, N. (2003) 'Making Peace or Doing Justice: Must We Choose?', in N. Biggar (ed.) *Burying the Past*, Washington, DC: Georgetown University Press.

Blimes, Randall J. (2006) 'The Indirect Effect of Ethnic Heterogeneity on the Likelihood of Civil War Onset', *Journal of Conflict Resolution*, 50, 4: 536–47.

Bourke, Joanna (2000) *An Intimate History of Killing*, London: Granta.

Bowcott, Owen (2006) 'Orangemen Want Ulster Parades to Become Carnivals', *The Guardian*, 23 June.

Brett, Rachel and McCallin, Margaret (1996) *Children: The Invisible Soldiers*, Växjö: Rädda Barnen.

Bringa, Tone (2002) 'Averted Gaze: Genocide in Bosnia-Herzegovina, 1992–1995', in Alexander Laban Hinton (ed.) *Annihilating Difference: The Anthropology of Genocide*, Berkeley: University of California Press.

Brinkerhoff, Jennifer M. (2006) 'Digital Diasporas and Conflict Prevention: The Case of Somalinet.com', *Review of International Studies*, 32, 1: 25–47.

Brockner, James and Rubin, Jeffrey Z. (1985) *Entrapment in Escalating Conflicts*, New York: Springer Verlag.

Brown, Michael E. (ed.) (1996) *The International Dimensions of Internal Conflict*, Cambridge, MA: MIT Press.

Brownmiller, Susan (1993) *Against Our Will: Men, Women, and Rape*, New York: Ballantine Books.

Buhaug, Halvard (2006) 'Relative Capability and Rebel Objective in Civil War', *Journal of Peace Research*, 43, 6: 691–708.

Buhaug, Halvard and Gates, Scott (2002) 'The Geography of Civil War', *Journal of Peace Research*, 39, 4: 417–33.

Calder, Angus (ed.) (1999) *Wars*, Harmondsworth: Penguin.

Calderisi, Robert (2006a) 'Africa: Better Off Without Us?', *New Statesman*, 26 June 2006, pp. 12–15.

Calderisi, Robert (2006b) *The Trouble with Africa: Why Foreign Aid Isn't Working*, New York: Palgrave Macmillan.

Carlson, Lisa J. (1995) 'A Theory of Escalation and International Conflict', *Journal of Conflict Resolution*, 39, 3: 511–34.

Carmody, Padraig (2002) 'The Liberalisation of Underdevelopment or Criminalisation of the State? Contrasting Explanations of Africa's Politico-Economic Crisis under Globalisation', in B. Logan (ed.) *Globalisation, the Third World State and Poverty-Alleviation in the Twenty-First Century*, Aldershot: Ashgate.

Castells, M. (1996) *The Information Age: Economic Society and Culture, vol. I, The Rise of the Network Society*, Malden, MA: Blackwell.

Central Intelligence Agency (2000) *Global Trends 2015*, Washington, DC: CIA.

Chadda, Maya (1996) *Ethnicity, Security, and Separatism in India*, New York: Columbia University Press.

Chalk, F. and Jonassohn, K. (1990) *The History and Sociology of Genocide*, New Haven, CT: Yale University Press.

Chandler, David (2002) *From Kosovo to Kabul*, London: Pluto Press.

Charter of the United Nations (1993) New York: United Nations.

Chege, Michael (2002) 'Sierra Leone: The State that Came Back from the Dead', *The Washington Quarterly*, 25, 3: 147–60.

Chesterman, Simon (2004) *You, The People: The United Nations, Transitional Administrations, and State Building*, Oxford: Oxford University Press.

Chopra, Jarat (2000) 'The UN's Kingdom of East Timor', *Survival*, 42, 3: 27–36.

Chua, Amy (2003) 'Venegeful Majorities', *Prospect*, 93: 26–32.

Cigar, Norman (1997) *Genocide in Bosnia: The Policy of 'Ethnic Cleansing'*, Austin, TX: Texas A&M University Press.

Clapham, Christopher (2002) 'The Challenge to the State in a Globalised World', *Development and Change*, 33, 5: 775–95.

Clausewitz, Carl von (1982) *On War*, Harmondsworth: Penguin.

Cohen, Robin (1999) 'The Making of Ethnicity: A Modest Defence of Primordialism', in Edward Mortimer (ed.) *People, Nation and State*, London: I.B. Tauris.

Cohn, Norman (1967) *Warrant for Genocide*, New York: Harper and Row.

Coicaud, Jean-Marc (2002) *Legitimacy and Politics: A Contribution to the Study of Political Right and Political Responsibility*, Cambridge: Cambridge University Press.

Colletta, Nat J. and Nezam, Taies (1999) 'The New Wars: From Reconstruction to Reconciliation', *Development Outreach*, Fall: 5–8.

Collier, Paul (2000a) *Economic Causes of Civil Conflict and Their Implications for Policy*, Washington, DC: World Bank.

Collier, Paul (2000b) 'Rebellion as a Quasi-criminal Activity', *Journal of Conflict Resolution*, 44, 6: 839–53.

Collier, Paul (2003) *Breaking the Conflict Trap: Civil War and Development Policy*, Oxford: Oxford University Press.

Collier, Paul and Dollar, David (2001) 'Can the World Cut Poverty in Half? How Policy Reform and Effective Aid Can Meet International Development Goals', *World Development*, 29, 11: 1787–802.

Collier, Paul and Hoeffler, Anke (2000) *Greed and Grievance in Civil War*, Washington DC: World Bank.

Collier, Paul and Hoeffler, Anke (2002) *Greed and Grievance in Civil War*, Working Paper 160, Oxford: Centre for Study of African Economies.

Collier, Paul, Hoeffler, Anke and Söderbom, Måns (2004) 'On the Duration of Civil War', *Journal of Peace Research*, 41, 3: 253–73.

Cooper, Neil (2005) 'Picking out the Pieces of the Liberal Peaces: Representations of Conflict Economies and the Implications for Policy', *Security Dialogue*, 36, 4: 463–78.

Cornett, Linda and Gibney, Mark (2003) *Tracking Terror: The Political Terror Scale. 1980–2001*, Vancouver: Human Security Centre, University of British Columbia.

Crawford, Neta (2002) *Argument and Change in World Politics: Ethics, Decolonisation and Humanitarian Intervention*, Cambridge: Cambridge University Press.

Crocker, Chester A. (1992*) High Noon in Southern Africa: Making Peace in a Rough Neighbourhood*, New York: W.W. Norton.

Crocker, Chester A., Hampson, Fen and Aall, Pamela (eds) (1999) *Herding Cats: Multiparty Mediation in a Complex World*, Washington, DC: United States Institute of Peace Press.

Danner, Mark (1997) 'America and the Bosnian Genocide', *New York Review of Books*, 44, 19: 6–11.

Darrow, Clarence (1972) *Crime: Its Cause and Treatment*, Montclair, NJ: Thomas Y. Crowell Company.

Davis, Garry (1995) 'The UN Can Do Nothing! Admits Secretary General Boutros-Ghali', *World Citizen News*, 9, 4, p. 1.

Dempsey, Gary and Fontaine, Roger (2001) *Fools Errands: America's Recent Encounters with Nation Building*, Washington: Cato Institute.

Denitch, Bogdan (1994) *Ethnic Nationalism: The Tragic Death of Yugoslavia*, Minneapolis: University of Minnesota Press.

DeRouen Jr, Karl R. and Sobek, David (2004) 'The Dynamics of Civil War Duration and Outcome', *Journal of Peace Research*, 41, 3: 303–20.

Deutsch, Karl (1961) 'Social Mobilisation and Political Development', *American Political Science Review*, 55, 3: 493–514.

De Varennes, Fernand (2002) 'Lessons in Conflict Prevention: A Comparative Examination of the Content of Peace Accords', *Global Review of Ethnopolitics*, 1, 3: 53–9.

De Waal, Thomas (2004) 'A War of Intended Consequences', *Index on Censorship*, 33, 4: 54–9.

Diamond, L., Dobbins, J., Kaufmann, C., Gelb, L.H. and Biddle, S. (2006) 'What to Do in Iraq: A Roundtable', *Foreign Affairs*, 85, 4: 150–69.

Dillon, Martin (1989) *The Shankill Butchers: A Case Study of Mass Murder*, London: Hutchinson.

Dobbins, James (2006) 'No Model War', *Foreign Affairs*, 85, 4: 153–6.

Dobbins, J., Jones, S.G., Crane, K., Rathmell, A., Steele, B., Teltschik, R. and Timilsina, A. (2005) *The UN's Role in Nation-Building: From the Congo to Iraq*, Santa Monica, CA: Rand Corporation.

Douma, Pyt (2003) *The Political Economy of Internal Conflict: A Comparative Analysis of Angola, Colombia, Sierra Leone, and Sri Lanka*, The Hague: Clingendael, The Netherlands Institute of International Relations,

Dowden, Richard (2004) 'Rwanda Ten Years on', *Prospect*, 97: 52–7.

Dowden, Richard (2007) 'ICC in the Dock', *Prospect*, 134, May: 11–13.

Doxtader, Erik and Villa-Vicencio, Charles (2003) *Through Fire With Water: The Roots of Division and the Potential for Reconciliation in Africa*, Claremont, Cape Town: David Philip / New Africa Books.

Doyle, Michael and Sambanis, Michael (2000) 'International Peacebuilding: A Theoretical and Quantitative Analysis', *American Political Science Review*, 94, 4: 779–801.

Duffield, Mark (1998) 'Post-modern Conflict: Warlords, Post-adjustment States and Private Protection', *Civil Wars*, 1, 1: 65–102.

Duffield, Mark (2001) *Global Governance and the New Wars*, London: Zed Books.

Dworkin, Anthony (1996) 'The World in Judgement: Do International War Crimes Tribunals Help or Hinder National Reconciliation?' *Index of Censorship*, 25, 5: 137–44.

Dyker, D.A. and Vejovda, I. (eds) (1996) *Yuglosavia and After: A Study in Fragmentation, Despair and Rebirth*, London: Longman.

Easterly, William (2006) *The White Man's Burden: Why the West's Efforts to Aid the Rest Have Done So Much Ill and So Little Good*, New York: Penguin.

Eckstein, Harry (1980) *Internal War: Problems and Approaches*, New York: Greenwood Press.

Economist, The (1999) 'Kalashnikov Kids', 8 July.

Economist, The (2002) 'Jonas Savimbi, an Angolan Rebel', 28 February.

Economist, The (2004) 'Multiculturalism: The Kindness of Strangers?', 26 February.

Economist, The (2006a) 'Macedonia and the European Union: Not so Fruity Salad', 21 October.

Economist, The (2006b) 'Spain's Historic Memory Law', 19 December.

Economist, The (2007) 'United Nations: Mission Impossible?', 6 January.

Enloe, Cynthia H. (1996) *Ethnic Soldiers: State Security in Divided Societies*, Harmondsworth: Penguin Books.

Enright, Robert D. and North, J. (eds) (1998) *Exploring Forgiveness*, Madison: University of Wisconsin Press.

Enzensberger, Hans Magnus (1990) 'Europe in Ruins', *Granta* 33: 113–40.

Eriksson, Mikael, Wallensteen, Peter and Sollenberg, Margareta (2003) 'Armed Conflict 1989–2002', *Journal of Peace Research*, 40, 5: 593–607.

Etzioni, Amitai (2004a) *From Empire to Community*, New York: Palgrave.

Etzioni, Amitai (2004b) 'A Self-Restrained Approach to Nation-Building by Foreign Powers', *International Affairs*, 80, 1: 1–17.

Evans, Graham and Newman, Jeffrey (1998) *Dictionary of International Relations*, Harmondsworth: Penguin.

Fearon, James D. (2004) 'Why Some Civil Wars Last So Much Longer Than Others', *Journal of Peace Research*, 41, 3: 275–301.

Fearon, James D. (2007) 'Iraq's Civil War', *Foreign Affairs*, 86, 2: 2–16.

Fearon, James D. and Laitin, David D. (2003) 'Ethnicity, Insurgency and Civil War', *American Political Science Review*, 97, 1: 75–90.

Feldman, Allen (1991) *Formations of Violence*, Chicago: University of Chicago Press.

Ferguson, Brian R. and Whitehead, Neil L. (2000) *War in the Tribal Zone: Expanding States and Indigenous Warfare*, New York: SAR Press.

Ferguson, Niall (2004) *Colossus: The Price of America's Empire*, New York: Penguin Press.

Fernandes, Walter (1999) 'Conflict in North-East: A Historical Perspective', *Economic and Political Weekly*, December 18, pp. 3579–82.

Fierke, Karin (2005) *Diplomatic Interventions: Conflict and Change in a Globalising World*, Basingstoke: Palgrave.

Fisher, Ronald J. (1990) *The Social Psychology of Intergroup and International Conflict Resolution*, New York: Springer-Verlag.

Flavin, William (2003) 'Planning for Conflict Termination and Post-Conflict Successes', *Parameters*, 33, 3: 95–112.

Flint, Julie and de Waal, Alex (2005*) Darfur: A Short History of a Long War*, London: Zed Books.

Flournoy, Michèle and Pan, Michael (2002) 'Dealing with Demons: Justice and Reconciliation', *Washington Quarterly*, 25, 4: 111–23.

Forman, Johanna Mendelson (2002) 'Achieving Socioeconomic Well-Being in Post-conflict Settings', *Washington Quarterly*, 25, 4: 125–38.

Fox, Jonathan (2004) 'The Rise of Religious Nationalism and Conflict: Ethnic Conflict and Revolutionary Wars, 1945–2001', *Journal of Peace Research*, 41, 6: 715–31.

Freeman, Michael (1995) 'Genocide, Civilisation and Modernity', *British Journal of Sociology*, 46, 2: 207–23.

Friedman, Jonathan (1994) *Cultural Identity and Global Process*, London: Sage.

Fuglerud, Oivind (1999) *Life on the Outside: Tamil Diaspora and Long Distance Nationalism*, London: Pluto.

Fukuyama, Francis (2005) *State Building: Governance and World Order in the Twenty-First Century*, London: Profile Books.

Fukuyama, Francis (2006) 'Nation-Building: Beyond Afghanistan and Iraq', Baltimore, MA: Johns Hopkins University Press.

Galbraith, Peter W. (2005) 'Iraq: Bush's Islamic Republic', *New York Review of Books*, 23, 13: 6–9.

Gallagher, Michael S. (2002) 'Soldier Boy Bad: Child Soldiers, Culture and Bars to Asylum', *International Journal of Refuge Law*, 13, 3.

Galtung, Johan (1996) *Peace by Peaceful Means: Peace, Conflict, Development and Civilisation*, London: Sage.

Gellner, Ernest (1983) *Nations and Nationalism*, Ithaca, NY: Cornell University Press.

Gellner, Ernest (1994) *Conditions of Liberty, Civil Society and Its Rivals*, Harmondsworth: Penguin.

Giddens, Anthony (1987) *The Nation-State and Violence*, Berkeley: University of California Press.

Gill, Bates and Reilly, James (2000) Sovereignty, Intervention and Peacekeeping: The View from Beijing', *Survival*, 42, 3: 41–59.

Gilley, Bruce (2004) 'Against the Concept of Ethnic Conflict', *Third World Quarterly*, 25, 6: 1155–66.

Girard, René (1977) *Violence and the Sacred*, London: Athlone.

Gleditsch, Kristian Skrede (2007) 'Transnational Dimensions of Civil War', *Journal of Peace Research*, 44, 3: 293–309.

Gleditsch, N.P., Strand, H., Eriksson, M., Sollenberg. M., and Wallensteen, P. (2002) 'Armed Conflict 1946–2001: A New Dataset', *Journal of Peace Research*, 39, 5: 615–37.

Goodhand, Jonathan (2007) 'Working 'in' and 'on' War', in Helen Yanacopulos and Joseph Hanlon (eds) *Civil War, Civil Peace*, Milton Keynes: Open University.

Goodman, Ryan (2006) 'Humanitarian Intervention and Pretexts for War', *American Journal of International Law*, 100, 1: 107–41.

Goose, Stephen D. and Smyth, Frank (1994) 'Arming Genocide in Rwanda: The High Cost of Small Arms Transfers', *Foreign Affairs*, 73, 5: 86–96.

Gottlieb, Gidon (1999) 'Between Union and Separation: The Path of Reconciliation', in Edward Mortimer (ed.) *People, Nation & State*, London: I.B. Tauris.

Gourevitch, Alex (2004) 'The Unfailing of the State', *Journal of International Affairs*, 58, 1: 255–60.

Gourevitch, Philip (1999) *We Wish to Inform You that Tomorrow We Will be Killed With Our Families*, London: Picador.

Gray, John (2001) 'Are There Global Political Values?' *Prospect*, 69, December.

Graybill, Lyn S. (1998) 'South Africa's Truth and Reconciliation Commission: Ethical and Theological Perspectives', *Ethics and International Affairs*, 12: 43–62.

Graybill, Lyn S. (2002) *Truth and Reconciliation in South Africa: Miracle or Model?*, Boulder, CO, and London: Lynne Rienner.

Graybill, Lyn S. (2004) 'Pardon, Punishment, and Amnesia: Three African Post-conflict Methods', *Third World Quarterly*, 25, 6: 1117–30.

Green, E.C and Honwana A. (1999) *Indigenous Healing of War-affected Children in Africa*, Washington, DC: World Bank IK Notes, 10.

Greene, Graham (1985) *The Lawless Roads*, Harmondsworth: Penguin.

Grossman, Herschel I. (1999) 'Kleptocracy and Revolution', *Oxford Economic Papers*, 51, 2: 267–83.

Gurr, Ted R. (1968) 'A Causal Model of Civil Strife: A Comparative Analysis Using New Indices', *American Political Science Review*, 62, 4: 1104–24.

Gurr, Ted R. (1971) *Why Men Rebel*, Princeton: Princeton University Press.

Gurr, Ted R. (1993) *Minorities at Risk: A Global View of Ethnopolitical Conflicts*, Washington, DC: United States Institute of Peace.

Gurr, Ted R. (1994) 'Peoples Against States: Ethnopolitical Conflict and the Changing World System', *International Studies Quarterly*, 38, 3: 347–77.

Gurr, Ted R. (2000) *People Versus States: Minorities at Risk in the New Century*, Washington, DC: United States Institute of Peace Press.

Haass, Richard N. (1999) *Intervention*, Washington, DC: Brookings Institution Press.

Haass, Richard N. (2005) *The Opportunity: America's Moment to Alter History's Course*, New York: Public Affairs.

Habermas, Jürgen (1991) *Between Facts and Norms*, Cambridge: Polity.

Halsan Hoiskar, Astri (2001) 'Underage and Under Fire: An Inquiry into the Use of Child Soldiers, 1994–1998', *Childhood*, 8, 3.

Hamilton, Alexander (1987) *The Federalist Papers*, edited by Isaac Kramnick, Harmondsworth: Penguin.

Hampson, Fen (1996) *Nurturing Peace: Why Peace Settlements Succeed or Fail*, Washington, DC: United States Institute of Peace.

Hanlon, Joseph (2006) 'Intervention', in Helen Yanacopulos & Joseph Hanlon (eds) *Civil War, Civil Peace*, Milton Keynes: Open University.

Harbom, Lotta and Wallensteen, Peter (2005) 'Armed Conflict and Its International Dimensions, 1946–2004', *Journal of Peace Research*, 42, 5: 623–35.

Harbom, Lotta, Högbladh, Stina and Wallensteen, Peter (2006) 'Armed Conflict and Peace Agreements', *Journal of Peace Research*, 43, 5: 617–31.

Hardin, Russell (1997) *One for All: The Logic of Group Conflict*, Princeton, NJ: Princeton University Press.

Harding, Susan F. (1984) *Remaking Ibieca: Rural Life in Aragon under Franco*, Chapel Hill: University of North Carolina Press.

Harff, Barbara and Gurr, Ted Robert (1988) 'Toward an Empirical Theory of Genocides and Politicides: Identification and Measurement of Cases since 1945', *International Studies Quarterly*, 32, 4: 369–71.

Hart, Peter (1998) *The I.R.A. and Its Enemies: Violence and Community in Cork, 1916–1923*, New York: Clarendon Press.

Hartzell, Caroline (1999) 'Explaining the Stability of Negotiated Settlements to Intra-state Wars', *Journal of Conflict Resolution*, 43, 1: 3–22.

Hartzell, Caroline and Hoddie, Matthew (2003) 'Institutionalising Peace: Power Sharing and Post-Civil War Conflict Management', *American Journal of Political Science*, 47, 2: 318–12.

Hasenclever, Andreas and Rittberger, Voeker (2003) 'Does Religion Make a Difference? Theoretical Approaches to the Impact of Faith on Politics Conflict', in Pavlos Hatzopoulos & Fabio Petito (eds) *Religion in International Relations*, Basingstoke: Palgrave.

Hatzfeld, Jean (2005) *A Time for Machetes*, London: Serpent's Tail.

Hatzopoulos, Pavlos and Petito, Fabio (2003) *Religion in International Relations*, Basingstoke: Palgrave.

Hechter, Michael (1975) *Internal Colonialism: The Celtic Fringe in British National Development, 1536–1966*, London: Routledge & Kegan Paul.

Hechter, Michael (2000) *Containing Nationalism*, Oxford: Oxford University Press.

Hegre, Håvard and Sambanis, Nicholas (2006) 'Sensitivity Analysis of Empirical Results on Civil War Onset', *Journal of Conflict Resolution*, 50, 4: 508–35.

Hilsum, Lindsey (2005) 'We Love China', *Granta* 92, *The View from Africa*.

Holloway, David and Stedman, Stephen J. (2002) 'Civil Wars and State Building in Africa and Eurasia', in Mark R. Bessinger and Crawford Young (eds) *Beyond State Crisis? Postcolonial Africa and Post-Soviet Eurasia in Comparative Perspective*, Washington, DC: Woodrow Wilson Press.

Holsti, Kalevi J. (1996) *The State, War, and the State of War*, Cambridge: Cambridge University Press.

Holzgrefe, J. L. and Keohane, Robert O. (eds) (2003) *Humanitarian Intervention Ethical, Legal and Political Dilemmas*, Cambridge: Cambridge University Press.

Homer-Dixon, Thomas F. (1999) *Environment, Scarcity, and Violence*, Princeton: Princeton University Press.

Honwana, Alcinda & Be Boeck, Filip (2005) (eds) *Makers and Breakers: Children and Youth in Postcolonial Africa*, Oxford: James Currey.

Hoole, M.R.R. (1998) 'The Tamil Secessionist Movement in Sri Lanka (Ceylon): A Case of Secession by Default?', in Metta Spencer (ed.) *Separatism: Democracy and Disintegration*, Lanham, MA: Rowman & Littlefield.

Horowitz, Donald L. (1985) *Ethnic Groups in Conflict*, Berkeley: University of California Press.

Horowitz, Donald L. (2001) *The Deadly Ethnic Riot*, Berkeley: University of California Press.

Hroch, Miroslav (1996) 'From National Movement to the Fully-formed Nation: The Nation Building Process in Europe', in Gopal Balakrishnan (ed.) *Mapping the Nation*, London: Verso.

Humphreys, Macartan (2005) 'Natural Resources, Conflict, and Conflict Resolution', *Journal of Conflict Resolution*, 49, 4: 508–37.

Hutt, Michael (ed.) (2004) *Himalayan 'People's War': Nepal's Maoist Rebellion*, London: Hurst & Co.

ICISS (International Commission on Intervention and State Sovereignty) (2001) *The Responsibility to Protect: Report of the ICISS*, Ottawa: International Development Research Centre.

Ignatieff, Michael (1996) 'Articles of Faith', *Index on Censorship*, 25, 5.

Ignatieff, Michael (1999) *The Warrior's Honour: Ethnic War and the Modern Conscience*, London: Vintage.

Ignatieff, Michael (2002) 'Nation-Building Lite', *New York Times*, 28 July.

Ignatieff, Michael (2003) *Empire Lite: Nation-Building in Bosnia, Kosovo and Afghanistan*, London: Vintage.

Ikenberry, G. John (2001) *After Victory: Institutions, Strategic Restraint, and the Rebuilding of Order After Major Wars*, Princeton, NJ: Princeton University Press.

Index on Censorship (1996) *Wounded Nations Broken Lives: Truth Commissions and War Tribunals*, 25, 5.

Issacharoff, Samuel (2004) 'Constitutionalising Democracy in Fractured Societies', *Journal of International Affairs*, 58. 1: 73–93.

Jackson, Robert H. (1990) *Quasi-Sates: Sovereignty, International Relations, and the Third World*, Cambridge: Cambridge University Press.

Jacobsen, Carl Gustav (1994) 'Bosnian War Crimes: Problems of Definition and Prosecution', *Security Dialogue*, 25, 2: 238–40.

Jalata, Isafa (2001) 'Ethno-nationalism and the global 'modernising' project', *Nations and Nationalism*, 7, 3: 385–405.

Jayawickrema, Nihal (1993) 'Self Determination', in *Report of the Martin Ennals Memorial Symposium on Self-Determination*, Saskatoon: International Alert and University of Saskatchewan.

Jeong, Ho-Won (2005) *Peacebuilding in Postconflict Societies: Strategy and Process*, Boulder, CO: Lynne Rienner.

Joffe, Josef (1992) 'The New Europe, Yesterday's Ghosts', *Foreign Affairs*, 72, 1: 29–43.

Judah, Tim (1997) *Serbs: History, Myth and the Destruction of Yugoslavia*, New Haven, CT: Yale University Press.

Judah, Tim (2005) 'The Waiting Game in the Balkans', *New York Review of Books*, 52, 13: 46–9.

Judt, Tony (2005) 'The New World Order', *New York Review of Books*, 52, 12: 14–18.

Juergensmeyer, Mark (1993) *The New Cold War? Religious Nationalism Confronts the Secular State*, Berkeley: University of California Press.

Kaldor, Mary (1999) *New and Old Wars: Organised Violence in a Global Era*, Cambridge: Polity.

Kalyvas, Stathis N. (2002) 'The Logic of Violence in Civil War', *Working Paper 1*, Universidad Autonoma de Madrid, www.uam.es/centros/derecho/cpolitica/wpapers. html.

Kane, John (2001) *The Politics of Moral Capital*, Cambridge: Cambridge University Press.

Kaplan, Robert D. (2000) *The Coming Anarchy*, New York: Random House.

Kapuściński, Ryszard (1984) *Another Day of Life*, Picador: London.

Kapuściński, Ryszard (1987) 'Outline of a Book', *Granta*, 21: 101–14.

Kapuściński, Ryszard (1989) 'Christmas Eve in Uganda', *Granta*, 26: 9–17.

Kapuściński, Ryszard (1990) 'Bolivia 1970', *Granta*, 33: 159–66.

Kapuściński, Ryszard (1991) *The Soccer War*, London: Granta Books.

Kapuściński, Ryszard (2007) *The Cobra's Heart*, Harmondsworth: Penguin.

Kaufman, Stuart J. (2006) 'Escaping the Symbolic Politics Trap: Reconciliation Initiatives and Conflict Resolution in Ethnic Wars', *Journal of Peace Research*, 43, 2: 201–18.

Kaufmann, Chaim (1996) 'Possible and Impossible Solutions to Ethnic Civil Wars', *International Security*, 20, 4: 136–75.

Kaufmann, Chaim (2006) 'Separating Iraqis, Saving Iraq', *Foreign Affairs*, 85, 4: 156–60.

Keegan, John (1993) *A History of Warfare*, London: Pimlico.

Keegan, John and Bull, Bartie (2006) 'Definition of 'Civil War' is Critical to Iraq', *Financial Times*, 19 November.

Keen, David (2000) 'Incentives and Disincentives for Violence', in Mats Berdal and David M. Malone (eds) *Greed and Grievance: Economic Agendas in Civil Wars*, Boulder, CO: Lynne Rienner, pp. 19–42.

Kemp, Walter A. (2004) 'The Business of Ethnic Conflict', *Security Dialogue*, 35, 1: 43–59.

Keohane, Robert O. (2002) *Power and Governance in a Partially Globalised World*, London: Routledge.

Khosla, Deepa (1999) 'Third World States as Intervenors in Ethnic Conflicts: Implications for Regional and International Security', *Third World Quarterly*, 20, 6: 1143–56.

King, Charles (2001a) 'The Benefits of Ethnic War: Understanding Eurasia's Unrecognised States', *World Politics*, 53, 4: 524–52.

King, Charles (2001b) 'The Myth of Ethnic Warfare: Understanding Conflict in the Post-Cold War World', *Foreign Affairs*, 80, 6: 165–70.

Kinzer, Stephen (2007) 'Big Gamble in Rwanda', *New York Review of Books*, 54, 5: 23–6.

Kirby, Arthur (2006) 'The Fate of Africa', *New Statesman and Society*, October.

Knight, Mark and Ozerdem, Alpaslan (2004) 'Guns, Camps and Cash: Disarmament, Demobilisation and Reinsertion of Former Combatants in Transitions from War to Peace', *Journal of Peace Research*, 41, 4: 499–516.

Kogan Iasnyi, Victor and Zisserman-Brodsky, Diana (1998) 'Chechen Separatism', in Metta Spencer (ed.) *Separatism: Democracy and Disintegration*, Lanham, MA: Rowman & Littlefield.

Kohli, Atul (1997) 'Can Democracies Accommodate Ethnic Nationalism? Rise and Decline of Self-Determination Movements in India', *Journal of Asian Studies*, 56, 2: 325–44.

Kolbert, Elizabeth (2006) 'Dead Reckoning: The Armenian Genocide and the Politics of Silence', *New Yorker*, 11.

Kolstø, Pål (2006) 'The Sustainability and Future of Unrecognised Quasi-States', *Journal of Peace Research*, 43, 6: 723–40.

Korf, Benedikt (2005) 'Rethinking the Greed-Grievance Nexus: Property Rights and the Political Economy of War in Sri Lanka', *Journal of Peace Research*, 42, 2: 201–17.

Krasner, Stephen D. and Pascual, Carlos (2005) 'Addressing State Failure', *Foreign Affairs*, 84, 4: 153–63.

Krause, Keith and Jütersonke, Oliver (2005) 'Peace, Security and Development in Post-Conflict Environments', *Security Dialogue*, 36, 4: 447–62.

Kriesberg, Louis (1992) *International Conflict Resolution*, New Haven, CT: Yale University Press.

Kriesberg, Louis (1998) *Constructive Conflicts: From Escalation to Resolution*, Oxford: Rowman and Littlefield.

Kristof, Nicholas D. (2006a) 'Genocide in Slow Motion', *New York Review of Books*, 53, 2.

Kristof, Nicholas D. (2006b) 'Aid: Can It Work?', *New York Review of Books*, 53, 15.

Kymlicka, Will (1995) *Multicultural Citizenship*, Oxford: Clarendon Press.

Laban Hinton, Alexander (2002) *Annihilating Difference: The Anthropology of Genocide*, Berkeley: University of California Press.

Lacina, Bethany (2004) 'From Side Show to Centre Stage: Civil Conflict after the Cold War', *Security Dialogue*, 35, 2: 191–205.

Lacina, Bethany (2006) 'Explaining the Severity of Civil Wars', *Journal of Conflict Resolution*, 50, 2: 276–89.

Lake, Anthony (1996) 'Defining Missions, Setting Deadlines: Meeting New Security Challenges in the Post-Cold War World', Plenary Speech at George Washington University, 6 March.

Lake, David A. and Rothchild, Donald (1998) 'Spreading Fear: The Genesis of Transnational Ethnic Conflict', in David A. Lake and Donald Rothchild (eds), *The International Spread of Ethnic Conflict: Fear, Diffusion and Escalation*, Princeton, NJ: Princeton University Press.

Lederach, John Paul (1997) *Building Peace: Sustainable Reconciliation in Divided Societies*, Washington, DC: United States Institute of Peace Press.

Leonard, David K. and Straus, Scott (2003) *Africa's Stalled Development: International Causes and Cures*, Boulder, CO: Lynne Rienner.

Leonard, Mark (2005) *Why Europe Will Run the 21st Century*, London: Fourth Estate.

Levi, Primo (1988) *The Drowned and the Saved*, London: Abacus.

Li, Quan and Schaub, D. (2004) 'Economic Globalisation and Transnational Terrorism: A Pooled Time-Series Analysis', *Journal of Conflict Resolution*, 48, 2: 230–58.

Lichbach, Mark I. (1990) 'Will Rational People Rebel Against Inequality? Samson's Choice', *American Journal of Political Science*, 34, 6: 1049–75.

Lichbach, Mark I. (1994) 'What Makes Rational Peasants Revolutionary: Dilemma, Paradox, and Irony in Peasant Collective Action', *World Politics*, 46: 383–418.

Licklider, Roy (ed.) (1993) *Stop the Killing: How Civil Wars End*, New York: New York University Press.

Licklider, Roy (1995) 'The Consequences of Negotiated Settlements in Civil Wars 1945–1993', *American Political Science Review*, 89, 3: 681–90.

Lieven, Anatol (2000) 'Nightmare in the Caucasus', *Washington Quarterly*, 23, 1: 145–59.

Lipschutz, Ronnie and Crawford, Beverly (1995) '"Ethnic" Conflict Isn't,' IGCC Policy Brief, 2, San Diego: Institute on Global Cooperation and Conflict, University of California.

Lobel, Jules and Ratner, Michael (1999) 'Bypassing the Security Council: Ambiguous Authorisations to Use Force, Cease-Fires, and the Iraqi Inspection Regime', *American Journal of International Law*, 93, 1: 124–53.

Long, William J. and Brecke, Peter (2003) *War and Reconciliation: Reason and Emotion in Conflict Resolution*, Cambridge, MA: MIT Press.

Lorenz, Konrad (1966) *On Aggression*, San Diego, CA: Harcourt Brace.

Luckham, Robin (2004) 'The International Community and State Reconstruction in War-torn Societies', *Conflict Security and Development*, 4, 3: 481–507.

Lumpe, Lora (2000) *Running Guns: The Global Black Market in Small Arms*, London: Zed Books.

Lundin, Iraé B. and Gaspar, Antonio da Costa (2003) 'Mozambique: Making Peace – The Roots of the Conflict and the Way Forward', in Erik Doxtader and Charles Villa-Vicencio (eds) *Through Fire With Water: The Roots of Division and the Potential for Reconciliation in Africa*, Claremont, South Africa: David Philip/New Africa Books.

Luttwak, Edward (1999) 'Give War a Chance', *Foreign Affairs*, 87, 4: 36–44.

Lyons, Terrence (2002) 'The Role of Post-settlement Elections', in Stephen John Stedman, Donald Rothchild and Elizabeth M. Cousens (eds) *Ending Civil Wars: The Implementation of Peace Agreements*, London: Lynne Rienner.

Lyons, Terrence (2005) *Demilitarising Politics: Elections on the Uncertain Road to Peace*, Boulder, CO: Lynne Rienner.

Lyons, Terrence (2006) 'Conflict-Generated Diasporas and Peacebuilding: A Conceptual Overview and Ethiopian Case Study', University for Peace Expert Forum on Capacity Building for Peace and Development: Roles of Diasporas, Toronto, 19–20 October, pp. 1–18.

McCaughey, Terence (2001) 'Northern Ireland: Burying the Hatchet, Not the Past', in Nigel Biggar (ed.) *Burying the Past: Making Peace and Doing Justice after Civil Conflict*, Washington, DC: Georgetown University Press, pp. 254–69.

McClelland, David C. (1975) *Power: The Inner Experience*, New York: Irvington Publishers.

MacCormick, Neil (1999) 'Does a Nation Need a State: Reflections on Liberal Nationalism', in Edward Mortimer (ed.) *People, Nation and State*, London: I.B. Tauris.

McDonald, Henry (2006) 'Peaceful Irish Learn New Hatreds', *Observer*, 25 June.

Macfarlane, S. Neil, Thielking, Carolin J. and Weiss, Thomas G. (2004) 'The Responsibility to Protect: Is Anyone Interested in Humanitarian Intervention', *Third World Quarterly*, 25, 5: 977–92.

Magnarella, P.J. (2000) *Justice in Africa: Rwanda's Genocide, Its Courts, and the UN Criminal Tribunal*, Aldershot: Ashgate.

Maiz, Ramón (2003) 'Framing the Nation: Three Rival Versions of Contemporary Nationalist Ideology', *Journal of Political Ideologies*, 8, 3: 252–67.

Malraux, André (1934) *Man's Fate*, New York: Modern Library.

Mamdani, Mahmood (2001) *When Victims Become Killers: Colonialism, Nativism and the Genocide in Rwanda*, Princeton, NJ: Princeton University Press.

Mamdani, Mahmood (2007) 'The Politics of Naming: Genocide, Civil War, Insurgency', *London Review of Books*, 29, 5, March.

Manguel, Alberto (1996) 'Argentina: Memory and Forgetting', *Index on Censorship* 5: 123–8.

Mani, Rama (2005) 'Rebuilding an Inclusive Political Community After War', *Security Dialogue*, 36, 4: 511–26.

Mann, Michael (1986) *The Sources of Social Power*, Cambridge: Cambridge University Press.

Mann, Michael (2005) *The Dark Side of Democracy: Explaining Ethnic Cleansing*, Cambridge: Cambridge University Press.

Marquez, Gabríel Garciá (1990) 'The Future of Colombia', *Granta*, 31: 85–95.

Mayall, James (1999) 'Sovereignty, Nationalism, and Self-determination', *Political Studies*, 47, 3: 474–502.

Mazower, Mark (2001) *The Balkans*, London: Phoenix Press.

Mead, Walter Russell (2004) *Power, Terror, Peace and War: America's Grand Strategy in a World at Risk*, New York: Alfred A. Knopf.

Migdal, Joel S. (2004) 'State Building and the Non-nation-State', *Journal of International Affairs*, 58, 1: 17–46.

Milliken, Jennifer (ed.) (2003) *State Failure, Collapse and Reconstruction*, Malden, MA: Blackwell.

Mishra, Pankaj (2005) 'The People's War', *London Review of Books*, 27, 12.

Misra, Amalendu (2001) 'The politics of secessionist conflict management in India', *Journal of Contemporary Security Policy*, 22, 2: 49–68.

Misra, Amalendu (2002) 'Subaltern and the Civil War: An Assessment of Left-wing Insurgency in South Asia', *Civil Wars*, 5, 4: 56–76.

Misra, Amalendu (2004a) *Identity and Religion: Foundations of Anti-Islamism in India*, Thousand Oaks, CA: Sage.

Misra, Amalendu (2004b) *Afghanistan: The Labyrinth of Violence*, Cambridge: Polity.

Moore, Margaret (2001) *The Ethics of Nationalism*, New York: Oxford University Press.

Moorehead, Caroline (2005) 'The Warrior Children', *New York Review of Books*, 52, 19: 46–7.

Murdoch, J. and Sandler, T. (2002) 'Economic Growth, Civil Wars, and Spatial Spillovers', *Journal of Conflict Resolution*, 46, 1: 91–110.

Murphy, Sean (1996) *Humanitarian Intervention: The United Nations in an Evolving World Order*, Philadelphia, PA: University of Pennsylvania Press.

Murshed, S. Mansoob (2002) 'Conflict, Civil War and Underdevelopment: An Introduction', *Journal of Peace Research*, 39, 4: 387–93.

Naimark, Norman N. (2001) *Fires of Hatred: Ethnic Cleansing in Twentieth Century Europe*, Cambridge, MA: Harvard University Press.

Naipaul, Vidiadhar S. (1989) *A Turn in the South*, London: Penguin.

Nasr, Vali (2006) 'When the Shiites Rise', *Foreign Affairs*, 85, 4: 58–74.

Neier, Aryeh (1998) *War Crimes: Brutality, Genocide, Terror, and the Struggle for Justice*, New York: Crown.

Newman, Edward (2004) 'The "New Wars" Debate: A Historical Perspective Is Needed', *Security Dialogue*, 35, 2: 173–289.

Newman, Edward and Schnabel, Albrecht (2002) 'Recovering from Civil Conflict', *International Peacekeeping*, 9, 2: 1–6.

Nieminen, Katja (2006) 'The Difficult Equation of Long-Term Peace and Post-Conflict Governance', *Security Dialogue*, 37, 2: 263–72.

Nordstrom, Carolyn (1997) *A Different Kind of War Story*, Philadelphia, PA: University of Pennsylvania Press.

Nordstrom, Carolyn (2004) *Shadows of War: Violence, Power, and International Profiteering in the Twenty-First Century*, Berkeley: University of California Press.

Norton-Taylor, Richard (2006) 'Bishops Seek Small Arms Curbs to Halt Spread of AK 47s', *Guardian*, 23 June.

Nussbaum, Martha (2007) *The Clash Within: Democracy, Religious Violence, and India's Future*, Cambridge, MA: Harvard University Press.

Oliver, Pamela (1984) 'Rewards and Punishments as Selective Incentives: An Apex Game', *Journal of Conflict Resolution*, 28, 1: 123–48.

Orr, Robert (2002) 'Governing When Chaos Rules: Enhancing Governance and Participation', *Washington Quarterly*, 25, 4: 139–52.

Ottaway, Marina (2002a) 'Rebuilding State Institutions in Collapsed States', *Development and Change*, 33, 5: 1001–23.

Ottaway, Marina (2002b) 'Nation Building', *Foreign Policy*, 9, 2, September–October: 16–20.

Oudraat, Chantal de Jonge (2000) 'Making Economic Sanctions Work', *Survival*, 42, 3: 105–27.

Paris, Roland (1997) 'Peacebuilding and the Limits of Literal Internationalism', *International Security*, 22, 2: 54–89.

Paris, Roland (2004) *At War's End: Building Peace After Civil Conflict*, Cambridge: Cambridge University Press.

Pascual, Carlos and Pollack, Kenneth M. (2007) 'The Critical Battles: Political Reconciliation and Reconstruction in Iraq', *Washington Quarterly*, 30, 3: 7–19.

Patrick, Stewart (2006) 'Weak States and Global Threats: Fact or Fiction', *Washington Quarterly*, 29, 2: 27–53.

Paul, T.V., Ikenberry, G. John and Hall, John A. (eds) (2003) *The Nation-State in Question*, Princeton, NJ: Princeton University Press.

Paz, Octavio (1985) *The Labyrinth of Solitude and Other Writings*, New York: Grove Press.

Pieterse, Jan Nederveen (1997) 'Sociology of Humanitarian Intervention: Bosnia, Rwanda and Somalia Compared', *International Political Science Review*, 18, 1: 297–359.

Politkovskaya, Anna (2003) *A Small Corner of Hell: Dispatches from Chechnya*, Chicago: University of Chicago Press.

Pouligny, Béatrice (2005) 'Civil Society and Post-Conflict Peacebuilding: Ambiguities of International Programmes Aimed at Building "New" Societies', *Security Dialogue*, 36, 4: 495–510.

Powers, Samantha (2001) 'Bystanders to Genocide', *The Atlantic Monthly*, September.

Powers, Samantha (2002) *A Problem from Hell: America and the Age of Genocide*, New York: Basic Books.

Pruitt, Dean G., Rubin, Jeffrey Z. and Kim, Sung Hee (1994) (2nd edn) *In Social Conflict: Escalation, Stalemate, and Settlement*, New York: McGraw Hill.

Prunier, Gérard (1995) *The Rwanda Crisis: History of a Genocide*, New York: Columbia University Press.

Prunier, Gérard (2005) *Darfur: The Ambiguous Genocide*, Ithaca, NY: Cornell University Press.

Psalidas-Perlmutter, Foulie (2000) 'Ethnic Conflicts: The Interplay of Myths and Realities', *Orbis*, 44, 2: 235–51.

Regan, Patrick (2000) *Users' Manual for Pat Regan's Data on Interventions in Civil Conflicts*, Mimeo, Binghamton, NY: Binghamton University.

Regan, Patrick M. and Aydin, Aysegul (2006) 'Diplomacy and Other Forms of Intervention in Civil Wars', *Journal of Conflict Resolution*, 50, 5: 736–56.

Regan, Patrick M. and Norton, Daniel (2005) 'Greed, Grievance and Mobilisation in Civil Wars', *Journal of Conflict Resolution*, 49, 3: 319–36.

Reilly, David (2004) 'The Growing Importance of the Failing State: Sovereignty, Security and the Return to Power Politics, *Journal of Conflict Studies*, Summer: 5–19.

Ricigliano, Robert (2003) 'Networks of Effective Action: Implementing an Integrated Approach to Peacebuilding', *Security Dialogue*, 34, 4: 445–62.

Rigby, Andrew (2001) *Justice and Reconciliation after Violence*, Boulder, CO: Lynne Rienner.

Rodenbeck, Max (2006) 'War Within War', *New York Review of Books*, 53, 14.

Roland-Gosselin, Louise (2006) 'Human Rights Violations in Darfur and the Issue of Genocide', in *Darfur: Genocide without Borders*, London: Waging Peace Publications.

Ron, James (2005) 'Paradigm in Distress? Primary Commodities and Civil War', *Journal of Conflict Resolution*, 49, 4: 443–50.

Rotberg, Robert I. (2004) 'Strengthening Governance: Ranking Countries Would Help', *Washington Quarterly*, 28, 1: 71–81.

Rotberg, Robert I. (ed.) (2003) *When States Fail: Causes and Consequences*, Princeton, NJ: Princeton University Press.

Rotberg, Robert I. and Thompson, Dennis (eds) (2000) *Truth v. Justice*, Princeton, NJ: Princeton University Press.

Rothstein, R.L. (ed.) (1999) *After the Peace: Resistance and Reconciliation*. London: Lynne Rienner.

Rubinstein, Robert A. (2005) 'Intervention and Culture: An Anthropological Approach to Peace Operations', *Security Dialogue*, 36, 4: 527–44.

Rupesinghe, Kumar (1998) *Civil Wars, Civil Peace: An Introduction to Conflict Resolution*, London: Pluto Press.

Sachs, A. (2000) *The Soft Vengeance of a Freedom Fighter*, London: Paladin.

Safire, William (2006) 'On Language – The Name Makes the News', *The New York Times Magazine*, 17 December.

Sambanis, Nicholas (2000) 'Partition as a Solution to Ethnic War: An Empirical Critique of the Theoretical Literature', *World Politics*, 52: 437–83.

Sambanis, Nicholas (2001) 'Do Ethnic and Nonethnic Civil Wars Have the Same Causes?: A Theoretical and Empirical Inquiry (Part 1)', *Journal of Conflict Resolution*, 45, 3: 259–82.

Sambanis, Nicholas (2003) *Using Case Studies to Expand the Theory of Civil War*, CPR Working Paper No. 5, Washington, DC: World Bank.

Sambanis, Nicholas (2004) 'What Is Civil War? Conceptual and Empirical Complexities of an Operational Definition', *Journal of Conflict Resolution*, 48, 6: 814–58.

Sandbrook, Richard and Romano, David (2004) 'Globalisation, Extremism and Violence in Poor Countries', *Third World Quarterly*, 25, 6: 1007–30.

Schulman, Miriam (1998) 'Neighbour to the Assassin: Transitional Justice in Guatemala', *Issues in Ethics*, 9, 3: 1–6.

Schwarz, Rolf (2005) 'Post-Conflict Peacebuilding: The Challenges of Security, Welfare and Representation', *Security Dialogue*, 36, 4: 429–46.

Sells, Michael (1997) *The Bridge Betrayed: Religion and Genocide in Bosnia*, Berkeley: University of California Press.

Seul, Jeffrey (1999) '"Ours is the Way of God": Religion, Identity, and Intergroup Conflict', *Journal of Peace Research*, 36, 5: 553–69.

Simonsen, Sven Gunnar (2005) 'Addressing Ethnic Divisions in Post-Conflict Institution-Building: Lessons from Recent Cases', *Security Dialogue*, 36, 3: 297–318.

Singer, P.W. (2005) *Children at War*, New York: Pantheon.

Singh, Gurharpal (2000) *Ethnic Conflict in India: A Case-Study of Punjab*, Basingstoke: Macmillan.

Sisk, Timothy D. (2004) 'Peacemaking in Civil Wars: Obstacles, Options and Opportunities', in Ulrich Schneckener and Stefan Wolff (eds) *Managing and Settling Ethnic Conflicts*, London: C. Hurst & Co.

Small, Melvin and Singer, David J. (1982) *Resort to Arms: International & Civil War, 1816–1980*, Thousand Oaks, CA: Sage.

Smith, Anthony D. (1986) *The Ethnic Origins of Nations*, Oxford: Blackwell.

Smith, Anthony D. (1991) *National Identity*, London: Penguin.

Smith, Anthony D. (1999) 'The Nation: Real or Imagined', in Edward Mortimer (ed.) *People, Nation and State*, London: I.B. Tauris.

Smith, D. (2004) *Towards a Strategic Framework for Peacebuilding: Getting Their Act Together*, Oslo: Ministry of Foreign Affairs, Evaluation Report 1.

Smith, Michael J. (1999), 'Humanitarian Intervention: An Overview of the Ethical Issues', in Joel H. Rosenthal (ed.), *Ethics and International Affairs: A Reader*, Washington, DC: Georgetown University Press.

Smith, Patrick (2001) 'Memory without History: Who Owns Guatemala's Past?', *Washington Quarterly*, 24, 2: 59–72.

Spencer, Metta (1998) 'When States Divide', in Metta Spencer (ed.) *Separatism: Democracy and Disintegration*, Lanham, MA: Rowman & Littlefield.

Staub, Ervin (1989) *The Roots of Evil: The Origins of Genocide and Other Group Violence*, Cambridge: Cambridge University Press.

Stedman, Stephen John (1991) *Peacemaking in Civil War: International Mediation in Zimbabwe*, Boulder, CO: Lynne Rienner.

Stedman, Stephen John, Rothchild, Donald and Cousens, Elizabeth (2002) *Ending Civil Wars: The Implementation of Peace Agreements*, Boulder, CO: Lynne Rienner.

Steele, Jonathan (2006) 'Iraqi Leader Unveils Reconciliation Plan . . .', *Guardian*, 23 June.

Stewart, Frances (2000) 'Crisis Prevention: Tackling Horizontal Inequalities', *Oxford Development Studies*, 28, 3: 245–65.

Stokke, Kristian (2006) 'Building the Tamil Eelam State: Emerging State Institutions and Forms of Governance in LTTE-Controlled Areas in Sri Lanka', *Third World Quarterly*, 27, 6: 1021–40.

Storey, Peter (1997) 'A Different Kind of Justice: Truth and Reconciliation in South Africa', *Christian Century*, 114, 25: 788–93.

Sulistiyanto, Pryambudi (2007) 'Politics of Justice and Reconciliation in Post-Suharto Indonesia', *Journal of Contemporary Asia*, 37, 1: 73–94.

Sutton, Amy (2006) 'Gendered Based Violence and Rape in Darfur', in Waging Peace, *Darfur: Genocide without Borders*, London: Waging Peace Publications.

Tabara, P. (1992) *Afrique, la face cachée*, Paris: La Pensée Universelle.

Tamir, Yael (1994) *Liberal Nationalism*, Princeton: Princeton University Press.

Tatla, Darshan Singh (1999) *The Sikh Diaspora: The Search for Statehood*, London: UCL Press.

Taylor, Christopher C. (2002) 'The Cultural Face of Terror in the Rwandan Genocide of 1994', in Alexander Laban Hinton (eds) *Annihilating Difference: The Anthropology of Genocide*, Berkeley: University of California Press.

Thant, U. (1970) *UN Monthly Chronicle*, 7, 2.

Thapa, Manjushree (2005) *Forget Kathmandu: An Elegy for Democracy*, New Delhi: Penguin.

Thomas, Hugh (1977) *The Spanish Civil War*, Harmondsworth: Penguin.

Thucydides (1974) *The Peloponnesian War*, Harmondsworth: Penguin.

Tierney, Dominic (2005) 'Irrelevant or Malevolent? UN Arms Embargoes in Civil Wars', *Review of International Studies*, 31, 4: pp. 645–64.

Tilly, Charles (1978) *From Mobilisation to Revolution*, London: Longman.

Tilly, Charles (1992) *Coercion, Capital, and European States, AD 900–1992*, Oxford: Blackwell.

Tilly, Charles (2003) *The Politics of Collective Violence*, Cambridge: Cambridge University Press.

Tremlett, Giles (2006) *Ghosts of Spain*, London: Faber & Faber.

United Nations (2000) *Sustainable Growth Report*, New York: United Nations.

Urquhart, Brian (2006) 'The Outlaw World', *New York Review of Books*, 53.

Uyangoda, J. (2005) *Conflict, Conflict Resolution and Peacebuilding*, Colombo: University of Colombo.

Van Creveld, Martin (1991) *The Transformation of War*, New York: Free Press.

Verdery, Katherine (1996) 'Whither "Nation" and "Nationalism"', in Gopal Balakrishnan (ed.) *Mapping the Nation*, London: Verso.

Verwey, Wilhelm (1992) 'Legality of Humanitarian Intervention after the Cold War', in E. Ferris (ed.) *The Challenge to Intervene: A New Role for the United Nations?*, Uppsala: Life and Peace Institute.

Vincent, R.J. (1974) *Non-intervention and International Order*, Princeton, NJ: Princeton University Press.

Volkan, Vamik (2000) 'Traumatised Societies and Psychological Care: Expanding the Concept of Preventive Medicine', *Mind and Human Interaction*, 11, 3: 177–94.

Von Hippel, Karin (2000) *Democracy by Force: US Military Intervention in the Post-Cold War World*, Cambridge: Cambridge University Press.

Wall, James, A. Jr., Stark, John B. and Standifer, Rhetta L. (2001) 'Mediation: A Current Review and Theory Development', *Journal of Conflict Resolution*, 45, 3: 370–91.

Wallensteen, Peter (2007) *Understanding Conflict Resolution*, London: Sage.

Walt, Stephen M. (1996) *Revolution and War*, Ithaca, NY: Cornell University Press.

Walter, Barbara F. (1997) 'The Critical Barrier to Civil War Settlement', *International Organisation*, 51, 3: 335–64.

Walter, Barbara F. (1999) 'Conclusion', in Barbara Walter F. and Jack Snyder (eds) *Civil Wars, Insecurity and Intervention*, New York: Columbia University Press.

Walter, Barbara F. (2004) 'Does Conflict Beget Conflict? Explaining Recurring Civil War', *Journal of Peace Research*, 41, 3: 771–88.

Walzer, Michael (2000) *Just and Unjust Wars: A Moral Argument with Historical Illustrations*, New York: Basic Books.

Weinstein, Jeremy (2002) 'The Structure of Rebel Organisations: Implications for Post-Conflict Reconstruction', *Conflict Prevention and Reconstruction Report*, 4, Washington, DC: World Bank.

Wendt, David (1994) 'The Peacemakers: Lessons of Conflict Resolution for the Post-Cold War World', *Washington Quarterly*, 17, 3: 163–78.

Wennmann, Achim (2005) 'Resourcing the Recurrence of Intra-state Conflict: Parallel Economies and Their Implications for Peacebuilding', *Security Dialogue*, 36, 4: 479–94.

Whelpton, John (2005) *A History of Nepal*, Cambridge: Cambridge University Press.

Williams, Paul D. (2005) 'International Peacekeeping: The Challenges of State-Building and Regionalisation', *International Affairs*, 81, 1: 163–74.

Wilson, Edmund (1967) *Europe without Baedeker: Sketches among the Ruins of Italy, Greece and England, with Notes from a European Diary: 1963–1964*, London: Rupert Hart-Davis.

Woodward, Susan L. (1995) *Balkan Tragedy: Chaos and Dissolution after the Cold War*, Washington, DC: Brookings Institution.

World Bank (1992) *Governance and Development*, Washington, DC: World Bank.

World Bank (2003) *Breaking the Conflict Trap: Civil War and Development Policy*, Washington, DC: World Bank/Oxford University Press.

Yanacopulos, Helen and Hanlon, Joseph (eds) (2006) *Civil War, Civil Peace*, Milton Keynes: Open University.

Zakaria, Fareed (2007) 'The Limits of Democracy', *Newsweek*, 29 January.

Zarkov, Dubravka (2001) 'The Body of the Other Man: Sexual Violence and the Construction of Masculinity', in Caroline O.N. Moser and Fiona C. Clark (eds) *Victims, Perpetrators or Actors? Gender, Armed Conflict and Political Violence*, London: Zed Books.

Zartman, I.W. (1989) *Ripe for Resolution: Conflict and Intervention in Africa*, New York: Oxford University Press.

Index

For Product Safety Concerns and Information please contact our EU
representative GPSR@taylorandfrancis.com
Taylor & Francis Verlag GmbH, Kaufingerstraße 24, 80331 München, Germany

www.ingramcontent.com/pod-product-compliance
Lightning Source LLC
Chambersburg PA
CBHW050652280326
41932CB00015B/2875